The Marquis
of Montrose

Prion Lost Treasures
Other titles in this series

Napoleon and his Marshals
A.G. Macdonell

The Atrocities of the Pirates
Aaron Smith

THE MARQUIS
OF MONTROSE

JOHN BUCHAN

PRION

This edition first published in Great Britain 1996 by
PRION
32-34 Gordon House Road
London NW5 1LP

Originally published 1913 by Thomas Nelson and Sons
Copyright by the Rt. Hon. The Lord Tweedsmuir, CBE, CD, LL.D.
All rights reserved.

A catalogue record of this book can be obtained from the
British Library

ISBN 1-85375-224-X

Cover design by Bob Eames
Cover image courtesy of the Bridgeman Art Library/Giraudon
Printed and bound by Biddles Ltd.,
Guildford & Kings Lynn

FRATRI DILECTISSIMO.

W. H. B.

When we were little wandering boys,
  And every hill was blue and high,
On ballad ways and martial joys
  We fed our fancies, you and I.
With Bruce we crouched in bracken shade,
  With Douglas charged the Paynim foes;
And oft in moorland noons I played
  Colkitto to your grave Montrose.

The obliterating seasons flow—
  They cannot kill our boyish game.
Though creeds may change and kings may go,
  Yet burns undimmed the ancient flame.
While young men in their pride make haste
  The wrong to right, the bond to free,
And plant a garden in the waste,
  Still rides our Scottish chivalry.

Another end had held your dream—
  To die fulfilled of hope and might,
To pass in one swift rapturous gleam
  From mortal to immortal light—
But through long hours of labouring breath
  You watched the world grow small and far,
And met the constant eyes of Death
  And haply knew how kind they are.

One boon the Fates relenting gave—
  Not where the scented hill-wind blows
From cedar thickets lies your grave,
  Nor mid the steep Himálayan snows.
Night calls the stragglers to the nest,
  And at long last 'tis home indeed
For your far-wandering feet to rest
  Forever by the crooks of Tweed.

In perfect honour, perfect truth,
  And gentleness to all mankind,
You trod the golden paths of youth,
  Then left the world and youth behind.
Ah no! I 'Tis we who fade and fail—
  And you from Time's slow torments free
Shall pass from strength to strength and scale
  The steeps of immortality.

Dear heart, in that serener air,
  If blessed souls may backward gaze,
Some slender nook of memory spare
  For our old happy moorland days.
I sit alone, and musing fills
  My breast with pain that shall not die,
Till once again o'er greener hills
  We ride together, you and I.

PREFACE

IN the following pages I have not attempted to write a complete biography of Montrose, but to tell simply and directly the story of a career which must rank among the marvels of our history, and to provide materials for the understanding of a mind and character which seem to me in a high degree worthy of the attention of modern readers. Hence I have passed rapidly over his early years, and told in detail only the incidents from his first raising of the Royal Standard in Scotland till his death. To avoid clogging the text, all references to the voluminous authorities and discussions of controversial points have been relegated to the notes at the end of the book. Every student of Montrose is in debt to a host of predecessors, and due acknowledgment will be found in the bibliographical note on page 213.

CONTENTS

CHAPTER I
YOUTH   1

CHAPTER II
THE STRIFE IN SCOTLAND   8

CHAPTER III
THE FIRST COVENANT WARS   15

CHAPTER IV
MONTROSE AND ARGYLL   24

CHAPTER V
THE RUBICON   33

CHAPTER VI
THE CURTAIN RISES   43

CHAPTER VII
TIPPERMUIR   51

CHAPTER VIII
ABERDEEN AND FYVIE   63

CHAPTER IX
INVERLOCHY   73

CHAPTER X
THE RETREAT FROM DUNDEE   85

CHAPTER XI
AULDEARN   95

CHAPTER XII
ALFORD   104

CHAPTER XIII
KILSYTH   113

CHAPTER XIV
THE WAR ON THE BORDER   124

CHAPTER XV
AFTER PHILIPHAUGH   138

CHAPTER XVI
THE YEARS OF EXILE   151

CHAPTER XVII
THE LAST CAMPAIGN   167

CHAPTER XVIII
THE CURTAIN FALLS   178

CHAPTER XIX
'A CANDIDATE FOR IMMORTALITY'   195

NOTES   213

INDEX   239

MAPS AND PLANS

THE CAMPAIGN OF TIPPERMUIR AND ABERDEEN
THE BATTLE OF ABERDEEN
THE CAMPAIGN OF INVERLOCHY
THE CAMPAIGN OF CARBISDALE

Publisher's Note

John Buchan wrote two versions of the life of Montrose. *The Marquis of Montrose* was published in 1913 and never reprinted. In 1928 Buchan substantially rewrote it, adding far more detail on the historical background, and published it as *Montrose*. We have chosen the first version as it is fresher, more vigorous and a better read. We consulted Bruce P. Lenman, Professor of History at St. Andrews University, and he endorsed our choice, calling this earlier work 'romantic adventure prose by a master of the genre.'

CHAPTER I

YOUTH
(1612–1636)

THE 'Highland Line' in the Scottish mainland, though often determined variously by political needs has been fixed by nature with sufficient clearness. The true battlement of the hills runs with a northeasterly slant from Argyll through the shire of Dumbarton, and then turns northwards so as to enclose the wide carselands of Tay. Beyond lie the tumbled wildernesses stretching with scarcely a break to Cape Wrath; south are the Lowlands proper around Forth and Clyde till these in turn end in the hills of Tweed and Galloway. Scotland had thus two Borderlands—the famous line of march with England, and the line, historically less notable but geographically clearer, which separated plain from hill, family from clan, and for centuries some semblance of civilization from its stark opposite. The northern Border may be defined as the southern portion of Dumbarton or Lennox, the shire of Stirling, and the haughs of the lower Tay. There for centuries the Lowlander looked out from his towns and castles to the blue mountains where lived his ancestral foes. Dwelling on a frontier makes a hardy race, and from this northern Border came famous men and sounding deeds. Drummonds, Murrays, Erskines, and Grahams were

1

its chief families, but most notably the last. What the name of Scott was in the glens of Teviot, the name of Graham was in the valleys of Forth and Earn. Since the thirteenth century they had been the unofficial wardens of the northern Marches.

The ancient nobility of Scotland does not show well on the page of history. The records of the great earldoms—Angus, Mar, Moray, Huntly—tell too often an unedifying tale of blood and treason. After the day of the Good Lord James, St. Bride of Douglas might have wept for her children. But the family of Graham kept tolerably clean hands, and played an honourable part in the national history. Sir John the Graeme was the trusted friend of Wallace, and fell gloriously at Falkirk. His successors fought in the later wars of independence, thrice intermarried with the royal blood, and gave Scotland its first primate. In 1451 the family attained the peerage. The third Lord Graham was made Earl of Montrose, when the short-lived Lindsay dukedom lapsed, and the new earl died with his king in the steel circle at Flodden. A successor fell at Pinkie; still another became viceroy of Scotland when James the Sixth mounted the English throne. The viceroy's son, apart from a famous brawl in the Edinburgh High Street, chose the quiet life of a country laird. He was a noted sportsman, a great golfer and a devotee of tobacco. His wife was Lady Margaret Ruthven, a daughter of the tragically fated house of Gowrie, who bore him six children, and died when her only son was in his sixth year. The family were rich as the times went, owning broad lands in Stirling, Perth and Angus, and wielding the influence which the chief of a house possesses over its numerous cadets. They had three principal dwellings—the tower of Mugdock in Strathblane, the fine castle of Kincardine in Perthshire where the Ochils slope to the Earn, and the house of old Montrose which Robert Bruce had given to a Graham as the price of Cardross on Clyde.

James Graham, the only son of the fourth earl and Margaret Ruthven, was born, probably in the town of Montrose, some time in the year 1612. Of his five sisters the two eldest were married young—Lilias to Sir John Colquhoun of Luss, and Margaret to a wise man of forty, the first Lord Napier of Merchiston. Their houses were open to the boy when he tired of catching trout in the little water of Ruthven, or wearing out horse-shoes on the Ochils, as the bills of the Aberuthven blacksmith testify. There was much in the way of adventure to be had at Rossdhu, Lady Lilias's new dwelling, and there the young Lord James may have learned, from practising on the roebuck and wild goats of Lochlomondside, the skill which made him later so noted a marksman.

At the age of twelve a certain Master William Forrett received the boy to prepare him for the University of Glasgow. To him Lord James journeyed with a valet, two pages, a quantity of linen and furniture, and his favourite white pony. He lived in the town house of Sir George Elphinstone of Blythswood; and the avenues to learning must have been gently graded, for he had always the happiest memory of those Glasgow days and of Master Forrett, who in later years became the tutor of his sons. He seems to have read Xenophon and Seneca, and an English translation of Tasso; but his favourite book, then and long afterwards, was Raleigh's *History of the World*, no doubt the splendid folio of the first edition.

In the second year of Glasgow study the old earl died, and Lord James posted back to Kincardine. Thither came the whole race of Grahams for the funeral ceremonies, which lasted some fifty days. A prodigious quantity of meat and drink was consumed, and if such mourning had its drawbacks, at any rate it introduced the new head of the family to those of his name and kin. He did not return to Glasgow, but presently was entered at St. Salvator's College, St. Andrews, of which one of his forebears had been a pious founder. Master Forrett brought his possessions from Glasgow, and with his own hands bestowed those valuable items, the books, in a proper cabinet. From the papers which Mark Napier has printed we know many of the details of the St. Andrews days. He began the study of Greek, and read widely in the classics, more especially Caesar and Lucan. Nor did he neglect romances, and no doubt he began the art of verse-making, of which his books contain many examples. In sport his tastes were catholic—hunting, hawking, horse-racing, archery, and golf claiming his attention in turn. His rooms at St. Salvator's were hung round with bows, and in his second year he won the silver medal for archery, which to the end of his college course he held against all comers. The Earl of Argyll, who was some years his senior, had carried off the same trophy. Happy and well dowered, popular with all classes, he varied his residence at St. Andrews with visits to his brothers-in-law and the cadet gentry of his name, and with entertainments on a generous scale at Kincardine. When his sister Dorothea married Sir James Rollo there was huge feasting in Edinburgh and Fifeshire, and the young earl returned to college only to fall sick. Two doctors were summoned, who charged enormous fees and prescribed cards, chess, and dieting. The barber shore away his long brown curls, and 'James Pett's dochter' attended to the invalid's food. It sounds high feeding for what was probably an attack of indigestion—trout, pigeons, capons, 'drapped eggs', calf's-foot jelly, grouse (out of season), washed down by 'liquorice, whey, possets, aleberry, and claret'. In those days the business of life crowded fast on boyhood. After the university came marriage as the next step in a gentleman's education. Not far from old Montrose stood Kinnaird Castle, where Lord Carnegie dwelt with six pretty daughters. There the young Montrose had visited, and there he fell in love with the youngest girl, Lady Magdalen. The match was too desirable for opposition either from the Carnegies or the young lord's guardians, and the two children—Montrose was scarcely seventeen—were married in the chapel of Kinnaird on November 10, 1629. According to the marriage contract, they were to spend the next four years at Kinnaird till the bridegroom came of age. They were years of quiet study, the leisurely preparation which is all too rare in youth for the necessities of manhood. The famous Jameson portrait, given by Graham of Morphie as a wedding gift to the young countess, shows us Montrose in those years of meditation, when he was scribbling his ambitions on his copy of Quintus Curtius. It is a charming head of a boy, with its wide, curious, grey eyes, the arched, almost fantastic, eyebrows, the delicate and mobile lips. Life was to crush out the daintiness and gaiety, armour was to take the place of lace collar and silken doublet; but one thing the face of Montrose never lost—it had always an air of hope, as of one seeking for a far country.

Early in the year 1633 Montrose, having just attained his majority, set out on a course of foreign travel. By doing so he missed the pageant of the king's coronation in Edinburgh, in which he would naturally have played a conspicuous part. Probably the reason is to be found in the scandal connected with his sister's husband, Colquhoun of Luss, which was then the talk of Scotland. The laird, in company with a 'necromancer' of the name of Carlippis, had fled from his lawful wife, carrying with him his sister-in-law, the little Lady Katharine, who had been for a time Montrose's comrade in his Glasgow lodgings. The malefactor was promptly outlawed, but the unhappy girl disappears from history. With such a tragedy in his memory Montrose may have welcomed the anodyne of new scenes and fresh faces.

We know little of his journey. He visited France and Italy with Basil Fielding—Lord Denbigh's son and Hamilton's brother-in-law—who flung in his fortunes later with the Puritan party. In the quaint old library at Innerpeffray there is still preserved a French Bible which he bought on his travels, scribbled throughout with mottoes which had caught his fancy, such as '*Honor mihi vita potior*' and '*Non crescunt sine spinis.*' In Rome he met Lord Angus, the future Marquis of Douglas, and others of the Scots gentry. He studied all the while—'as much of the mathematics as is required of a soldier,' wrote his faithful adherent, Thomas Saintserf, 'but his great study was to read men and the actions of great men.' It is a phrase which aptly describes the attitude of high dedication in which the young lord passed his youth. He went gravely about the business of life, and already had made certain of renown, though careless enough about happiness. To Cardinal de Retz long afterwards he seemed like one of the heroes of Plutarch, and there was something even in his boyish outlook of the old Roman manner. The descriptions of his person and habits at this date are familiar: of middle stature, and beautifully made; chestnut hair; a clear fresh colour; keen grey eyes; a mighty horseman; and an adept at every sport which needed a lithe body and a cool head.[1] On his manners all accounts are agreed, and most accounts are critical. He was very stately and ceremonious, even as a young man: in no way prepared to forget that he was a great noble, except among his intimates. To servants and inferiors he was kindly and thoughtful, to equals and superiors a little stiff and hard. 'He was exceeding constant and loving,' a friend wrote, 'to those who did adhere to him, and very affable to such as he knew; though his carriage, which indeed was not ordinary, made him seem proud.' He knew himself destined for great deeds, and his boyish stateliness was his advertisement to the world of the part he had set himself to play.

He returned three years later in his twenty-fourth year—a figure of intense interest to the Scottish faction-leaders, and of some moment to the king's court. He was altogether too remarkable to please the Marquis of Hamilton, who was the interpreter of Scottish business to the royal ears. When Montrose reached London he appeared at court, and naturally asked Hamilton to be his sponsor, announcing his wish 'to put himself into the king's service.' Hamilton did his best to dissuade him by representing Charles as the foe of Scottish rights, and then promptly sought out the king to tell him that Montrose, by reason of his royal descent, was a danger to the royal interests, and should be discouraged. The upshot was that the traveller was received by Charles with marked coldness. The king spoke a few chilly words, gave him his hand to kiss, and turned away. It was enough to discourage the most ardent loyalist. But, indeed, Montrose was no sentimental king's man; he was a loyalist on constitutional not on personal grounds. He may have returned to Scotland with small affection for his monarch, but it is certain that the rebuff played little part in determining that momentous policy upon which he was now called to enter.

CHAPTER II

THE STRIFE IN SCOTLAND
(1636–1638)

BEFORE we can understand the course which Montrose now followed, it is necessary to look for a moment at the storm which was slowly gathering to a head in the north. The weakness of the Reformation in Scotland was not that it was too drastic, but that it was not nearly drastic enough. It was a change of creed, ritual, and Church government, but there was no reform in morals or in society. It had the weakness of all movements engineered by an aristocracy. The Scottish nobles from the fourteenth to the sixteenth century were probably the most turbulent, rapacious, and independent in Europe. Resolute champions of indefensible privileges, they resisted all the reforming efforts of their kings, and were the death of more than one sovereign. They had not even the merit of patriotism, for if they were consistently against the common people, they were not infrequently against their own land, and Scottish history is stored with ugly tales of treason. Their prime foes were the King and the Church, and they cast longing eyes at the fat abbeys and the rich glebes of their clerical rivals. The Reformation gave them their chance. Two-thirds of the Church plunder fell into their hands, and their Protestantism grew with their self-interest. Knox complained, not without reason, that in all the Lords of the Congregation there was not one righteous man. A few no doubt were dogmatic enthusiasts, but the majority cared as little for the difference between priest and minister as for the Ten Commandments.

James the Sixth, having spent his youth in Scotland, was wise enough to leave this hornets' nest alone. The new Kirk, though its braver leaders protested, had some difficulty in quarrelling with those who had fought with it the battle of the Reformation. Moreover, it saw in the nobility a bulwark against what it was growing to fear—the Episcopalian tendencies of the throne; for the nobles, having overthrown the authority of Rome, had no mind to set up Canterbury in its stead. The common people, living in dire poverty under harsh laws, had little means of making their voice heard. While Montrose was growing to manhood, the tithe—to take one instance only—had become a crying scandal. It had passed from the old Church to the feudal lords, who could levy it in kind pretty much as they pleased and when they pleased. The tenant could not get in his harvest till the lord had taken his toll. The bonnet-lairds and the farmers the labourers and the shepherds, even the burghers in the little towns, groaned under a tyranny as harsh as the darkest period of the Middle Ages. It was remembered by elderly folk that the old abbots with the same powers had been far more merciful in their dealings. Had the thing gone on, Scotland might have been in danger of a counter-Reformation.

If one storm centre was the nobles, the other was the Kirk. As conceived by its authors, Scottish Presbyterianism was to be a noble democracy, the sanctuary of the true Word, and not a museum of pedantries. It began its career under the aegis of John Knox, a man of alert and masculine genius; and its spirit was admirably suited to his close-reasoning and independent countrymen. Unhappily, like all things built of new materials by human hands, it contained the elements of strife and decay. Seeking its warrant directly from on high, it made of the Bible a manual of government, not only for Church but for State. While it repudiated Rome, it revived the claims of Rome, and imposed a far more merciless discipline. 'New presbyter,' in Milton's phrase, was, 'but old priest writ large.' The Kirk had, indeed, become possessed of weapons too terrible for plain men to use with safety to themselves or others. It sought to make rules for daily life out of the fierce ritual of early Israel. It forgot the spirit in the letter and religion in its mechanical forms. We need not blame the Scottish ministers unduly. Their fashion was the fashion of their age. If a man believes that his heart is desperately wicked, that he is doomed to eternal fires but for the interposition of God's grace, and that to walk in grace it is necessary to observe half-understood precepts from the Scriptures without any attempt to rethink them in the light of new conditions—nay, that such an attempt is in God's eyes the unpardonable sin—it is small wonder if he forge such an instrument as the seventeenth-century Scottish Kirk. To him tolerance must be only another name for lukewarmness, and reason only the temptation of the devil. If he is right, all those who differ from him must be wrong, and it is his duty to enforce his faith with fire and sword. Since God orders all things, no part of life is beyond the province of His servants, and the Kirk must rule not only in general assemblies but in court and camp and parliament. And from all this it is only a little step to a kind of Jesuitism—the belief that in the performance of so great a work a sin or two will not be remembered against the worker. Fanaticism is curiously apt to forget its original goal, and to run for running's sake.

Scotland was thus in danger of two tyrannies—the material domination of the nobles and the more deadly spiritual and moral despotism of the Kirk. There was no Knox with his clear, far-reaching mind to see the perils.

He had, indeed, laid the foundation, but it was narrower men, such as Andrew Melville, who had raised the structure. There was not even a Moray with a reasonable share of patriotism and political wisdom. The country was in the hands of men neither great nor wise—nobles desperately intent on holding what they had won, and Churchmen desperately in earnest about their spiritual prerogatives. The two sects agreed in one thing only—their stubborn conservatism. It was a very pretty powder-magazine for the inevitable spark.

The spark came from the king. Charles took up the question of Scottish reform with the sincere intention of setting things straight. But the strange fatality of his race pursued him, and he mingled in his policy what was just and sensible, and what was unjust and foolish. He undertook the business of reforming some of the feudal tenures, particularly the vexed matter of tithes, and in the most modern way he appointed a Royal Commission. The result was a genuine reform, acceptable alike to the commons and clergy of Scotland. It was far from acceptable to the nobles, but their mouths were stopped; they bided their time till their chance came. They had not long to wait. Fanaticism always produces a counter-fanaticism, and it was the dearest wish of the king's heart to make the worship of God uniform throughout his dominions. When he came to Edinburgh in 1633 to be crowned, he and Laud arranged a ceremony which to the onlookers seemed very like the ritual of Rome. Next year he created a See of Edinburgh, filled the Privy Council with bishops, and gave the Chancellorship to a Churchman, Archbishop Spottiswoode. A Book of Ecclesiastical Canons was issued under the supervision of the Scottish bishops. Last and worst, in the summer of 1637 came Laud's new Service Book, ordered to be read in all churches. It was the true counter-fanaticism. Charles gave to his bishops precisely that impossible position which the Presbyterian

ministers were beginning to claim for themselves—a position which in the long run makes civilized government
impossible. It was a proposal as repugnant to the reasonable loyalist as to the hot-gospeller of the Kirk. 'That
Churchmen have competency,' Lord Napier wrote, 'is agreeable to the law of God and man; but to invest them into
great estates and principal offices of the State, is neither
convenient for the Church, for the King, nor for the
State . . . Histories witness what troubles have been raised
to kings, what tragedies amongst subjects, in all places
where Churchmen were great. Our reformed Churches,
having reduced religion to the ancient primitive truth
and simplicity, ought to beware that corruption enter
not into their Church in the same gate.'[2] They did not
beware. They were only too ready to welcome this particular corruption for themselves, but they were resolutely
determined that the Episcopal Church in Scotland should
be kept free from temptation.

Laud's Service Book was the last straw. The devout
women of Edinburgh rose in their wrath, and the first
attempt to read it in St. Giles's Kirk was the signal for a
riot. The flame ran fast over Scotland, for the grievance
was indeed intolerable. To endure such interference
with private rights of worship was to stultify the whole
Reformation principle. Every post to England carried a
supplication or a remonstrance to his Majesty, and early in
the autumn public meetings began to be held. Montrose
returned from his travels with his head full of academic
politics, and his mind fired with dreams of military glory,
to find his country in the throes of a petty and yet vital
strife. He could not avoid taking sides, and both parties
in Scotland angled feverishly for his support. To the
amazement of many he chose for the malcontents, and in
November 1637 appeared publicly on their side. Early in
the new year a Committee of Sixteen, representing the
Estates of the Realm, was appointed to deal with the present discontents, and Montrose was one of them. He

appeared to protest against the proclamation of the Liturgy, mounted in boyish enthusiasm upon a barrel, so that the prophetic Rothes was led to observe: 'James, you will never be at rest till you are lifted up above the rest in three fathoms of a rope.' Meantime Johnston of Wariston and Alexander Henderson had drafted a document which they called a Covenant—an old device, for when the Scottish nobles chose to walk in the paths of rebellion they used to enter into 'ane band.' On the last day of February 1638, in Greyfriars' Churchyard in Edinburgh, came the reading of the protest with its solemn appeal— 'that religion and righteousness may flourish in the land, to the glory of God, the honour of the king, and the peace and comfort of us all.' The National Covenant had been consummated, and Montrose was sworn among the leaders.

His reasons are not far to seek. No doubt something must be set down to personal grounds, for he was little more than a boy. He had been unkindly received by Charles and snubbed by Hamilton, and such treatment may have disposed him to listen to Rothes and Loudoun when they respectfully solicited his opinion and his help. But, apart from personal feelings, there were good grounds for a man of his temper approving the principle of the Covenant. He could not see that, whatever its professions might be, its supporters made it impossible. He could not read the factious hearts of Loudoun and Balmerino, and see how little they cared for 'religion' or 'righteousness' or the 'glory of God.' He could not see that the Kirk was dreaming at the back of its mind of a tyranny which would annihilate all government. He looked only at the Covenant; he had not the experience to judge the Covenanters. And on the face of it the Covenant was sound policy. It protested against the despotic and illegal infliction of the Prayer Book upon people who preferred to address their Maker in their own words. It protested against the appointment of

Churchmen to civil offices. Montrose, being a good Presbyterian and true to the spirit of that faith, did not like the ecclesiastic in politics. In his dying declaration he repeated: 'Bishops, I care not for them. I never intended to advance their interests.' All these views were held by Napier, his brother-in-law; but Napier did not sign the Covenant, and Montrose did. The explanation is that Montrose looked only at the document, while Napier, older and wiser, looked at the men behind it. He knew that the letter is little and the spirit much, and he did not like the spirit. Montrose stood for what seemed to be the liberties of the Scottish people. When he found that the Covenant had become the cause of a selfish oligarchy of nobles and a tyrannical Kirk, he was to cast it behind him. Like a true statesman, he sought the reality of things, not the name.

CHAPTER III

THE FIRST COVENANT WARS
(1638-1639)

THE Covenant was an act of rebellion, and its makers were aware of the consequences of their deeds. The Tables, as the Committee of Sixteen was named, set about organizing a provisional government. Its leaders subscribed largely to the war chest, and a general tax was levied of a dollar for every thousand merks of rent. The king, who had at times no mean capacity for judging a situation, estimated the events in Scotland more shrewdly than his advisers. He looked forward sooner or later to an appeal to force, but he wished to gain time till he could make use of it conveniently; so he sent the Marquis of Hamilton as a commissioner with power to treat with the malcontents. One thing he demanded: the Covenant, the sign—manual of rebellion—must be dropped before any concessions were made.

Hamilton set off on a task for which he had little liking. A vain, tortuous being, a diligent tramper of backstairs, and a master of intrigue, he was probably the most futile of the many schemers of his day. Scotland he hated, as he told the king, 'next to hell;' but visions of the Scottish crown and memories of his royal descent were the will-o'-the-wisp to his shallow and inconstant brain.

He arrived in Edinburgh early in June 1638, and found sullen looks and little of the welcome due to a Royal Commissioner. The Tables appointed a committee of three nobles and three ministers to confer with him, and one of the six was Montrose. Their demands were simple and reasonable. They asked for the withdrawal of the obnoxious Liturgy and Book of Canons; the summoning of a free General Assembly; and, finally, of a Parliament to decide the various questions at issue. The Scottish Church was to shape its own ecclesiastical policy, and a Scottish Parliament was to give such policy the validity of the civil law. It was a moderate assertion of a justifiable nationalism.

Hamilton hummed and hawed, promised and withdrew, and finally left Edinburgh in despair. But before he went he vindicated his character for doubledealing. He privately told the Covenanters, as we know on Montrose's evidence, that if they took a firm stand they were likely to win. Then ensued a war of king's proclamations and Covenanting protests. Hamilton flitted between London and Edinburgh, carrying royal concessions, till all the demands of the Covenanters had been met. But the concessions came too late. The king proposed a new covenant of his own, the chief point of which was the abjuration of Popery; but the Covenanting leaders, whose detestation of Popery needed no advertisement, very naturally described it as a 'mockery of God.' Their demands were now nothing less than the complete suppression of Episcopacy in Scotland. Everywhere except in Aberdeen the National Covenant had been enthusiastically received. Montrose was sent with a bevy of ministers to convert those northern burgesses; but the preaching of Mr. Alexander Henderson, Mr. David Dickson, and Mr. Andrew Cant was without effect. His future visits to Aberdeen were to be to better purpose.

On the 21st of November the General Assembly met in the old cathedral church of Glasgow. Laymen were admitted as members in accordance with the law and spirit of

Presbyterianism. Hamilton and the ministers opposed this admission—the latter with some justice, for they saw that laymen meant nobles, and they knew well enough the motives of these gentry in their interference with Church affairs. The scene must have been a curious one. Hamilton sat uneasily on a high chair of state, with the Privy Council below him. Opposite him sat the Moderator, Henderson, with Wariston as his clerk. Then came the Covenanting nobles, and then, in a confused mass, the clergy and the other lay delegates. Baillie, an extreme Covenanter, was so shocked at the pandemonium that he observed that his brethren 'might learn from Canterbury or the Pope, or even from Turks or pagans,' for the members 'made such a din and clamour in the house of the true God that if they minded to use the like behaviour in his chamber he would not be content till they were down the stairs.'

The session was one long and dreary wrangle, during which Montrose in his youthful zeal came into conflict with the Moderator. Hamilton stood on the king's prerogative, and questioned the legality of the whole assembly, a foolish move which intensified the bitterness. He departed after trying to dissolve the house, and on his way to the king saw to the garrisoning of Edinburgh Castle. The Assembly, left to its own devices, deposed all the bishops, some on false charges of immorality; abolished all Charles's Episcopalian innovations; and excommunicated a number of ministers who had shown leanings to the royal faith. Scotland had made it abundantly clear that in Church matters she would have her own way, and that that way was not the king's. The issue could only be war. The unity of the nation was proved by the accession to the Covenant party of the head of the House of Campbell, who was a shrewd judge of the likely winner in every dispute. In a speech of portentous length he announced his adherence to the good cause, and he was the leader in the summary handling of the episcopate. The Assembly closed with thanks to God and to the Earl of Argyll.

Up in the north, Aberdeen stood for the king. Charles would soon be marching to the Border, and the Council could not go out to meet him with an enemy in the rear. Besides, there was always the danger that Strafford might land Irishry in the west who would join their Gordon co-religionists. Whatever the faults of the Tables, they were no sluggards in war. The castles of Edinburgh, Dumbarton, and Dalkeith were surprised, the Hamilton strongholds in Clydesdale were taken, and soon in the south of Scotland only the castle of Caerlaverock remained hostile. Aberdeen must be reduced, and the command of the army for the purpose was given to Montrose. But, to correct the inexperience of the young earl, he was given as his lieutenant a little, crooked soldier of fortune, Alexander Leslie, who had won fame in the wars of Gustavus. With Leslie had come over many Scottish mercenaries of the Dugald Dalgetty type, who, finding their occupation gone on the Continent, welcomed the chance of turning an honest penny in their native land. Such men cared as little about prayer books and general assemblies as they cared for the international quibbles of a German princeling, but they were to provide the Covenant with what it sorely lacked—a body of experienced and cool-headed professional soldiers.

The course of the First Bishops' War was not glorious or swift, but it gave Montrose his first lesson in that art of which he was to become a consummate master. The House of Gordon was the great family of north-east Scotland. Till a few years earlier it had been Catholic, and, while strong in loyalty to the throne, had stubbornly resisted the Reformation. But the Huntly of the day had married Argyll's sister, and had compromised on the Episcopalian variety of Protestantism. The old royalism, however, was maintained, and he sent off the Covenant envoys with the word that his house had risen with the kings of Scotland and would ever stand by them. 'If the event be the ruin of my sovereign, then shall the rubbish

that belongs to it bury beneath it all that belongs to mine.'
He was now appointed royal lieutenant in the north, but
bidden take instructions from Hamilton and engage in no
fighting without his assent. The result of these impossible
orders might have been foreseen. Montrose spent the
beginning of the year 1639 in beating up recruits in his
own Braes of Angus, where he had high words with Lord
Southesk, his father-in-law, who not unnaturally asked
him for his warrant. Presently he summoned the northern
Covenanters—chiefly Frasers and Forbeses to meet him at
the little town of Turriff. Huntly heard of the rendezvous,
and, resolved to prevent it, marched thither with two
thousand of his clansmen. But Montrose was to give the
first proof of his amazing power of annihilating distance.
When Huntly arrived he found the churchyard garrisoned with several hundred muskets, and Montrose and
his friends ensconced in the church. Huntly could do
nothing, for he could not fight without Hamilton's
instructions. He withdrew to Inverurie, and disbanded
most of his men.

A few days later Leslie arrived with the rest of the
Covenant army, and Montrose marched on Aberdeen.
Ever in love with the spectacular side of things, he found
a rival colour for the royal scarlet, and decorated his men
with knots of blue ribbon. It is curious to remember that
the Covenant received its famous blue badge from the
man who was to prove its chief opponent. The city,
deserted by Huntly, had no power of resistance, and
opened its gates. Montrose, to the disgust of his followers, was merciful, and contented himself with imposing
a fine for recusancy. Then he departed for Huntly's castle in the Bog of Gight.

Now follows a curious tale, on which it is hard to form
an opinion. Huntly and Montrose met in the camp at
Inverurie, and came to terms. Huntly signed a modified
version of the Covenant, binding himself 'to maintain the
king's authority, together with the liberties both of

19

Church and State, Religion and Laws'—probably a version dictated by Montrose himself, whose principles it exactly represented. The Gordons would be allowed to sign the Covenant if they pleased, and the Catholic members of the clan were to be protected so long as they stood by Scottish liberty. Then Montrose repaired to Aberdeen, where he was joined by certain of the Covenanting nobles. A council was held, and the general was severely chidden for his leniency to Huntly. Apparently the command in the field did not carry any superior powers at the council board, for Huntly was promptly bidden to attend under a safe conduct. Montrose had promised more than he could perform, and the chief of the Gordons found himself in a trap. He was told that he must accompany the Covenanting lords to Edinburgh. He asked if he was to go as a prisoner or as a free man. Montrose, according to Spalding, bade him take his choice; and the marquis replied that he would go as a volunteer. To Edinburgh they went, and Huntly's suspicions proved to be only too well founded. He refused to subscribe any other covenant than that he had taken, and the Tables promptly sent him and his son, Lord Gordon, to Edinburgh Castle. The simple explanation seems to be that Montrose was overruled; but, knowing as we do his natural temper, it seems strange that he should permit his promise to be violated by his colleagues and still retain his command. One point alone is clear: that Huntly was bitterly aggrieved. He never forgave Montrose, though his clan was to fight by his side. Had the Gordon been a different man, or had this unfortunate incident never happened, the history of Scotland might have been written otherwise.

These events befell in April. On May Day, Hamilton arrived in the Forth with nineteen ships of war and five thousand men. He found the approaches to Edinburgh strongly fortified, and both shores of the Firth in arms. His mother, the terrible old dowager-countess, arrived from the west with pistols in her holsters and the resolve to shoot her son if he set foot on Scottish soil. The king's commissioner proved as futile in war as in diplomacy. He contented himself with landing his men on the islands of the Firth, and writing melancholy letters to his master.

But up in the north the Gordons had taken matters into their own hands. In a one-sided engagement called the Trot of Turriff they drove out a small Covenanting garrison, and marched on Aberdeen, which they occupied on the 15th of May. Meanwhile, Huntly's second son, Lord Aboyne, had made his way to Charles at Newcastle, and had offered his services on the royal side. He was sent back to Hamilton to get troops, but Hamilton gave him nothing save a few field-pieces and the services of Colonel Gun, who had fought in the German wars. The main Covenanting army, under Leslie, was already marching to the Border accompanied by a cohort of ministers, one of whom, Mr. Robert Baillie, described the temper of his brethren as 'a sweet, meek, humble, yet strong and vehement spirit.' Hamilton sent off two of his three regiments to the king, and himself remained snugly in the Forth.

At the first word of the Gordon rising Montrose had marched north again with 4,000 men. He reached Aberdeen on the 25th of May, to find that the city had already fallen to the Earl Marischal on or about the 20th. His ministers pressed him to make an example of the place, but he declined. The next day was Sunday, and while the officers were in church the soldiers made short work of every dog that had been decked in scorn with the blue ribbon of the Covenant. They also came to blows with the fisher-folk over sundry essays in salmon-poaching. But beyond a fine of ten thousand merks levied by the victors, the city suffered little.

On the 30th of May Montrose marched into the Gordon country and laid siege to Huntly's castle of Gight. But two days later he got news which changed his plans. He heard that Aboyne with a large force was on the sea, and he assumed that Hamilton was with him. He must keep his communications open at all costs, so after a day's rest in Aberdeen he hastened south. On the 5th of June Aboyne arrived with his field-pieces, Gun, and a few young adventurers of his own class. His brother, Lord Lewis, who had attained the mature age of thirteen, rode into the city with a thousand of the clan, and so aroused the spirit of the burghers that by the 14th of June Aboyne had 4,000 men at his back.

Montrose had met the Earl Marischal,[3] the head of the house of Keith, at Stonehaven, and when news came of Aboyne's landing he went north to meet him. Aboyne's following showed the inclination, common to Highland levies, to melt mysteriously away; but he had six hundred Gordon cavalry, and he had the citizen forces of the twice-captured Aberdeen, who could expect little in the way of mercy if the war went against them. He had a strong position, for the Dee was in flood, and the narrow bridge might be held by resolute men against great odds. Had all his officers been of the stamp of Colonel Johnston, the provost's son, it would have gone ill with Montrose. The muskets at the bridge-head bit fiercely into the Covenant ranks, the spirit of the townspeople rose high, and the first day's fighting left their defences intact. But in the night Montrose brought up his heavier cannon and sent his horse up the river to find a ford. Gun induced the Gordons to move upstream also, and as soon as they had gone the Covenanters made a general attack. Gun, having made nothing of his ride, fell into a panic which communicated itself to the rest. The Gordons fled with the unwilling Aboyne to their own country, and the citizens, deprived of their allies, broke at last.

Marischal, with the cordial assent of the ministers, would have burned and pillaged the city, but Montrose pled for a respite. Luckily for Aberdeen, events had taken place in the south which made the truce a peace. On the 18th of June there had been signed the Pacification of

Berwick, the most hollow treaty ever made. Under it both armies were to be disbanded. Montrose imposed another fine upon Aberdeen, released his prisoners, and dismissed his men to their homes; and a few days later set out himself for the south. He had won his first battle, and proved conclusively his gift for war; but as he journeyed Edinburgh-wards he can have had little of the joy of victory in his heart. He was no professional soldier like Leslie, but a perplexed and patriotic statesman, and he saw small hope for the future of that loyalty and that liberty which were the twin principles of his life.

CHAPTER IV

MONTROSE AND ARGYLL
(1639-1642)

WE leave Montrose on his way south to glance at that other Scottish noble whose name was now on the lips of everybody. The Earl of Argyll was some thirty-four or thirty-five years of age, a lean, narrow-chested man, more noted in debate than in war. Close-set, squinting eyes, a thin, drooping nose, and a sinister mouth were the outward characteristics of this new 'Archibald the Grim.' The head of the great House of Campbell, he had the widest possessions and largest revenues of any Highland chief, save Huntly, and at his back stood a powerful and well-organized clan. Till the Glasgow Assembly of 1638 he had played little part in public life. But he was widely known as assiduous, wily, and infinitely patient. Hamilton, no bad judge of intriguers, told Charles that he was the most dangerous man in Scotland. Another opinion is that of the old Argyll, his father, who having turned Catholic in his dotage was compelled by the king to make over his estates to his son and leave the country. 'Sir,' he wrote to Charles, 'I must know this young man better than you can do. You may raise him, which I doubt you will live to repent, for he is a man of craft, subtlety, and falsehood, and can love no man, and if ever he finds it in his power to do you a mischief, he will be sure to do it.'[4] Of his ability there can be no question. Mr. Gardiner thinks him as much superior to Montrose in statesmanship as he was inferior in the art of war; and Clarendon, who detested him, said that Argyll wanted only courage and honesty to be a very great man. Montrose despised him, but then Montrose was apt to despise those whom he did not love.

In every national crisis there is some personal antagonism, where the warring creeds seem to be summed up in the persons of two protagonists. Caesar and Pompey, Pym and Strafford, Fox and Pitt, are familiar instances. So stood Montrose and Argyll, secular types of conflicting temperaments and irreconcilable aims. Argyll must always remain one of the mysteries of history. We can see the man and his doings, but we cannot see the dream at the back of that patient head. He had a grim piety of the ascetic kind, but the mainspring of his actions was not piety. Nor was it a political ideal, for he had no theory of state-craft worth the name. He was the eternal fisher in troubled waters, the creature of a mediaeval twilight. He had the chief's inordinate love of power, and visions of a crown may have haunted one who boasted that he was the 'eighth man from Robert Bruce.' But above all he loved the exercise of his admirable brain, using the raw material of fanaticism in the ministers and of gross self-interest in the nobles to serve his own most unfanatical ends.

Physically he was a coward, though like many cowards he plucked up courage to make a good ending. This shrinking made him a poor general, and predisposed him to win his purpose by peaceful means. But, though pacifically inclined, he had no gentleness or humanity, and many of the barbarities of the Covenant must be laid to his account. He had no enthusiasm, though he could use its catchwords, and few principles which were not priced. This freedom from the common foibles of mankind made him a terrible antagonist, but it left one chink in his armour. He could not realize a motive other than fanaticism or self-interest, and in failing to understand, he undervalued and miscalculated. Small wonder that he did not love Montrose, who represented something beyond his ken. Single-heartedness did not come within the scope of his capacious understanding. He was puzzled, and, being puzzled, he was compelled to hate one who had no personal ambition in the common sense, who was a civic enthusiast as Wariston and Guthrie were religious enthusiasts, and who, as he knew well, would sooner or later force the appeal to that which Argyll hated above all things—the sword.

The next four years of Montrose's life are a tale of a slow disillusionment, the gradual ripening of the antagonism with Argyll, and repeated bouts with his opponent in that field of parliaments, assemblies, and subterranean intrigues in which the chief of the Campbells was most at home. At the date of the Treaty of Berwick, Montrose, though looked askance at by some of the extremists for his clemency in the northern campaign, was still a trusted leader of the Covenanters. But events were soon to shake him in their estimation. Before the year was out the King and the Covenant were at loggerheads again. Charles, blundering by the letter of the agreement, broke in the opinion of the Covenanters its spirit, and the Scottish army was not disbanded. Traquair, the royal treasurer, was mobbed in the Edinburgh streets, and when Charles summoned the Covenanting leaders to Berwick to explain the proceedings, most of them ignored the command. Among the few who obeyed was Montrose, and the interview with the king marked, probably, an epoch in his life. He fell for the first time under the spell of Charles's personality. He heard for the first time the case of the king. He seems to have been convinced for the first time of the royal *bona fides,* convinced that Charles, for all his earlier follies, would not go back from the path of constitutional monarchy to which he now stood pledged. Montrose was never one to disguise his thoughts, and the paper with the words '*Invictus armis verbis vincitur,*' presently found pinned to his door, showed the view of his new attitude held by the inner circle of the Covenant.

On his return to Scotland he was persuaded of another fact, the unconstitutional ambitions of the Earl of Argyll. The new Assembly sat in August, and made short work of Scottish Episcopacy. On the last day of that month the new Parliament met to ratify their decision, and an important question at once arose as to the gap left by the bishops. With them one of the estates of the realm had disappeared, and the Lords of the Articles—the committee which provisionally licensed all Bills before their presentation to Parliament—were sadly depleted. The problem was how to fill up the vacancies. Charles would have had ministers take the bishops' place, but the jealousy of nobles and clergy alike made this solution impossible. Montrose proposed the nomination by the king of a number of laymen—an odd suggestion for one of his views. Perhaps he hoped to secure as royal nominees some of the wiser and more moderate nobles, such as Napier, who had little interest in party intrigues. Argyll's scheme, which was carried by one vote, allowed each estate to elect its own lords—eight from the nobles, sixteen from the lairds and the burghers. It was probably the best expedient, and it had the advantage, from the point of view of its author, that it gave his unique talents for intrigue a fair field. He was what we should call today a brilliant electioneer, and he could exercise this gift more profitably among the Covenanting middle classes than among his jealous and unruly peers. The reform, whatever its grounds, abolished the royal influence in the Scottish Parliament, and substituted for it the mastery of Argyll.

The next stage in Argyll's advance revealed the hand less of a master of statecraft than of a feudal baron with grievances to avenge. The Parliament which met in the following summer (June 1640) set up a general

committee of public safety with powers over the army.
Montrose was one of its members, and went north to
raise men for the force which Leslie a second time was
to lead across the Border. He had to effect the reduction
of various Royalist fortresses, among others that of Airlie,
the seat of the Ogilvys. The castle was peaceably surrendered and a small garrison left behind. But Argyll had
also gone north on the same errand, though in a very different spirit. He had old scores to pay off, for Campbells
and Ogilvys had been long at feud. The burning of the
'bonny house of Airlie' is too well known from the ballad
to need retelling. He turned Lord Ogilvy's young wife out
of doors in wild weather on the eve of her confinement.
Hastening into Badenoch and Lochaber he wreaked his
ill-will on those ancient foes of his clan, the Macdonalds,
and he trapped Atholl by a subterfuge and sent him prisoner to Edinburgh. Returning in triumph the hero
obtained from Parliament an indemnity for his deeds—
'for any violence whatsoever done to the liberty of the
subject, or freedom taken with their property, houses, or
castles, for burning the same or putting fire there into, or
otherwise destroying the same howsoever, or by putting
whatsomever person or persons to torture or question,
or of putting any person or persons to death'—a fairly
comprehensive catalogue which sheds some light upon his
campaign. He had also the audacity to charge Montrose
with treason for dealing too leniently with rebels, a charge
which honest old Leslie would have none of. Montrose
went southward with the army, and was the first to lead
his division across the Tweed at Coldstream to English soil.

Meantime he had had news which showed him something of Argyll's heart. He was privately approached with
a suggestion to depose the king, and to place the government of Scotland in the hands of three dictators, two of
whom were ciphers and the third Argyll. The scheme
must have revealed to him how far the Covenant had
strayed from its original intention to do nothing 'to the

diminution of the king's greatness and authority.' Such a plot would set an end forever to all his hopes of a constitutional monarch, a popular government, and a free and loyal Presbyterian Church. He was convinced that many in Scotland had no desire to depose a Stuart and set up a Campbell, and he resolved to appeal to the moderate Covenanters. During the year 1640 some of them met at Cumbernauld, the house of Montrose's uncle, Lord Wigton, and signed a bond. It protested against the 'particular and indirect practising of a few,' and bound the signatories to uphold the letter and spirit of the National Covenant 'to the hazard of our lives, fortunes, and estates.' It was signed among others by Marischal, Atholl, Boyd, Mar, Perth, Erskine, and Almond. In November Boyd fell ill, and in the delirium before his death revealed something of his doings. Word was carried to Argyll, who denounced the bond to his colleagues of the Council. Montrose was summoned to Edinburgh to answer to the Estates on a charge of treason, frankly avowed the whole business, and defended it as an honest statement of the constitutional policy for which the Covenant had been originally framed. It was idle for the ministers to describe as a 'damnable bond'[5] what was obviously no more than their own declared intentions, and Argyll regretfully had to let the matter drop. It was enough for the present by hints and rumours to spread abroad the impression that the late Covenanting general was a traitor to the cause of true religion.

A man of active temper and complete honesty, if he cannot see his way plain, is apt to make a sorry business of waiting. Perplexities thickened about the path of the undecided Montrose. He saw clearly the necessity of asserting the royal power if Scotland was to be saved from anarchy, and he saw no less clearly the direction of Argyll's thoughts; but he still believed that the Covenanters as a whole were willing to listen to moderate counsels, and that if he bided his time he might yet lead his countrymen into reasonable ways. He had seen the fiasco at Newburn and the ready capitulation of Newcastle; now, he may have argued, Scotland has sufficiently asserted her rights as against the king, and the time is ripe for insisting that the royal rights in turn shall be safeguarded. He did not realize how closely the interests of the Covenant were linked with Pym and his followers in the English Parliament, whose maxim it was rapidly becoming that 'the king could do no right.' Meantime he was zealous in discussing public affairs and winning adherents for his views, and presently he gave Argyll his chance. This is not the place to discuss at length the details of what is called the 'Plot'— details which are still for the most part obscure. Montrose, his brother-in-law Napier, their nephew Sir George Stirling of Keir, and Keir's brother-in-law, Sir Archibald Stewart of Blackhall, used to meet and discuss public affairs, and the upshot of their deliberations was that the king must come to Scotland and meet Parliament. They resolved to communicate their views to Charles, and for the purpose selected a certain Walter Stewart, of the Traquair family, who happened to be journeying to London. A little later Montrose went to Scone to visit Lord Stormont, and there met Atholl, smarting under recent indignities, and John Stewart of Ladywell, the Commissary of Dunkeld. Some Covenanting ministers came to the house, among them the minister of his own parish of Auchterarder, and most unwisely Montrose unburdened himself in their presence on public discontents, and especially on the intentions of Argyll. Argyll, he said, had often spoken against the king, and even now was plotting a dictatorship. Argyll heard of these speeches and brought the matter before the committee. Montrose avowed responsibility and named his evidence. His witnesses, he said, were Lord Lindsay of the Byres, Stewart of Ladywell, Cassilis, and Mar. The witnesses were summoned, and proved unsatisfactory. Lindsay remembered the conversation, but said he had not named Argyll.

Ladywell at first stuck to his words, and then in a sudden fit of fear repudiated them. He was convicted under an old Scottish statute of leasing-making[6] and put to death. But the committee had made a better capture, no less than that Walter Stewart who had carried to the king the letter of Montrose and his friends. Stewart produced the letter, which in its tone was irreproachable; but he also produced papers written in a strange jargon, which was probably the product of his own half-witted fancy, but which to the committee had an ugly look of a secret cipher. Montrose and his three friends were arrested and lodged in Edinburgh Castle.

The chief prisoner refused to answer any questions before the committee, and demanded a public trial. His houses were broken into and his private papers examined, but nothing could be found more dangerous to the peace of the realm than some boyish love-letters. He was brought before the bar of Parliament, but his accusers could adduce no proof of guilt or extract any damning admission. The summer passed, and the king arrived in Edinburgh on August 14, 1641. On the surface his reception was magnificent. He went to church, discoursed courteously with the ministers, and was seen in public with old Leslie, who had lately led an army against him. But presently Argyll tightened his grip. Acts were passed, making the king's choice of ministers dependent upon the will of Parliament—a piece of modern constitutionalism, admirable in itself, which, lacking the machinery and safeguards of modern government, was simply to set a premium upon sectarian tyranny—and it was added that no one who had taken the king's side should be eligible for office. Well might Perth exclaim, 'If this be what you call liberty, God give me the old slavery again!' There were others in Scotland besides Montrose who saw the drift of these measures, and among one class of the nobles Argyll and his two jackals, Hamilton and Lanark, became the objects of hostile demonstrations. Montrose wrote twice from his prison praying for an interview with the king, and the third time he put his cards on the table and offered to prove that Argyll and Hamilton were traitors to the commonwealth. Charles, himself beginning to be of the same opinion, laid the letter before his chancellor and others of the nobles, and asked their advice.[7]

Now comes the curious performance known in history as the 'Incident.' On the evening of the 11th of October, so ran the gossip in the Edinburgh streets, Argyll, Hamilton, and Lanark were warned that their lives were in danger, and early next morning fled from the city. We shall never know the truth of the business. No doubt there were nobles, such as Ker and Crawford, with bands of retainers at their heels, who would gladly have taken the old Scots way of settling matters with their enemies. There were others, such as Carnwath, who made no secret of their view that there were now three kings of Scotland, and that two of them could be dispensed with. Parliament held an inquiry, but few facts emerged, for it was not conducted with much seriousness. The likeliest explanation is that Argyll and his friends took this way of escaping from the awkward corner in which Montrose's third letter had placed them. Argyll was a master of electioneering tricks; he knew that the suspicion of being in peril is a supreme asset to a leader. He returned to Edinburgh to be made a marquis, and to dictate the recipients of the great offices of state. Montrose and his friends were released a few weeks later on probation, after the king had bound himself not to employ them again or suffer them to approach his presence. The case against them was finally closed on March 16, 1642, and the four gentlemen, who had lain five months in prison without trial, or indeed without any specific charge, were informed that they owed their happy escape only to Argyll's clemency. The new marquis could afford to be generous to an antagonist whom in a game of plots and counterplots he had so signally outplayed.

CHAPTER V

THE RUBICON
(1642–1644)

SOMETIME during these years Montrose set down his views on government, and the paper still survives in the Advocates' Library, and is printed by Mark Napier in his 'Memoirs of Montrose.' It is in the form of a letter to a 'Noble Sir,' who may or may not have been Drummond of Hawthornden, but in its essence it is one of those confessions of faith by which sorely perplexed men have at all times striven to ease their souls. It may be questioned if the seventeenth century produced a more searching political treatise. It reveals, indeed, a capacity for abstract thought rare in all ages in a man of action, but especially rare in that turbid era when men fought for half-truths and died for fictions. He begins by laying down, almost in the words of the nineteenth-century John Austin, the true doctrine of 'Sovereign Power.' He had none of the contemporary faith in Divine Right, he had no brief even for the monarchy; he saw that sovereignty must ultimately reside in a free people, but might be delegated to a king, a council of nobles, or a parliament as was found most convenient. In the case of a monarchy this delegated sovereign power is limited by three other authorities—the law of God, the law of nature, and the law of the land;[8] an

33

advanced doctrine for Scotland in the year 1640. But no other limitation is possible. No section of the people can seize a part of sovereignty; for if sovereignty be divided, then follows anarchy, the oppression by subjects, which, as he says, is 'the most fierce, insatiable, and unsupportable tyranny in the world.' He desires free and frequent parliaments and stern measures with any law-breaking king; but he insists that when sovereignty has been granted on conditions, it must be inviolable so long as these conditions are observed. Then he goes on; he is speaking to the commons of Scotland,—

> 'Do you not know, when a monarchical government is shaken, the great ones strive for the garland with *your* blood and *your* fortunes? Whereby you gain nothing . . . but shall purchase to yourselves vultures and tigers to reign over your posterity, and yourselves shall endure all those miseries, massacres, and proscriptions of the Triumvirate of Rome—till the kingdom fall again into the hands of One.'

It is the old profound lesson of history, always taught and always forgotten. After anarchy comes the tyrant. The successors of the Gracchi are the Caesars; the blood and fury of the French Revolution are stamped out by Napoleon. Even in England at that moment the 'One' of whom Montrose prophesied was walking about in his sober country clothes and great buff boots, the man who was soon to clear out parliaments, and rule by force in an absolutism of which no Tudor ever dreamed.

To the holder of such views the way was becoming plain. To a man so far-sighted, so modern in his conception of the State, it was growing clear that the Covenant and its allies were in a fair way to restore the Middle Ages. Argyll and the ministers between them would have established a theocracy on a feudal basis, an omnipotent Kirk and a free licence to the worst aristocracy with which any country has been cursed, provided that aristocracy remained orthodox. Toleration was as remote from them as practical wisdom. They adopted a mediaeval creed of religious uniformity, and would have compelled it at the point of the sword. In 1640, after the fall of Newcastle, they demanded the abolition of Episcopacy in England, and the establishment of Presbyterianism against the will of at least three-fourths of the inhabitants. 'In the Paradise of Nature,' so ran the request, 'the diversity of flowers and herbs is useful, but in the Paradise of the Church different and contrary religions are unpleasant and hurtful: it is therefore to be wished that there were one Confession of Faith, one form of Catechism, one Directory, for the parts and public worship of God, as prayer, etc.; and one form of Church government in all the churches of his Majesty's dominions.' This was the view of Laud, though he favoured a different form from the Scots. Later they were to make the same demand in more ecstatic words, promising that the issue would be 'the voice of harpers harping with their harps, which shall fill the whole island with melody and mirth.' Between such a temper and Montrose's practical statesmanship there must be war to the death.

What of the people of Scotland? '*Quicquid delirant reges, plectuntur Achivi.*' Their condition had never been more wretched. The land was impoverished by petty wars and miserably and corruptly governed. Throughout all Montrose's writings and speeches there rings a note of pity for the common folk, who had to bear the brunt of their rulers' folly. 'Ye have oppressed the poor, and violently perverted judgment and justice,'—so ran his last tremendous indictment. Nor was there any revival of true spiritual life, such as has at other times attended a season of religious wars.[9] The hungry sheep were fed with windy politics. Let us take one witness, the famous Mr. Robert Law, author of Law's *Memorials,* a stout Covenanter who was ejected from his church in 1662. 'From the year 1652-1660,' he writes, and his words are notable, 'there was great good done by the preaching of the Gospel in the west of Scotland, more than was observed to have been for twenty or thirty years before; a great many brought into Christ Jesus by a saving work of conversion, which was occasioned by ministers preaching nothing through all that time but the Gospel, and had left off to preach up Parliaments, Armies, Leagues, Resolutions, and Remonstrances.'[10] The use of the Lord's Prayer was condemned by some zealots as being too much of a 'set form.' Private meetings for devotion were discouraged as savouring of Brownism—a strange policy for a Church which owned Livingstone and Samuel Rutherford. Religion, in a word, had ceased to be a quickening spirit, and become a *hortus siccus* of withered pedantries. Of the Kirk, now dominant in Scotland, Cromwell after Dunbar had certain truths to proclaim. 'By your hard and subtle words,' he told the ministers, 'you have begotten prejudice in those who do too much in matters of conscience—wherein every soul has to answer for itself to God—depend upon you. Your own guilt is too much for you to bear. . . Is it therefore infallibly agreeable to the word of God, all that you say? I beseech you in the bowels of Christ, think it possible that you may be mistaken. There may be a Covenant made with Death and Hell.'[11]

Montrose had a season of leisure before the storm burst. This, the last taste he was to have of peace with his wife and children, he spent probably in his house of Kincardine. Thither came a pleasant company of neighbours and kinsfolk, Napiers, Erskines, and Stirlings, and in the old halls by the Ruthven water children's play and the gossip of young voices varied the grave talk about the future of the land. In these months he may have written the lyric by which his name is best known in our literature. It is no song to the eyebrow of a mortal Sylvia, but one in which the ardour of the patriot is joined to the passion of the lover in singing of his mistress, Scotland, and what he will do for her if she trusts him. It breathes the same spirit as his 'Discourse on Sovereignty,' a hatred of sectarian war, a plea for that unity which had long fled from his distracted land. These verses are the confession of a soul which thought no risk too high for a noble end.

'My dear and only love, I pray
    That little world of thee
Be governed by no other sway
    Than purest monarchy;
For if confusion have a part
    (Which virtuous souls abhor),
And hold a synod in thine heart,
    I'll never love thee more.

'Like Alexander I will reign,
    And I will reign alone;
My thoughts did evermore disdain
    A rival on my throne.
He either fears his fate too much,
    Or his deserts are small,
That dares not put it to the touch,
    To win or lose it all.

'And in the empire of thine heart,
    Where I should solely be,
If others do pretend a part
    Or dare to vie with me,
Or if Committees thou erect,
    And go on such a score,
I'll laugh and sing at thy neglect,
    And never love thee more.

'But if thou wilt prove faithful then,
    And constant of thy word,
I'll make thee glorious by my pen,
    And famous by my sword;
I'll serve thee in such noble ways
    Was never heard before;
I'll crown and deck thee all with bays,
    And love thee more and more.'[12]

He was soon to be called to this test of manhood. Sir John Hotham had shut the gates of Hull in the king's face, and the English rebellion was begun. The General Assembly which sat in Edinburgh in July made it clear that the Covenant would side with Pym in the quarrel. On the 22nd of August, Charles raised the royal standard at Nottingham, and on the 23rd of October was fought the battle of Edgehill. Montrose set out for England to warn the king that the Scottish army, so far from being his bulwark as Hamilton had promised, was certain to join forces with his enemies. When he reached Newcastle he heard that the queen was in Yorkshire, and hastened to Bridlington Bay to inform that distracted lady, who had just been fired on by the Parliament fleet, of the graver menace in the north. He urged the immediate need of a royal warrant to authorize a Scottish loyalist rising. But the queen would not listen, Hamilton was still too powerful at court, and Montrose returned home with the reputation of an alarmist.

He did not wait long for his vindication. Under Charles's grant of triennial parliaments the next fell due in June 1664; but Argyll had business on hand and desired one a year earlier. Charles declined, so Argyll called a Convention of Estates on his own authority. Here was an act of rebellion, more final than that of Sir John Hotham's. Hamilton attended to watch, as he said, the royal interests, but Montrose and his friends stayed away. Instead they held a meeting of their own in the north, which was attended by loyalist nobles like Huntly, Marischal, and Ogilvy. Argyll took alarm, and the capture of Antrim in Ireland with a budget of letters from Aboyne and Nithsdale gave him the chance to raise the cry of a Popish invasion. Scotland was to be overrun by Irish kerns, and the 'true Protestant faith' was in danger. Commissioners from London had arrived, among them the younger Vane, to ask on behalf of the Parliament for 11,000 Scots. The troops were readily granted, Lanark using the royal seal for a warrant which levied war against its owner, and a new Covenant was devised by Vane and Henderson to bind still closer the Scottish and English Parliaments. This bond, the Solemn League and Covenant, was accepted by the Estates and ratified at Westminster by what was left of the English House, being thereafter solemnly subscribed in St. Margaret's Church on September 25, 1643. The old National Covenant had been drawn up by earnest men in defence of rational liberties; the new Covenant was a pact to destroy the Church of England, and force Presbytery down the throat of every man and woman in Britain. It was signed by English Parliamentarians because it was the price of the sorely needed Scottish help. It was extensively signed in Scotland, because the Covenanters saw to it that those who did not sign should suffer in person and estate.

War was inevitable, and Argyll never showed his astuteness more than in his last bid for Montrose's support. If others were blind to the powers of this young man of thirty, the dictator of Scotland knew capacity when he saw it. He knew that Montrose had been snubbed by the queen, and he hoped to catch him on the rebound. It was a mistake natural in one who recognized no loyalty but self-interest. Lord Leven, as Leslie had now become, had an army ready to march, and Montrose was offered the position of second in command. The offer was not at once refused, but it was hinted that certain scruples stood in the way. To solve them the Moderator of the Kirk, Alexander Henderson, was dispatched to interview the doubter. Henderson, one of the inspirers of the National Covenant, was a man of singular uprightness and purity of soul, but he held the impossible creed of Presbyterian domination as a law divinely established, and, as Clarendon said, he meddled more in temporal affairs than all the bishops together. Sometime during June 1643 he met Montrose on the banks of the Forth near Stirling. It was a curious meeting, the embarrassed Sir James Rollo,[13] Montrose's brother-in-law, acting as Henderson's second, and Napier, Keir, and Ogilvy being present as witnesses. The Moderator, taking Argyll's view of human nature, assumed that he was talking to a man only too anxious to be convinced, and frankly avowed that the Covenanters were about to send an army to England in support of the Parliament. He offered on behalf of the Estates to pay Montrose's debts, mainly incurred in legal expenses; and to give him any terms he asked for. Montrose replied that he could not come to an immediate decision, asked for time, and took a friendly leave of the strange embassy.

It was all that was needed to clinch his resolution. Now he knew that in truth he could look for no support from his old allies. The Covenant, as he read it, had chosen the path of rebellion and anarchy, and out of the anarchy must come in the long run Argyll's dictatorship, and the pitiless tyranny of Kirk and nobles. The one safety lay in Charles. He sent a report of the interview to the queen at Oxford and the king at Gloucester, and then set out himself for the south. With him went other of the loyalists, Crawford, Ogilvy, Kinnoul,[14] Nithsdale, and Aboyne. Against such a testimony Hamilton's smooth words could not stand. Presently Hamilton himself confessed the truth: Leven was about to cross the Border, and the Covenant had cast in its lot with Pym. He and Lanark came to Oxford to brazen it out, but Charles's eyes were open. Hamilton was arrested and sent a prisoner to Pendennis Castle in Cornwall, and his brother escaped, first to London and then to the Covenant army. At long last the king turned to the only man who could offer him any hope.

For six months Montrose stayed with the court at Oxford and prepared his plans. They seemed a desperate remedy. The only project he could offer was to 'raise Scotland for the king,' but it seemed as if Scotland had effectively risen for the king's opponents. Leven was over the Border, and the whole line of the Marches was commanded by the Covenant. They held every city and town in Scotland; Parliament and General Assembly alike were their creatures; the revenue of the country was in their hands; the great part of the nobles had joined their standard. A year ago there had been a chance; now it seemed the wildest of wild ventures. If the Scottish people were tired of their taskmasters, they had given no sign of it, and the supposed loyalists, with a few shining exceptions, had proved broken reeds at the best. But in the small inner circle of the royal councils, among men like Endymion Porter and Hyde and Digby, the grave purpose of the young Scottish earl commanded respect. They had the wit to recognize that a certain kind of spirit may win against all odds. In any case, it was no season for prudence. 'I will not,' said Montrose, 'distrust God's assistance in a righteous cause; and if it shall please your Majesty to lay your commands upon me for this purpose, your affairs will at any rate be in no worse case than they are at present, even if I should not succeed.'

He asked for little help. Antrim was to raise troops in Ireland and land in the west of Scotland to keep Argyll occupied in his own country. A body of horse from Newcastle's army would assist him to cut his way through the Lowlands to the Highland line. The King of Denmark might lend some German cavalry, and by hook or by crook a sufficient store of arms and ammunition must be transported to the north. Charles consented, and Antrim was dispatched to Ulster with instructions to land 2,000 troops in Argyll by April 1, 1644. Montrose was offered the commission of viceroy and captain-general of the royal forces in Scotland, but very wisely he declined; the title was bestowed on the king's nephew, Prince Maurice, and Montrose was content to be known as his lieutenant-general. He knew something of the jealous temper of the northern peers, and he had no desire to wreck his expedition on an empty name.

The six years of waiting were ended. The fates had cleared the stage, and the waverer had an issue of his perplexity. Words were to give place to deeds, the narrow streets of Edinburgh and the heavy air of conventions and assemblies to the clean winds and wide spaces of the hills. He had before him a straight path of duty, and little it troubled him that it ran into dark shadows. Once more he had recaptured his boyish ardour, and there was no happier man in the world than Montrose when on that March morning, with the ash-buds black in Magdalen gardens, he rode north out of Oxford to win a kingdom.

CHAPTER VI

THE CURTAIN RISES
(MARCH 1644–AUGUST 1644)

ST. THERESA, when she set out as a child to convert the
Moors, was engaged in an adventure scarcely less hopeful
than that which Montrose had now set himself. It seemed
the wildest of gambles against impossible odds. He was to
'raise Scotland for the king,' but where was he to find an
army? The best of the semi-professional levies were with
Leven in the north of England. The soldiers of fortune
from the German wars were few, and were already most-
ly under Leven's banner. He could get nothing from the
towns and villages of the Lowlands, for, whatever the feeling of the people, the Kirk and the Estates had a firm
control of the machinery of enlistment. There were the
nobles and gentry, of course; but most of the former, certainly the most powerful, were Covenanters, and, even if it
had been otherwise, were far too jealous and self-centred
to follow one of no higher rank than their own in a cause
which at the best was forlorn. Did he hope that his words
of wisdom, his far-seeing political doctrines, would carry
conviction to a backward peasantry, harassed by temporal
want on the one side, and the fear of eternal damnation
on the other? Besides, was he not planning to bring
Antrim's Irishry to his aid? and Antrim's Irishry, though

43

most of them were Scots, seemed to the Lowlanders so many emissaries of the Pope and the devil! With such allies he would not attach a single doubting Presbyterian to his standard.

The truth seems to be that, as in most great adventures, there was no solid hope save in the soul of the adventurer. In a desperate case the man who risks most is probably the wisest, and Montrose staked everything on the speed and gallantry of his spirit. It seems impossible that he can at this time have intended to raise the Highlands. He relied on his kinsmen and friends in Perth and Angus, and he had some hope of the Gordons. It was the gentry of the northern Lowlands in whom he trusted—if he trusted in any one besides himself—and not in the clans of the hills. Probably at the time he knew very little about the Highlands, and his experience in the First Bishops' War would not prepossess him in favour of the desultory bands who accompanied Huntly's Lowland levies to battle. Had he known more he would not have been greatly encouraged. There were no ordinary politics among the hills. The chiefs were Royalists only in as much as they were not Covenanters. He could, indeed, have counted on the assistance of all those who hated the name of Campbell—the Clan Chattan, the Clan Donald, the Stewarts, the Camerons, and the Macleans. But Seaforth and his Mackenzies would never fight on the same side as a Macdonald, and, if he enlisted the Gordons, he might look to find the Grants in the other camp.

If Montrose's mission was desperate in purpose, it was no less desperate in its lack of a base. He flung himself into the midst of a hostile country to improvise his army. Nothing could be looked for from the king. Even had Charles been that ideal monarch whom Montrose, out of a few interviews, had created in his fancy, he could have done little to help his champion. As it was he passed from blunder to blunder, enraging by his duplicity both friend and foe. The man who fought for a

Stuart must be content to wage war without reserves. His life and his reputation alike must be in his own keeping.

Accompanied by Ogilvy and others of his friends, Montrose made for Newcastle's camp. He found that unfortunate and by no means skilful general at Durham, and in the worst of spirits. Leven was at his gates, and Fairfax and Manchester were closing up on him from the south. He received Montrose with courtesy, but gave him little help. A hundred ill-mounted troopers and two brass cannon were the most the perplexed nobleman could spare for the conquest of Scotland. Another disappointment was in store, for old Carnwath, who happened to be in Newcastle's camp, refused to accept from Montrose's hands the king's commission as lieutenant of Clydesdale. It was a foretaste of the spirit of even the loyal among the Scots nobles. Newcastle, however, called out for him the militia of the northern counties, and sundry local gentlemen joined his standard. It was with a force of some thirteen hundred men that he crossed the Border on the 13th of April and marched towards Dumfries. But he had not forded the Annan before trouble began. The English militia, worked upon by Sir Richard Graham of Netherby, deserted. With his few hundred followers he reached Dumfries, and occupied the town without opposition. The provost, a Maxwell, welcomed him gladly, and a few months later swung for it in Edinburgh.

It was very soon apparent that nothing could be done in the Lowlands. The Maxwells and Johnstones of the Dumfries neighbourhood were in no mood to rise, and their heads, Nithsdale and Hartfell, were jealous of the new commander. Annandale, Morton, Roxburgh, and Traquair, though nominally Royalists, refused, like Carnwath, the king's commission of lieutenancy, by means of which Montrose had hoped to organize a powerful opposition.[15] Further east, Lothian was hot for the Parliament, and the 'bauld Buccleuch' was commanding— with little credit to himself—a regiment under Leven.

The peasantry round about were under the thumb of the ministers and fickle noblemen like Glencairn. Montrose issued a declaration explaining that he was now in arms for the king, on the same principle as he had once been in arms for the Covenant—'for the defence and maintenance of the true Protestant religion, his Majesty's just and sacred authority, the fundamental laws and privileges of Parliament, the peace and freedom of oppressed and enthralled subjects.' 'Knew I not perfectly,' he added, 'his Majesty's intention to be such, and so real as is already expressed, I should never at all have embarked myself in his service. Nor did I but see the least appearance of his Majesty's change from these resolutions or any of them, I should never continue longer my faithful endeavour in it.'[16] But he was talking a language which the burghers of Dumfries, and for that matter the Scots people, did not understand. 'It was not,' in Mr. Gardiner's words, 'for the restoration of a dead past that he drew his sword. He stood up for that which was, in some sort, the hope of the future.'[17] And the language of the future is always strange in contemporary ears. Montrose lingered on, waiting for news of Antrim's men; which seems to argue that Galloway, instead of Argyll, may have been one of their possible objectives. But no news came. He received, however, a message of another kind from his niece, Lady Stirling of Keir, inviting him on behalf of the commander, Lord Sinclair, to take possession of the castle of Stirling and the town of Perth. Sinclair and his second in command, Sir James Turner, were probably sincere in their offer; but it was lucky for Montrose that he did not attempt to accept it. For the Covenant had got wind of the intentions of the pair, and while Montrose was reading the letter, Callander, with Sinclair and Turner in tow, was marching south. Callander—who had once been Almond and a party to the Cumbernauld Bond—presently occupied Dumfries, while Montrose and his handful recrossed the Border. Meanwhile two events had befallen the Royalist leader. He had received his patent of marquis from the king, and had been excommunicated by the Kirk in Edinburgh. The latter honour was also conferred at the same time upon Huntly, who had just been attempting an aimless and ill-managed rising in the north, and was now hiding in Strathnaver.

For two months Montrose waited for Scottish news and kept Callander busy on the western Marches. Meantime Newcastle had flung himself into York, where he was closely beset by Leven, Fairfax, and Manchester. The centre of the war was shifting northward, but Montrose had no better share in it than desultory Border fighting. He got together a few troops, and captured Morpeth after a siege of twenty days. This exploit, performed without a single cannon, has scarcely been given the credit it deserves.[18] He collected supplies in Northumberland, and succeeded in getting them into Newcastle-on-Tyne. Presently he received a summons from Prince Rupert, then marching through Lancashire to the relief of York. He set off to join him, but before they met the king's cause had suffered its first crushing disaster. Rupert indeed relieved York, but on the 2nd of July, about five in the afternoon, he met the Parliamentary forces on Marston Moor, and discovered that new thing in England—the shock of Cromwell's horse. His army was scattered, Newcastle fled overseas, and he himself with some six thousand troops rode west into the hills. Two days after the battle, Montrose found him in an inn at Richmond, but Rupert had nothing to give; on the contrary, he stood much in need of Montrose's scanty recruits. So with a sad heart the new marquis rode by Brough and Appleby to Carlisle, to indite his report to the king.

Four months had passed and nothing had been done. Ogilvy and Sir William Rollo had journeyed secretly into Scotland, and had returned with ill news. The land lay quiet under the Covenant, and Antrim's levies seemed to have vanished into the air. The nobles, headed by Traquair, were tumbling over each other in their anxiety to swear fealty to Argyll. There seemed nothing to be done except to surrender the royal commission, and go abroad to wait for a happier time. So his friends advised, and Montrose made a pretence of acquiescing. He set out for the south with the others, having taken Ogilvy into his confidence. A little way from Carlisle he slipped behind, but as his servants and baggage went on it was presumed that he was following. Had he continued he would have shared in the capture of the whole party by Fairfax at Ribble Bridge.

He had resolved on the craziest of ventures. He would break through the Covenanting cordon in the Lowlands and win to his own country. There, at any rate, were loyal hearts, and something might be devised to turn the tide. He chose as his companions the lame Sir William Rollo (who had been on Ogilvy's expedition a month before) and an officer who had fought under him in the Bishops' War, Colonel Sibbald. They wore the dress of Leven's troopers, while Montrose followed behind as their groom, riding one ill-conditioned beast and leading another.

It was a dangerous road to travel. The country was strewn with broken men and patrolled by Covenanting horse, and a gentleman in those days was not so easily disguised. At first all went smoothly. Passing through the woods of Netherby, they learned that Sir Richard Graham had joined the Covenant, and in its interests had constituted himself Warden of the Marches. His servant, from whom they had the news, spoke freely, as if to Leven's troopers. A little further on they fell in with a Scot, one of Newcastle's soldiers, who disregarded the troopers, but paid great attention to their groom, hailing him by his proper title. Montrose tried to deny it; but the man exclaimed, 'What, do I not know my Lord Marquis of Montrose well enough? But go your way, and God be with you.' A gold piece rewarded the untimely well-wisher.

The journey must have grown daily more anxious till the Forth was passed. 'It may be thought,' says Patrick Gordon, 'that God Almighty sent His good angel to lead the way, for he went, as if a cloud had environed him, through all his enemies.' We do not know the road they travelled–whether by Annandale and then by Tweed or Clyde, or up Eskdale and thence over the Tweedside range to the Lothians. The safest way was probably to follow the belt of moorland which runs north by Carnwath almost to the Highland hills. The distance from Carlisle to Perth can be little short of a hundred miles, and the party made good progress, riding both by day and night. On the fourth day they came into the Montrose lands in Stirling and Strathearn, but they did not draw rein till they reached the house of Tullibelton between Perth and Dunkeld. Here lived Patrick Graham of Inchbrakie, one of the best loved of all the Montrose kinsmen, and here was safe shelter for the traveller while he spied out the land and looked about for an army.

The curtain rises, and the first act of the great drama reveals a forlorn little party late on an August evening knocking at the door of a woodland tower above the shining reaches of Tay. The king's lieutenant-general makes a very modest entry on the scene. Two followers, four sorry horses, little money and no baggage, seem a slender outfit for the conquest of a kingdom; but in six months he was to see Scotland at his feet.

CHAPTER VII

TIPPERMUIR
(SEPTEMBER 1644)

FOR six days the royal lieutenant lay close in hiding, while his comrades scoured the country for news. Tullibelton was too near the Lowland town of Perth, and its laird too noted a loyalist, for his guest to run needless risks, and Montrose spent most of his time in the woods and hills, sleeping at night in hunters' bothies. The scouts returned with a melancholy report. Huntly had made a mess of it in the north, and the Gordons were leaderless and divided, while the influence of their uncle, Argyll, was driving Huntly's sons to the Covenant camp. Some of the Graham and Drummond kinsmen, even, with the alternative of prison and fines before them, were in arms for the Estates. There were rumours of Covenant levies in Aberdeenshire, and Argyll in the west had his clan in arms. Montrose in his despondency may well have wondered at this strange activity. The tide of war had rolled over the Border, and with Scotland in so iron a grip such precautions may well have seemed odd to one who knew the economical spirit of the Estates.

He was soon to learn the reason, and at the same time recognize his opportunity. The incident is best told in the words of Patrick Gordon, who had the story from Montrose's own lips:—

'As he was one day in Methven Wood, staying for the night, because there was no safe travelling by day, he became transported with sadness, grief, and pity to see his native country thus brought into miserable bondage and slavery through the turbulent and blind zeal of some preachers; and now persecuted by the unlawful and ambitious ends of some of the nobility, and so far had they already prevailed that the event was much to be feared, and by good patriots to be lamented. And therefore, in a deep grief and unwonted ravishment, he besought the Divine Majesty, with watery eyes and a sorrowful heart, that His justly kindled indignation might be appeased and, His mercy extended, the cause removed; and that it might please Him to make him a humble instrument therein, to His Holy and Divine Majesty's greater glory. While he was in this thought, lifting up his eyes, he beholds a man coming the way to St. Johnston (Perth) with a fiery cross in his hand. Hastily stepping towards him, he inquired what the matter meant? The messenger told him that Coil Mac Gillespick—for so was Alexander Macdonald called by the Highlanders—was entered in Athole with a great army of the Irish, and threatened to burn the whole country if they did not rise with him against the Covenant, and he, the messenger, was sent to advertise St. Johnston that all the country might be raised to resist him.'

Antrim's levies had come out of the mist at last. Presently he received a letter from Alastair Macdonald himself, directed to the king's lieutenant-general at Carlisle. The messenger who carried it asked directions from Inchbrakie, who took the dispatch and promised to deliver it. In the letter Macdonald announced his arrival and begged for instructions. If Montrose needed help, no less did the Irish commander.

Alastair Macdonald was of the ancient stock of Dunyveg in Islay, the son of a Colonsay Macdonald, commonly called Coll Keitach, or 'Coll who can fight with either hand.' The name was corrupted into Colkitto, and transferred by the Lowlanders from the father to the son.

Sorley Boy Macdonald, the father of the first Earl of Antrim, had been his father's great-uncle. The Macdonnells of Antrim were near blood relations of Alastair's own people, the Macdonalds of Islay and Kintyre, and the Campbell oppression of the latter clan had left bitter memories on both sides of the North Channel.

When Antrim, after many difficulties with the Supreme Council, had by the end of June raised 1,600 recruits, he turned to Alastair, a man of vast size and proved courage, to lead them against his ancestral foe. Early in July the invaders landed in Ardnamurchan, an old territory of the Macdonalds, and proceeded to exact vengeance on the unfortunate Campbell settlers. The king's quarrel was forgotten in a more intimate and personal strife. Alastair ravaged the peninsula with fire and sword, and seized as a base the castle of Mingaray and the old keep of Lochaline, which still stands where the little river Aline enters the sea. He sent messengers through the West Highlands to summon the other Macdonalds to help him in his task. But the hand of Clan Diarmaid lay heavy on Glencoe and the Isles, and he got few recruits. Soon his position became desperate, for Argyll was raising an army for revenge; so he swept back to his base, only to find that all his ships had been destroyed. Alastair, though an indifferent general, was a bold fighter, and he resolved to bid for Gordon support, though it meant marching across the breadth of Scotland. He led his troops through Morvern and round by the head of Loch Eil to the glens of Lochaber, the western fringe of Huntly's country. Here he had his second piece of ill-tidings. Huntly's revolt was over, and the Gordons had made their peace with the Covenant. There was nothing for it but to try the more northern clans, and his next venture was Kintail. But the Mackenzies, little though they loved the Campbells, had a long memory of Macdonald misdeeds, and their chief, Seaforth, warned off the intruders. Headed back on all sides Alastair decided that the boldest course was the safest. He marched south again to Badenoch on the head waters of the Spey, and himself issued a summons calling on the clans to rise in the name of the king and Huntly. This brought him some five hundred recruits, most of them Gordons; but he could get no nearer the heart of that powerful clan, for the Grants, Forbeses, and Frasers blocked the road down Spey, and 1,000 of Seaforth's Mackenzies lent their aid. Alastair now seemed in a fair way to be exterminated. The Campbells intercepted his retreat to the sea, and Argyll was hot-foot on his track. Seaforth cut him off from the north and east, the new Badenoch levies were mutinous and distrustful, and south lay the unfriendly Lowlands and clans like the Stewarts of Atholl, who would never serve under any leader of an alien name. He had proved that whoever might band the Highlands into an army, it would not be a man of Highland blood. Hence his despairing letter to the king's lieutenant-general asking for help and instructions. He can scarcely have hoped for much from his appeal, for Carlisle was a far cry from Badenoch, and he had the enemy on every side.

Montrose sent back an answer, bidding Alastair be of good heart and await him at Blair. It must have seemed a hard saying to a man who believed that his correspondent was still at Carlisle, but he obeyed and marched into the braes of Atholl. The local clans resented his intrusion, the fiery cross was sent round, and at any moment there was the likelihood of a desperate conflict between two forces who alike detested the Covenant and followed the king. The Irish levies were stout fellows in hard condition, but they were uncouthly dressed, wild-eyed from much travel, and, after their custom, attended by a mob of half-starved women and children. The Atholl clans living on the fringe of the Lowlands may well have looked askance at such outlandish warriors.

The situation was saved by a hairbreadth. Montrose, accompanied by Patrick Graham the younger of Inch-brakie—Black Pate, as the countryside called him—set off on foot over the hills to keep the tryst. He had acquired, probably from Inchbrakie, a Highland dress—the trews, a short coat, and a plaid round his shoulders. He wore, we are told, a blue bonnet with a bunch of oats as a badge, and he carried a broadsword and a Highland buckler. Thus accoutred he entered upon the scene in the true manner of romance, unlooked for and invincible. Alastair and his ragged troops were waiting hourly on battle, when across the moor they saw two figures advancing. Black Pate was known to every Atholl man, and there were many who had seen Montrose. Loud shouts of welcome apprised the Ulsterman that here was no bonnet-laird, and when he heard that it was indeed the king's lieutenant he could scarcely believe his eyes. He had looked for cavalry, an imposing bodyguard, and a figure more like his own swashbuckling self than this slim young man with the quiet face and searching grey eyes.

In a moment all quarrels were forgotten. Montrose revealed his commission and Alastair gladly took service under him, thankful to be out of a plight which for weeks had looked hopeless. The Atholl Highlanders were carried off their feet by the grace and fire of their new leader. The Stewarts and Robertsons, to the number of 800, brought to his standard those broadswords which that morning had been dedicated to cutting Ulster throats. Montrose slept the night at the house of Lude, and next morning unfurled the royal standard on a green knoll above the Tilt. The king's lieutenant had got him an army.

At first sight it seemed an indifferent force. At the most it numbered 2,500 men. The Highlanders were active fellows, accustomed to an outdoor life, but their equipment was fantastic, for only a few carried claymores, and most were armed with pikes, sticks, and bows and arrows. Alastair's Ulstermen were regular soldiers, inured to discipline, and seasoned by hard campaigns, and they had the advantage of bearing firearms. But these firearms were old match–locks, and the stock of ammunition was so low that only one round remained for each man. There was no artillery, and, since horses were scarce in the Highlands, the only cavalry mounts were three of the unfortunate beasts that had carried Montrose and his friends from Carlisle. If a blow was to be struck it must be at once, for the Council was arming against the invaders, though as yet Edinburgh had no news of Montrose. Elcho was at Perth with a large force of burghers and men from Fife and the Perthshire Lowlands. Lord Balfour of Burleigh had another army at Aberdeen, with the young Gordons serving under him; while from the west Argyll was leading his formidable clan to avenge the smoking homesteads of Morvern and Ardnamurchan. Montrose had no supplies, no reserve of ammunition, no means of increasing his force except by victory. He must fight at once, and he chose the nearest enemy.

On the 30th day of August he led his men from Blair through the hills to Loch Tummel, and thence by the eastern side of Schiehallion to Aberfeldy. The same night they crossed the Tay. At dawn next morning Black Pate led on the Atholl men as an advance guard, and the army marched with Highland swiftness across Strathbran and by the Sma' Glen to the Almond. There at the Hill of Buchanty they fell in with an unexpected reinforcement. Lord Kilpont, the eldest son of the Earl of Menteith: David Drummond, the Master of Maderty: and Sir John Drummond, Lord Perth's younger son, had raised 500 bowmen at the order of the Estates to oppose Alastair's invasion. The leaders were kin to the Graham house, and when they knew that it was Montrose who was advancing their purpose changed. They gladly joined the royal general, and brought him a welcome accession of stalwart peasants, who, living on the border line between Highlands and Lowlands, had some of the virtues of both. The force crossed the ridge to Strathearn, and spent the night on the moor of Fowlis.

It was now Sunday, the 1st of September. Elcho had nearly seven thousand men, including a body of seven hundred horse, and nine pieces of artillery. He had ample munitions of war, and his troops were fortified by the Sabbath-morning exhortations of a convoy of ministers. To give these latter their due, says Wishart, 'they plied their lungs stoutly in the performance of that work; they most freely promised them, in the name of Almighty God, an easy and unbloody victory. Nay, there was one Frederick Carmichael . . . who was not afraid to deliver this passage in his sermon, "If ever God spake word of truth out of my mouth, I promise you in His name assured victory this day."' With Elcho, too, was the flower of the neighbouring Covenanting gentry, including Lord Murray of Gask,[19] and some who were not Covenanting, like Lord Drummond; and he had the assistance of at least one experienced professional soldier, Sir James Scott of Rossie, who had just come from serving under the flag of Venice. Little wonder that the Covenant forces were in good heart. They had seen something of the Highlander in the First Bishops' War, and thought little of his prowess. They knew that Alastair's troops were in rags—as one of the ministers described them, 'naked, weaponless, ammunitionless, cannonless men.' Their view was that of Elspeth's ballad in *The Antiquary*:—

'My horse shall ride through ranks sae rude,
As through the moorland fern;
Then ne'er let gentle Norman blude
Grow cauld for Highland kerne.'

Besides, they outnumbered the enemy by nearly three to one. So, early in the day, Elcho with his army marched three miles out to Tippermuir, accompanied by many of the Perth citizens who were not unwilling to see a surprising judgment fall upon their ancient foes.

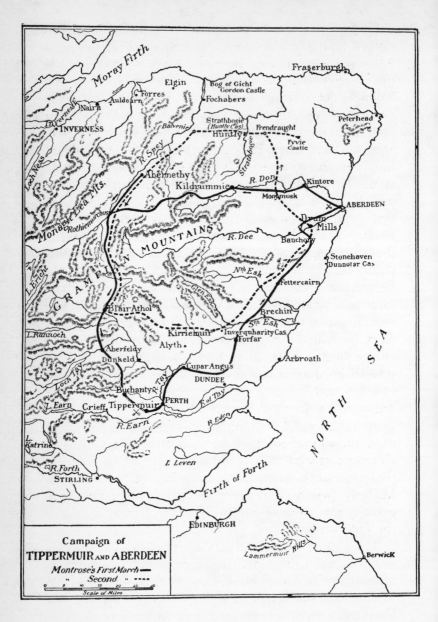

Campaign of
TIPPERMUIR AND **ABERDEEN**

Montrose's First March ————
Second " - - - - -

Scale of Miles

He took up a good position in open ground where his cavalry had room to move. Montrose had at the most 3,000 men—including probably 1,200 Ulstermen, 500 of Alastair's Badenoch recruits, 800 Atholl men, and Kilpont's 500 bowmen. His cavalry, as we have noted, was confined to the three lean horses from Carlisle. The most pressing lack was ammunition, for only the Irish had guns, and they had but one round apiece. On Tippermuir, however, there were plenty of stones, and with these as missile-weapons he bade the rest arm themselves. He put the Irish under Alastair in the centre of his little force, and Kilpont with his bowmen on the left, while he himself led his Atholl men on the right flank, where they were opposed to Sir James Scott's horse. He saw clearly that Elcho with his cavalry would surround him if he did not strike straight at his heart. Further, he knew something of the temper of the unwilling Lowland levies —men drawn from the counter and the plough-tail to a work for which they had little stomach. To such the wild charge of the clans would be a new experience. Then, true to his duty as a constitutional commander, he sent Maderty with a flag of truce to inform Elcho that he was acting under the royal commission, that he wished above all things to avoid shedding Scottish blood, and to summon him to remember his due and lawful allegiance. The Covenanters were to show at all times a curious dislike of the etiquette of civilized warfare. They promptly made Maderty prisoner and sent him to Perth, telling him genially that they would attend to his beheading when the fight was over.

The contest began with a skirmish. Lord Drummond rode out from the Covenant army with a squadron, in order to entice Montrose into one of those partial attacks to which an undisciplined army is prone. It was the one glimmer of tactical knowledge that Elcho displayed. But Montrose was ready. He had drawn up his men in a long line only three deep, with instructions to the Irish to kneel and fire their pieces when they were within range, and to the ranks behind to deliver a volley of stones. The volley sent Drummond flying and halted Elcho's advance. Then Montrose gave the order to charge. From behind the smoke came the fierce kerns of Ulster and Badenoch, with pike and claymore and Lochaber axe. The shouts of men who had to win or perish struck terror into the Lowland hearts. Elcho's centre crumpled like paper, and in a few minutes was racing back on the road to Perth. On the Covenant left alone was there any serious resistance. There stood Scott with his horse on rising ground, and for a little he and the Atholl men disputed the hill. But Montrose soon won the crest, and the cavalry fled with the others. The place was littered with lathered horse and panting foot.[20]

Then followed a grim slaughter. Scarcely a dozen fell in the battle, but nearly two thousand died in the rout; some from the swords of Montrose, some from sheer fatigue, for we are told that nine or ten Perth burgesses succumbed unwounded to their unusual exertions. Presently the enemy were at the gates of Perth, and the city surrendered without a word. Cannons, arms, supplies, tents, colours, drums, baggage, all were the spoil of the victors. Montrose kept his wild force in check. He refused to allow the captured guns to be turned against the fugitives, and he would not permit his men to rob or slay within the walls. He contented himself with fining the burghers £50, which went to Alastair, who was in desperate straits for money, and he levied a large contribution of cloth to amend the raggedness of his army.

For three days Montrose tarried at Perth. He took up his quarters in the town, in the house of one Margaret Donaldson, and sent to Kinnaird for his old tutor, William Forrett, and his two elder sons, Lord Graham and Lord James. Like Cromwell, he had the ministers to dinner, and one of them was afterwards taken to task by the Presbytery for saying grace at his table. Meantime his victory did not bring him the recruits he had hoped for, Lord Dupplin[21] being the only man of note who arrived at his camp. The Highlanders, according to their custom, made off to their homes to secrete their booty, and his force was soon reduced to little more than Alastair's Irishry. There were two other armies waiting to be met, and one of them, Argyll's, was approaching rapidly from the west. Montrose decided that his force was not sufficient to oppose Argyll, and at that time he does not seem to have been aware of the existence of Lord Balfour at Aberdeen. His immediate aim was to collect recruits in his own county of Angus, and, if possible, capture Dundee.[22] On the 4th of September he left Perth, and crossing the Tay, reached the neighbourhood of Coupar-Angus.

That night the camp was stirred by a tragedy. Young Lord Kilpont shared a tent with James Stewart of Ardvoirlich. A quarrel arose in the small hours, and Stewart stabbed Kilpont to the heart, killed two sentries, and with his son and some friends escaped to the Covenanters. Argyll procured him a pardon from the Estates, and, to give further proof of his partiality for assassination, issued a proclamation offering a sum of money to any one who would slay Montrose and exhibit his head to the Parliament in Edinburgh. The murderer was also to have a free pardon for any crimes he might have been unfortunate enough to commit in the past. Mr. Gardiner dryly points out the inconsistency of this course. 'When Argyll desolated the Highland glens with fire and sword, he was but inflicting due punishment on barbarians. When Montrose gathered the Highlanders to the slaughter of the burghers and farmers of the Lowlands, he placed himself outside the pale of civilized warfare.'[23] The natural presumption from Argyll's reception of Stewart was that Stewart had been endeavouring to anticipate the wishes of the Estates, and had tried to persuade Kilpont, who had refused. For such a view there is no evidence, and it is intrinsically unlikely. Kilpont would have offered barren soil for such a proposal, and Stewart knew this as well as anybody. It is more probable that the account given in Stewart's official pardon is the true one. He had proposed to desert, and Kilpont, divining his intention, tried to prevent him and was slain. Or, if we like, we can take the family tradition referred to by Scott in his *Legend of Montrose,* that Stewart had challenged Alastair, that Kilpont had them both arrested, and that afterwards in their cups Kilpont and Stewart had words which ended in the fatal blow. Argyll and the Estates have so many deeds of violence on their shoulders that the impartial historian is glad to relieve them of one.

CHAPTER VIII

ABERDEEN AND FYVIE
(SEPTEMBER-DECEMBER 1644)

DUNDEE proved out of the question. It was too well garrisoned for 1,500 men to take, and the guns captured at Tippermuir were no siege-pieces. Montrose moved accordingly to the upper waters of the Esks in the hope of enlisting some of the loyal gentlemen of Angus. Here he had definite word of Lord Balfour's army at Aberdeen, which determined his next step. The Angus recruits came in slowly. Lord Airlie indeed appeared, the father of Lord Ogilvy who bad been captured at Ribble Bridge. No Ogilvy was ever anything but a king's man, and two of the sons, Sir Thomas and Sir David, accompanied their father. With the Gordons Montrose fared no better than had Alastair Macdonald. Huntly was still lurking among the bogs of Strathnaver. Aboyne, the second son, was fighting for the king in the garrison at Carlisle, and Lord Gordon, the heir, and his younger brother, Lord Lewis, were with Balfour at Aberdeen. The clan, however, was not wholly unrepresented in the royal army. Nathaniel Gordon had stood with Huntly in his rising, and now rode joyfully to join the new king's lieutenant. He was an intrepid and seasoned soldier, but as rash as any subaltern of Alastair's. It is a pity that no romancer has made him the subject of a tale, for his career, both early and late, offers rich material. Before he took part in politics, brigandage, piracy, and the rabbling of Mr. Andrew Cant had been among the simple diversions of his life. With Airlie had come forty-four horsemen, so the little army was not without its cavalry.

Keeping to the skirts of the hills Montrose marched through the Mearns, and crossed the Dee about midway between Banchory and the Mills of Drum. Crathes Castle, the stronghold of the Burnets of Leys, lay on the north bank, and was peacefully surrendered. Burnet was a staunch Covenanter, but he entertained the royal lieutenant hospitably, and indeed offered him a sum of money. The following day, the 12th of September, the army advanced down the river to within two miles of the town of Aberdeen, where they found Balfour awaiting them. Montrose had avoided the main road, having no desire to dispute the strongly-fortified bridge of Dee, but the Covenanters had had ample warning, and had taken up a good position on the slope of a hill. A lane ran downwards from their centre, and around the foot of it were houses and gardens, which were strongly held. Balfour had some 2,000 foot, 500 cavalry, and better artillery than the guns brought from Tippermuir. The cavalry seem to have been chiefly the gentry of the northern Lowlands, like the Forbeses, Frasers, and Crichtons, and twenty horse were under the separate command of Lord Lewis Gordon. The infantry were the usual Covenanting levies, including a proportion of Aberdeen townspeople, and the remnants of Elcho's Fife regiment. It was Montrose's business to beat this force as soon as possible, for Argyll was lumbering in his wake, and Fabian tactics would land him between two fires.

On the morning of the 13th, according to his custom, he sent in an envoy to the magistrates of the city summoning them to surrender, and advising them, at any rate, to send the women and children to a place of safety. It was a merciful act, which was ungenerously requited, for a drummer-boy who accompanied the messenger was brutally slain by one of the Fife troopers. A breach of the laws of war always offended Montrose, and this was a peculiarly wanton breach. He vowed to make the enemy pay dearly for the misdeed, and promised Alastair the sack of the city if the day was won. Without delay he drew up his forces for battle. The Irish as before held the centre, and on the right wing Sir William Rollo and Colonel James Hay commanded, while Nathaniel Gordon led the left. He divided his cavalry into equal portions, and placed one on each wing, while in both cases he stiffened the score of horsemen with musketeers and bowmen interspersed among them. The little force was the nearest approach to a regular army that he had yet commanded, for every one was adequately armed, and nearly all had some experience of war. Balfour, who was nothing of a general, was content with his superior position, heavier guns, and more numerous cavalry. He had little authority and no plan of battle, and his lieutenants followed their own devices.

The fight began with an attack on the houses and gardens that protected the Covenant centre. Alastair had little difficulty in driving the enemy out of these and advancing up the slope. Presently Lord Lewis Gordon charged with his twenty horse on Montrose's left, and Lord Fraser and Crichton of Fren draught[24] followed, but they knew nothing of the value of shock tactics, and sporadic assaults of this sort were easy to repulse. On the Covenant's left wing the cavalry had apparently no orders, and at first sat staring at the battle.

Soon, however, an unexpected danger threatened Montrose. Some wiser head among the Covenanters had sent 100 horse and 400 foot round his left wing by a mill road which was out of sight of the combatants. The device all but succeeded. They turned the Royalist flank, and in a few minutes would have taken Nathaniel Gordon in the rear. But they were too slow, and Montrose had time to bring up Rollo's horse from his own right, and to push 100 musketeers against them. In a little the attackers became the attacked, their cavalry fled, and few of the infantry returned to tell the tale. Sir William Forbes of Craigievar had charged Montrose's right when Rollo had been drawn off to the left wing. The attack fell wholly upon Alastair's infantry, and gallantly they met it. They opened their ranks and let the troopers sweep through; then facing round they pursued them with volleys. The Covenant horse were soon out of action.[25]

It was the turning-point of the fight, which had now lasted for several hours. Montrose, who had darted from flank to flank, reinforcing and cheering his troops, called on his men for a general charge. The Irish responded with enthusiasm, the whole force swept forward, and the Covenanting centre broke and fled. The ground between the battlefield and the city walls was a scene of heavy slaughter, and Alastair's men, mindful of Montrose's promise before the fight, burst into the streets in pursuit. No doubt the horrors of that sack have been greatly exaggerated, and the evidence in particular of the killing of women is far from conclusive;[26] but enough is established to convict Montrose of a share in a grievous barbarity. It was the only time in his life that he was guilty of needless bloodshed, and natural indignation at the boy's murder, and a rash promise to Alastair, are no defence for one who must be judged by the highest standards. He seems indeed to have repented, and tried at the last moment to save the city,[27] but the mischief had been done. The sack of Aberdeen was not only a crime, it was a gross blunder. It was no Covenanting city, and the majority of those who perished had been forced into the fight—as Spalding says, 'harllit out sore against their wills to fight against the King's lieutenant.' He had spoiled his chance of getting recruits for the king among the burghers of Deeside. All over Scotland, too, the tale, zealously disseminated by the

Covenanters, and of course wildly exaggerated, must have deterred moderate men from casting in their lot with one whose methods seemed more like a Tilly or a Wallenstein than a kindly Scot.

After waiting three days, on Monday, the 16th of September, Montrose left the city and marched by Kintore and Inverurie up the Don valley. Two days later the heavy-footed Argyll entered Aberdeen, and proceeded to exact contributions from the surviving citizens. Soon the news of the battle reached Edinburgh, and began to disquiet the Estates. Argyll might be a pillar of the Kirk, but he was very slow in bringing the malefactors to book. The Scottish Covenanters in London held an edifying debate, according to Baillie, as to whether their misfortunes were due 'to the sins of the Assembly, the sins of the Parliament, the sins of the army, or the sins of the people.' Requisitions were sent to Leven at Newcastle, who dispatched 1,000 of his best troops, including a body of cavalry. Lothian, Argyll's master of horse, apparently received the reinforcements under Marischal somewhere in Aberdeenshire. Meanwhile Montrose had made another desperate appeal to the Gordons, but the clan was dumb. They would not stir without Huntly's word, and Huntly, jealous of a royal commission which interfered with his own lieutenancy of the north, and not forgetful of his treatment by Montrose in the First Bishops' War, refused to give it. The place was getting unhealthy for a loyalist with Argyll a day's march off, so Montrose retreated into the hill country around Rothiemurchus, and somewhere on the road be buried the cannon which he had captured in Aberdeen.[28] Here Alastair left him on an expedition of his own, to raise recruits among the Clan Donald, and to see to the security of his castles of Mingary and Lochaline. Montrose had probably now little more than five hundred men behind him.

At Rothiemurchus he fell seriously ill; it was rumoured in the south that he was dead; and from Lowland pulpits the Almighty was publicly thanked for espousing the Covenant's quarrel. But the illness was short, and by the 4th of October he was getting his men south into Atholl. Now began what Baillie calls a 'strange coursing,' Montrose leading the dance, and Argyll some seven or eight days behind footing it heavily from Spey to Tay and from Tay to Don. Montrose darted eastward, and, clinging to the flanks of the hills, crossed the Dee at his old ford on the 17th of October. Here he sanctioned the burning of the lands of Covenanting owners, like the Frasers and Crichtons, in retaliation for the fire and sword which Argyll had borne to every one suspected of loyalty. By the 20th he was in Strathbogie, busy once more with fruitless appeals to the Gordons. Here he had word of Argyll's approach, and retired to Fyvie Castle on the Ythan. He thought Argyll was scarcely yet over the Grampians, when in reality he was almost within musket-shot. For once the king's lieutenant was caught napping.

Fyvie, an old seat of the Earls of Dunfermline, had become more of a seventeenth-century dwelling-house than a feudal tower. On three sides lay bogs with strips of hardened ground too narrow for the approach of an army. On the eastern side was a long low ridge of hill, thickly wooded on one face, and here Montrose drew up his men. He was short of ammunition, and melted down the pewter vessels of the castle to make bullets; for powder he looked to the pouches of the enemy. Argyll, thinking that at last he had driven his nimble foe into a blind alley, and strong in the consciousness of a force at least four times as large, attacked the position with—for him—considerable spirit. The omens were propitious, for a handful of Gordon horse, who had been enlisted in Strathbogie, deserted at the first shot. The Covenanting centre advanced up the little hill, and was half-way to the top before Montrose saw his danger. He called to a young

Ulsterman, O'Kean,[29] whom Alastair had left behind him, and bade him drive the enemy from the slope. The gallant Irish charged with pike and broad-sword, drove back the Covenanters, and obtained a supply of powder for their famished muskets. It is recorded that one of them, looking at the booty, said, 'We must at them again; the stingy rogues have left us no bullets.' Mean-while Lothian's horse had assaulted Montrose's position on the flank. But the powder-flasks were now replenished, and the fire of the musketeers, whom Montrose led round the brow of the hill, was too much for the lowland cavalry. Argyll drew off his men, and put the Ythan between himself and the enemy.

But Fyvie was no place to linger at, since 500 men cannot for ever defy an army. For three more days desultory attacks were made, in one of which Lord Marischal's brother was slain on the Covenant side. On the fourth night, under cover of darkness, Montrose slipped away, and was presently heard of in Strathbogie. Here he hoped for news of Alastair and his western men, but no news came. His aim is clear; he had still hopes of the Gordons, and was loath to leave their country. This Argyll knew very well, and he too followed to Strathbogie, keeping up a show of attacks which were easily repulsed. But the Campbell chief was engaged on work more suited to his genius than fighting, and busied himself with making overtures to Montrose's Lowland officers. He did not ask them to betray their cause; he only offered, of his generosity, free passes to any who wished to go home, asking no payment in return. it was an ingenious plan, and it largely succeeded. Sibbald, a companion on the ride from Carlisle, left, and the seeds were sown of further discontent. A council of war was called, and it was resolved to retreat into the hills. The Royalists marched by moorland roads to Balvenie on the Spey, out of reach of Argyll's horse, and there took stock of their position. Argyll, wisely avoiding the mountains, marched south again by an easier road, and lay with his army in the neighbourhood of Dunkeld.

At Balvenie matters came to a crisis. The Lowland gentlemen had no love for a campaign in midwinter, conducted at Montrose's incredible pace, and offering little hope of finality. They feared for their estates and families now at the mercy of the Covenant. Moreover, Highland and Lowland are ill to mix, and they may have disliked their associates. Montrose accordingly proposed a descent on the Lowlands, the plan which he had always held in view, for his aim was to relieve the king by drawing back Leven from England. But the scheme found little favour. The Lowlanders may well have argued that success in hill warfare was no warrant for victory against regulars in a settled and hostile country, and the Highlanders had grievances of their own to avenge, which they thought of far greater moment than any royal necessities. Men like Kinnoul, Colonel Hay, and Sir John Drummond slipped away to make a temporary peace with the Covenant. Almost alone of the gentry old Airlie and his gallant sons refused to leave. They, like Montrose, fought not for safety or revenge, but for an ideal of statesmanship.

It was now the end of November. In the levels the heavy rains told of the beginning of winter, and the hills were whitening with snow. Argyll was at Dunkeld, busy with attempts on the loyalty of Atholl, and he may well have believed that no general in his senses would continue the war in such inclement weather. Montrose resolved to disappoint his expectations, and led his handful of troops through the Badenoch passes for a descent on Dunkeld. But long ere he reached the Tay Argyll had news of him, and wisely decided that he at any rate would end the campaign. He dismissed his Campbells to their homes, sent his regulars into winter quarters, and himself repaired with all speed to Edinburgh, where he surrendered his commission into the hands of the Estates.

Lothian and Callander refused the thankless post, and Baillie, one of the best of Leven's lieutenants, was summoned to Scotland to take up the command.

At Blair, Montrose met Alastair returning from his western expedition. The meeting changed his plans. He had now the rest of the Ulstermen, and a large levy of the western clans. The Macdonalds had not forgotten Argyll's commission of fire and sword in 1640, and the Macleans had long scores to settle with the secular enemy of their name. Five hundred Macdonalds—of Glengarry, Keppoch, and Clanranald—had flocked to his standard. With them came Macleans from Morvern and Mull, Stewarts from Appin, Farquharsons from Braemar, and Camerons from Lochaber. John of Moidart, the captain of Clanranald, brought his fierce spirit and devoted following to Montrose's side. The middle Highlands, for the first time since Harlaw, were united, but it was not in the king's service. The hatred of every clansman was directed not at the Covenant but at the house of Diarmaid. Now was the time to avenge ancient wrongs, and to break the pride of a chief who had boasted that no mortal enemy could enter his country. The hour had come when the fray must be carried to Lorn.

Montrose had that supreme virtue in a commander which recognizes facts. He could not maintain his army without war, and Lowland war they would not listen to. If he looked to their help in the future he must whet their valour and rivet their loyalty by fresh successes. In return for their assistance in the king's quarrel they must have the help of the king's lieutenant in their own. Besides, a blow at the Campbells in their own country would put fear into the heart of the Covenant, and shatter Argyll's not too robust nerve. It was a wild venture, but wild ventures have their psychological value in war. In a sense it had always been Montrose's second line of strategy, for in the previous March, we find him writing to Sir Robert Spottiswoode from York: 'We intend to make all possible dispatch to follow him (Argyll) at the heels, in whatever position we can.' There may have been a further reason. The Estates had confiscated his lands, and taken captive his friends. Wishart, his chaplain, and Lord Ogilvy, his dearest companion, were in the Edinburgh Tolbooth; the ladies of his family had been seized and consigned to squalid prisons. A blow at the arch-enemy would be some little solace to a heart that was only too prone to the human affections.

CHAPTER IX

INVERLOCHY
(DECEMBER 1644–FEBRUARY 1645)

IN seventeenth-century Scotland the Clan Campbell stood by itself as a separate race, almost a separate state, whose politics were determined by the whim of its ruling prince. Built upon the ruins of many little septs, it excelled in numbers and wealth every other Highland clan; indeed, if we except the Gordons, it surpassed all the rest put together. It was near enough to the Lowlands to have shared in such civilization as was going, including the new theology. On the other hand, its territory was a compact block of land, well guarded on all sides from its neighbours, so that it enjoyed the peace and the self-confidence of a separate people. With its immense seacoast its doors were open to the wider world, and the Campbell gentry acquired at foreign universities and in foreign wars the training which few landward gentlemen could boast; while Spanish velvets and the silks and wines of France came more cheaply and readily to its little towns than to the burghers of Perth or Edinburgh. The country, though less fertile than the Lowlands, was a champaign compared to Lochaber or Kintail. Thousands of black cattle flourished on its rich hill pastures, and farms and sheilings were thick along the pleasant glens that sloped to Loch Fyne and Loch Awe. In the town of Inveraray the clan had its natural capital, and from Inveraray ran the Lowland road through Cowal and Dumbarton for such as preferred a land journey. Compared with other clans the Campbells were prosperous and civilized, and accordingly they were detested by their neighbours. They had eaten up the little peoples of Benderloch and Morvern, and their long arm was stretching north and east into Lochaber and Perth. Every Maclean and Stewart and Macdonald who could see the hills of Lorn from his doorstep had uneasy thoughts about his own barren acres. The Campbells had a trick of winning by bow and spear, and then holding for all time by seal and parchment.

It was not without reason that Argyll boasted that his land was impregnable. Strategically it had every advantage. On the eastern side, where it looked to the Lowlands, there were the castles of Roseneath and Dunoon to keep watch and deep sea-lochs to hinder the invaders. Besides, the Lowlands and Argyll were always at peace. South and west lay the sea, and the Campbells had what little navy existed in Scotland at the time. The Macleans in Mull were too small and broken to take the offensive, and in any case it was a long way from the coast at Knapdale to the heart at Inveraray. North lay a land of high mountains and difficult passes, where no man could travel save by permission of the sovereign lord. Moreover, the Campbells of Lochow and Glenorchy had flung their tentacles over Breadalbane and held the marches around the head waters of Tay. There might be a raid of Macgregors or Maclarens on the east, or a foray from Appin on Loch Etive side, but not even the king and his army could get much beyond the gates. 'It is a far cry to Lochow,' so ran the Campbell ower-come, and it was a farther one to Inveraray.

When Montrose assented to Alastair's wishes he resolved to strike straight at the enemy's heart. He would wage war not in the outskirts but in the citadel. From

Blair there was little choice of roads. To go due west by
Rannoch and the springs of Etive would mean a march
among friendly clans, but a few score Campbells could
hold the narrows of Loch Etive or the Pass of Brander
against the strongest army. The Lowland road by Dumbarton and Loch Lomond meant a dangerous proximity
to the Covenanting westlands and the narrow and difficult
pass of Glencoe. But midway through Breadalbane ran a
possible route among wild glens and trackless bogs which
at this winter season would be deep in snow. This was the
old raiding road out of Lorn, and Argyll flattered himself
that his clan alone had the keys of it. But with Montrose
were men who had made many a midnight foray into the
Campbell country, and who knew every corrie and scaur
as well as any son of Diarmaid. A Glencoe man, Angus
MacAlain Dubh, is named by tradition as the chief guide,
and he promised Montrose that his army could live well
on the country, 'if tight houses, fat cattle, and clear water
will suffice.' Accordingly, with Airlie and the Ogilvys and
his eldest boy, Lord Graham, as his Lowland staff, the
king's lieutenant ordered a march to the west. The army
travelled in three divisions, led respectively by Montrose,
by Alastair, and by John of Clanranald.

The road from Blair was the same as that taken in the
march to Tippermuir. The lands of the Menzieses, a
small and uncertain clan, were first traversed, and the
laird of Weem taken prisoner. Then past the shores of
Loch Tay swept the advance till the confines of Breadalbane
were reached and a country that owned Campbell sway.
Up Glen Dochart[30] they went, following much the same
road as the present railway line to Oban, past Crianlarich
and Tyndrum and into the glens of Orchy. It was a raid of
vengeance, and behind them rose the flames of burning
roof-trees. Presently Loch Awe lay before them, under a
leaden winter sky, and soon the little fortresses of the
lochside lairds smoked to heaven. It was a bloody business,
save that the women and children were spared. All

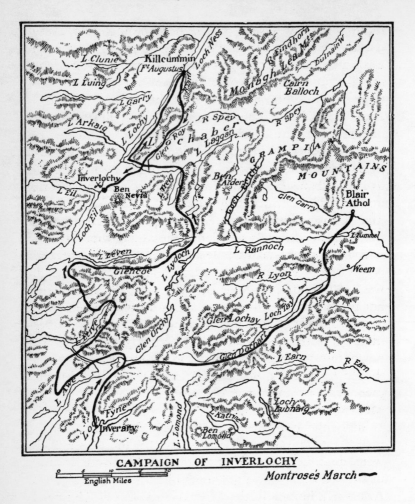

CAMPAIGN OF INVERLOCHY

English Miles

Montrose's March ⌐

fighting men were slain or driven to the high hills, every cot and clachan was set alight, and droves of maddened cattle attested the richness of the land and the profit of the invaders. It was Highland warfare of the old barbarous type, no worse and no better than that which Argyll had already carried to Lochaber and Badenoch and the Braes of Angus.

Argyll was well served by his scouts, and to him at Edinburgh word was soon brought of Montrose's march to Breadalbane. He must have thought it a crazy venture; now at last was his enemy delivered into his hands. No mortal army could cross the winter passes, even if it had the key; and the men of Glenorchy would wipe out the starving remnants at their leisure. Full of confidence he posted across Scotland to Inveraray. There he found that all was quiet. Rumours of the foray in Lorn were indeed rife, but the burghers of Inveraray, strong in their generations of peace, had no fear for themselves. Argyll saw to the defences of the castle, and called a great gathering of the neighbouring clansmen to provide reinforcements, if such should be needed, for the Glenorchy and Breadalbane men, who by this time had assuredly made an end of Montrose.

Suddenly came the thunderbolt. Wild-eyed herds rushed into the streets with the cry that the Macdonalds were upon them. Quickly the tale flew. Montrose was not in Breadalbane or on the fringes of Lorn; he was at Loch Awe—nay, he was in the heart of Argyll itself. The chief waited no longer. He found a fishing-boat and, the wind being right, fled down Loch Fyne to the shelter of his castle of Roseneath. The same breeze that filled his sails brought the sound of Alastair's pipes, and he was scarcely under way ere the van of the invaders came down Glen Shira.

Then began the harrying of Clan Campbell. Leaderless and unprepared they made no resistance to Montrose's army of flushed and battle-worn warriors. Macleans and

Macdonalds, Stewarts and Camerons, satiated their ancient grudges with the plunder of Inveraray. The kerns thawed their half-frozen limbs at the warmth of blazing steadings, and appeased their ravenous hunger at the expense of the bakers and vintners and fleshers of the burgh. Never had the broken men of Lochaber and the Isles fared so nobly. For some happy weeks they ran riot in what for them was a land of milk and honey; while the townsmen, crouching in cellars and thickets, or safe behind the castle gates, wondered how long it would be before their chief returned to avenge them. There seems to have been no special barbarity about the business. Here and there a refractory Campbell was dirked, but Alastair's men preferred victual and cattle to human blood.

Meantime word had gone from the exile at Roseneath to the Estates in Edinburgh. William Baillie of Letham, the new commander-in-chief, was a natural son of Sir William Baillie of Lamington. An old soldier of Gustavus, he had done good service at Marston Moor and at the siege of Newcastle, and he brought to Scotland some of the pick of Leven's infantry, which he increased by local levies. He was now ordered by the Estates to repair to Roseneath and consult with Argyll on the best way of crushing Montrose. But at Roseneath he found the exile in a difficult humour. There must be no stranger general in the Campbell fastness. It was for Argyll, and Argyll alone, to avenge the shame of his clan. Accordingly the Estates ordered Baillie to transfer to Argyll 1,100 of his best foot, representing the flower of the Scottish militia. Baillie himself was sent to Perth, with Sir John Hurry (who was a Royalist a year before and was to be a Royalist again) as his second in command. He was bidden keep in touch with the Covenanting garrison that had been left in Aberdeen and with Seaforth's northern army at Inverness. Argyll sent hastily to the army in Ireland to summon back his kinsman, Sir Duncan Campbell of Auchinbreck, the best soldier that the clan could boast. The dislocated shoulder, which he had given to the Estates as the reason of his flight from Inveraray, was now happily mended. It looked as if the Royalists had walked into a certain trap. Montrose would be caught between Argyll and Seaforth, and if he tried to escape to the right Baillie and Hurry would await him. It seemed the certainty on which Argyll loved to stake. 'If we get not the life of these worms chirted out of them,' wrote the agreeable Mr. Robert Baillie, the general's ministerial cousin, 'the reproach will stick on us for ever.'

Midwinter that year was open and mild. Had it been otherwise Clan Campbell must have been annihilated, and Montrose could never have led his men safely out of Argyll. About the middle of January[31] 1645 he gave the order for the march. He had as yet no news of Argyll's preparations, but he must have realized that the avenger would not be slow on his track. His immediate intention was to come to an account with Seaforth, who not only barred him from the Gordon country, but was responsible for the whole opposition of the Moray and Speyside gentry and the powerful clan of Mackenzie. He had guides who promised to show him an easy way out of Lorn into Lochaber, whence the road ran straight by the Great Glen to Inverness. Laden with miscellaneous plunder and cumbered no doubt with *spreaghs* of cattle, the Highlanders crossed from Loch Awe to the shore of Loch Etive. Since they had nothing to fear in front of them they continued up the steep brink of that loch to the site of the present house of Glen Etive. Crossing the *beallach* by the old drove road they marched through Appin and up Glencoe to the neighbourhood of Corrour. The shorter road by Kingshouse and the Moor of Rannoch was no place for a heavily-laden force in midwinter. From Corrour their route was that now taken by the West Highland Railway. Passing Loch Treig, they descended the valley of the Spean to the shores of Loch Lochy and the opening of the Great Glen. By the evening of Thursday, the 30th of January, Montrose was at Kilcumin at the head of Loch Ness. Most of the Atholl men and the bulk of Clanranald had left him, after their custom, to deposit their booty. No more than 1,500 remained—Alastair's Irish, a handful of Stewarts, Macdonalds, Macleans, and Camerons, and sufficient cavalry to mount the Lowland gentry and provide an escort for the standard.

At Kilcumin Montrose had definite news of Seaforth. He was thirty miles off at Inverness with 5,000 men—Frasers, Mackenzies, and regulars from the Inverness garrison; a disorderly multitude, says Wishart, for, apart from the old soldiers of the garrison, it was 'newly raised out of husbandmen, cowherds, tavern boys, and kitchen boys.' Montrose was preparing to make short work of Seaforth when he received graver tidings. Ian Lom Macdonald, the bard of Keppoch, arrived to tell of Argyll at his heels. The Campbells were only thirty miles behind at Inverlochy, 3,000 men-at-arms eager to avenge the wrongs of Lorn. They were burning and harrying Glen Spean and Glen Roy and the Lochaber braes, and their object was to take Montrose in the rear what time Seaforth should hold him in the front.

At Kilcumin Montrose had prepared a bond to which all the chiefs set their names. Such bonds and manifestoes were favourite devices of the general. They were his Covenants, the only means by which he could advertise to the world the principles for which he fought. The signatories swore to fight to the death for their sovereign and his legitimate authority against 'the present perverse and infamous faction of desperate rebels now in fury against him,' and never to swerve from their oath as they 'would be reputed famous men.' The little army had much need of all the heartening it could get, for its plight seemed hopeless. Fifteen hundred very weary men were caught between two forces of 5,000 and 3,000. There was no way of escape to west or east, for the one would lead them to a bare seacoast and the other into the arms of Baillie's foot. Of the two hostile forces the Campbells were the more formidable. Montrose knew very well that the fighting spirit of Clan Diarmaid was equal to any in the Highlands, and, now that they were commanded by a skilled soldier and infuriated by the burning of their homes, he could not hope to fight them at long odds. But it is the duty of a good general when he is confronted by two immediate perils to meet the greater first. Montrose resolved to fight the Campbells, but to fight them in his own way.

Early on the morning of Friday, the 31st of January, began that flank march which is one of the great exploits in the history of British arms.[32] The little river Tarff flows north from the Monadliadh Mountains to Loch Ness. Up its rocky course went Montrose, and the royal army disappeared into the hills. Scouts of Argyll or Seaforth who traversed the Great Glen on that day must have reported no enemy. From Tarff Montrose crossed the pass to Glen Turritt and following it downwards reached Glen Roy. Pushing on through the night he came to the bridge of Roy, where that stream enters the Spean, on the morning of Saturday, the 1st of February. The weather had been icily cold, the upper glens were choked with snowdrifts, and the army had neither food nor fire. The road led through places where great avalanches yawned above the adventurers, and over passes so steep and narrow that a hundred men could have held an army at bay. As they struggled along at the pace of a deerstalker, Montrose walked by his men, shaming them to endurance by the spectacle of his own courage.

From Roy Bridge to Inverlochy is some thirteen miles. But to take Argyll in the flank a circuit was necessary, and Montrose followed the northern slopes of the wild tangle of mountains, the highest in Britain, that surround Ben Nevis.[33] In the ruddy gloaming of the February day the vanguard saw beneath and before them the towers of Inverlochy 'like a scowl on the fringe of the wave,' and not a mile off the men of Clan Diarmaid making ready their evening meal. Shots were exchanged with the pickets, but no effort was made to advance. Montrose waited quietly in the gathering dusk till by eight o'clock the rest of his famished columns had arrived. There, supperless and cold, they passed the night, keeping up a desultory skirmishing with the Campbell outposts, for Montrose was in dread that Argyll should try to escape. It was a full moon, and the dark masses of both armies were visible to each other. Argyll thought the force he saw only a contingent of Highland raiders under O'Kean or Keppoch or some petty chief. But opportunely his wounded shoulder began to trouble him, so with his favourite minister, an Edinburgh bailie or two, and Sir James Rollo, he retired to a boat on Loch Eil.

At dawn on Candlemas Day his ears were greeted by an unwelcome note. It was no bagpipes such as Keppoch might use, but trumpets of war, and the salute they sounded was that reserved for the royal standard. The king's lieutenant, who two days ago was for certain at Loch Ness, had by some craft of darkness taken wings and flown his army over the winter hills. There was no alternative but to fight. Till Montrose was beaten the Campbells could neither march forward to join Seaforth nor backward to their own land.

Auchinbreck drew up his forces with the fighting men of Clan Campbell in the centre, and the Lowland regiments borrowed from Baillie on each wing. Montrose himself led the Royalist centre, with Alastair on the left and O'Kean, who since Fyvie had held high command, on the right. Sir Thomas Ogilvy commanded the little troop of horse which had managed to make its way with the infantry over the terrible hills. This was the one advantage Montrose possessed. Otherwise his men were on the point of starvation, having had scarcely a mouthful for forty-eight hours. He himself and Lord Airlie breakfasted on a little raw oatmeal mixed with cold water which they ate with their dirks.

The battle began with a movement by Ogilvy's horse which gravely disquieted the Lowland wings. Then the Campbell centre fired a volley, and immediately the whole Royalist front responded and charged. We may well believe that the firing of famished men was wild, but it mattered little, for soon they were come, as Montrose wrote, 'to push of pike and dint of sword.' Alastair and O'Kean had little difficulty with the Lowland levies. In spite of the experience of many of them with Leven, a Highland charge was a new and awful thing to them, and they speedily broke and fled. Inverlochy was won by strategy. Of tactics there was little, and that little was as elementary as at Tippermuir. The gallant Campbell centre, indeed, made a determined stand. They knew that they could hope for no mercy from their hereditary foes, and they were not forgetful of the honourable traditions of their race. But in time they also broke. Some rushed into the loch and tried in vain to reach the galley of their chief, now fleeing to safety; some fled to the tower of Inverlochy. Most scattered along the shore, and on that blue February noon there was a fierce slaughter from the mouth of Nevis down to the narrows of Loch Leven. The Lowlanders were given quarter, but in spite of all his efforts Montrose could win no mercy for the luckless Campbells. The green Diarmaid tartan was a badge of death that day. On the Royalist side only four perished, but one of them was Sir Thomas Ogilvy, who died shortly after the battle. On the Covenant side the slain outnumbered the whole of Montrose's army. At least fifteen hundred fell in the battle and pursuit, and among them were the gallant Auchinbreck and forty of the Campbell barons.[34] Well might Keppoch's bard exult fiercely over the issue!

'Though the bones of my kindred, unhonoured, unurned,
Mark the desolate path where the Campbells have burned—
Be it so! *From that foray they never returned.*'[35]

Inverlochy was in one respect a decisive victory. It destroyed the clan power of Argyll. From its terrible toll the Campbells as a fighting force never recovered. Alastair's policy was justified and the Macdonalds were amply avenged; the heather, as the phrase went, was above the gale at last. To Montrose at the moment it seemed even more. He thought that with the galley of Lorn fell also the blue flag of the Covenant. He wrote straightway to the king, giving him a full account of the fight, and ending on a high note of confidence:—[36]

'Give me leave, in all humility, to assure Your Majesty that, through God's blessing, I am in the fairest hopes of reducing this kingdom to Your Majesty's obedience. And, if the measures I have concerted with your other loyal subjects fail me not, which they hardly can, I doubt not before the end of this summer I shall be able to come to Your Majesty's assistance with a brave army which, backed with the justice of Your Majesty's cause, will make the rebels in England, as well as in Scotland, feel the just rewards of rebellion. Only give me leave, after I have reduced this country to Your Majesty's obedience, and conquered from Dan to Beersheba, to say to Your Majesty then, as David's general did to his master, "Come thou thyself, lest this country be called by my name."'

CHAPTER X

THE RETREAT FROM DUNDEE
(FEBRUARY–APRIL 1645)

IT was not till March that Charles received tidings of Inverlochy. By that time he had already rejected the proposals of the Treaty of Uxbridge, one of which was that Montrose should be exempted from the act of oblivion, and the news of the fall of Argyll gave him hopes of a diversion in the north. He wrote to Montrose telling him that he was sending 500 horse under Sir Philip Musgrave, and announcing that he himself with his army would make his way to Scotland as soon as possible. It was a scheme of Digby's which Cromwell was soon to render abortive. Meanwhile Inverlochy had a different effect upon the temper of the Estates in Edinburgh. Argyll arrived there ten days after the battle, with his arm in a sling, to be publicly thanked for his services. Baillie and Hurry were exhorted to fresh efforts, and further levies were made on Leven's army. James Graham, sometime Earl of Montrose, was declared an excommunicated traitor and his life and his estates forfeited. The Kirk, not to be outdone in martial zeal, proposed, since it was so hard to lay hold of the chief malefactor, to make a beginning with those in its power. Did not Crawford and Ogilvy and Wishart lie fast in the Tolbooth? Mr. David Dickson,

Mr. Robert Blair, Mr. Andrew Cant, Mr. James Guthrie, and Mr. Patrick Gillespie attended as a deputation from the General Assembly to urge their immediate execution. Parliament commended the 'zeal and piety' of the clergy, but hinted that with Montrose victorious in the field it would be well to wait a little before destroying his hostages.

After resting a few days at Inverlochy, Montrose marched northward again. Had it been possible, his wisest course would have been an immediate descent upon the capital. But for Lowland warfare he needed cavalry, and cavalry could not be manufactured in Lochaber. To get it he must go where alone in the north it could be had—among the Gordon gentry. He found that the opposition had melted away. Having no war chest, he was compelled to provide for his forces by fines and requisitions from the Covenanting lairds, and where these were not forthcoming there was burning and pillage. By the middle of February he had entered Elgin with no sign of Seaforth, or indeed of any opponent. The Mackenzies had disappeared into the fastnesses of Kintail. At Elgin, to his joy, he found that recruits began to come in. The first was the laird of Grant with 300 men, and at the plundering of the houses of certain Covenanting absentees it is said that the new convert showed himself highly assiduous. Then came a far greater ally, no less than Huntly's son, Lord Gordon, who, tired of the ways of his uncle Argyll, rode over from the castle of Gight to offer his sword to the king. He was accompanied by his brother, Lord Lewis, whom we have already seen twice arrayed against Montrose at Aberdeen, first with Aboyne and then with Balfour of Burleigh. He was still in his teens, a fiery and perverse young man, of undoubted gallantry, but of an excitable and fantastic mind. With the Gordons, as an earnest of Gordon support, came 200 well-mounted troopers, a sight to gladden Montrose's heart, for cavalry could alone make possible that Lowland campaign on which his soul was set. Lord Gordon was more than a comrade in arms ; he was to prove for the short space of life that remained to him Montrose's tenderest and truest friend. Last of all came Seaforth to make his peace. He had never been much of a Covenanter, but Mackenzie and Macdonald could not be expected to see eye to eye. Montrose received him cordially, and dispatched him to hold his own countryside for the king. At Elgin or at Gight, which was the next halting-place of the royal army, the bond prepared at Kilcumin received further signatures. It is odd to find in the document, which is still preserved in the Montrose charter-chest, the names of Grant and Seaforth beside the scrawls of Alastair, Lochiel, and Clauranald, and to remember that, when the latter signed, the former were the foes against which the bond was aimed.

He had now a compact force of 2,000 foot and about two hundred horse. The nucleus of the infantry was still Alastair's Irish, who may have numbered from a thousand to twelve hundred men. The Lochaber and Badenoch clans had probably gone home with their booty after Inverlochy, and the rest were the remnant of the Atholl levies, chiefly Robertsons, the 300 Grants, and small contingents from Moray, Nairn, and the Gordons. The cavalry, with the exception of the few who had been with Ogilvy, was wholly Gordon. Montrose may well have believed himself strong enough, what with the hope of further Gordon aid, and the certainty of more recruits from Atholl, to meet Baillie on equal terms south of the Tay.

At Gight he suffered a sore bereavement. His eldest boy, Lord Graham, now in his sixteenth year, had been his father's companion ever since William Forrett brought him to Perth after Tippermuir. The swift marches over the winter hills had worn him out, and his life was part of the price for that miraculous descent at Inverlochy. He died in the early days of March, and was buried in the neighbouring kirk of Bellie. Shortly after, old Lord Airlie fell dangerously sick, and was sent to Huntly's castle of Strathbogie with a guard of several hundred men, whom the royal army could ill afford. Montrose had to lock up his grief in his heart, for there was no time to spare for sorrowing. He marched east, and by the 9th of March was in the neighbourhood of Aberdeen. A deputation of burgesses met him at Turriff and, remembering with regret his last visit, he undertook that his Irish should not come within eight miles of the city. There, however, a grave misfortune befell him. Nathaniel Gordon with eighty cavaliers rode into Aberdeen from the camp at Kintore on a friendly errand of amusement. Word was sent by certain local Covenanters to Hurry, who with the Covenanting cavalry was in the Mearns, and Sir John made a dash on the city in the evening. Such Royalists as he found in the streets were promptly cut down, most of the horses were driven off; and among the dead was the chief of the Farquharsons, one of Montrose's best commanders. Hurry, on his way back, took prisoner the new Lord Graham, who was with his tutor at Montrose, and carried him to Edinburgh. The king's lieutenant waited in Aberdeen to bury the dead Farquharson, and on Monday the 18th of March began his southward journey.

On the 21st he burned the lands and town of Stonehaven, and the outbuildings of Dunnottar Castle. Marischal, who like so many Scots nobles blew hot and cold in turn, was for the present by way of being a Covenanter, and in the company of sixteen ministers watched from his impregnable keep the destruction of his lands, finding what comfort he could in the consolation of Mr. Andrew Cant that the smoke of his barns was 'a sweet-smelling incense in the nostrils of the Lord.' By the end of March Montrose was at Fettercairn, with Hurry and his 600 horse only six miles off. Here he all but made an end of Hurry. That general, confident in his cavalry, came out to battle near Halkerton Castle, and believing that only 200 horse were opposed to him charged them gaily. But behind the horse Montrose had concealed his best musketeers in the den of a burn, and Hurry was received with a fire which emptied his saddles and put his cavalry to confusion. Then the Royalist horse turned and charged, and Hurry fled incontinent across the South Esk, never drawing rein till he had covered the twenty-four miles to Dundee. Next day the Royalists occupied Brechin, which was plundered, and the town of Montrose, which was spared by the general for the sake of old times. Here he heard of the advance of a more formidable opponent than Hurry. Baillie, with 3,000 of the best and most seasoned infantry in Scotland, was blocking the road to the south.

Montrose hastened to meet him and found him in the neighbourhood of Coupar-Angus. But Baillie was a cautious commander and he respected his enemy. He was determined to fight only on the most favourable ground, and he knew that Fabian tactics were the likeliest to wear out an army with no base, no reserves, and no coherence save the personal influence of its leader. The river Isla flowed between the two forces, and Montrose dared not try to wrest the passage in the face of superior strength. So in the true cavalier fashion he sent Baillie a challenge, offering to cross and fight him, if the passage were permitted, or to let him cross unhindered, if he preferred the other bank. Baillie wisely replied that he would fight at his own pleasure, and not to suit his adversary's convenience.

Seeing that it was hopeless to wait longer Montrose devised a new plan. He struck camp and marched west to Dunkeld, with the intention of descending on the Lowlands by another road. At Dunkeld he could cross the Tay with safety, and after that he had a straight road to the Forth. Baillie could not keep up with him, and retired south, as it was reported, on his way to Fife. Now was the chance for that avalanche from the hills which should

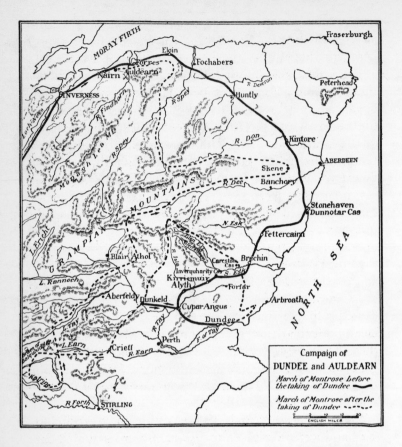

Campaign of
DUNDEE and AULDEARN

*March of Montrose before
the taking of Dundee* ———

*March of Montrose after the
taking of Dundee* -------

0   5   10   15   20
ENGLISH MILES

sweep the Covenanting Lowlands, and gather up with it all the disaffected and anti-Covenant elements which Montrose believed to be rife in the south of Scotland.

But at Dunkeld he was to be reminded of the nature of the Highland army which he led. Once more his forces began to melt away. The Atholl men slipped back to their homes, and so did the recent levies from the north of the Grampians. The Gordon cavalry, led by Lord Lewis Gordon, began to grumble, and though they did not desert yet awhile he knew that he could not long count on their assistance.[37] Presently his troops had shrunk so gravely that any attempt on the Lowlands was out of the question.

Something must be done if only to keep his remnant together. Twenty-four miles off lay the town of Dundee, an ancient stronghold of rebellion and the chief base of the Covenant in Angus. To read Dundee a lesson might be a profitable employment till he saw his way more clearly. He had now no infantry but Alastair's Irish. Of these he sent the weaker half on to Brechin with the baggage, and with 600 foot and 150 horse left Dunkeld at midnight on the 3rd of April. By ten next morning he was under the walls of Dundee.[38]

Dundee in the year 1645 was a little town, with a big kirk and a market-place in the centre, from which four or five streets radiated. Though it had no garrison at the time it had substantial walls, and inside the walled area was a mound called the Corbie Hill, long since levelled, on which cannon had been set. Montrose sent a trumpeter to summon the citizens to surrender, but after the Covenanting fashion the envoy was made prisoner and ultimately hanged. Thereupon the assault began. Dundee was a strong place, but the walls were being mended in one part, and there the Royalists soon made a breach. The guns on the Corbie Hill were captured and turned against the town, and presently the church and the market-place were in the invaders' hands. Several houses were set on fire, but pillage rather than burning was the order of the day. The booths of the merchants were turned inside out, and the plenishing of many a well-doing citizen took to the streets on Highland backs. Ale and wine were discovered, and soon many of the assailants, who had marched all night without a halt, were in that state of bodily and mental ease which Wishart describes as *'vino paululum incalescentes.'*[39]

It was now late afternoon, and as Montrose stood on the Corbie Hill watching the ongoings in the town, his breathless scouts brought him startling news. Baillie and Hurry had not crossed the Tay on their way to Fife. With 3,000 foot and 800 horse they were now within a mile of the west port of Dundee. It was as perilous a position as any commander ever stood in, and his colonels gave counsels of despair. Some urged him to leave his half-drunken troops to their fate and save himself, on the plea that another army could be found, but not a second Montrose. Others of a more heroic temper cried that all was lost but honour, and were for dying in a desperate charge. Only Montrose kept his head. He was determined to escape, not alone, but with his army—a determination which, by itself, shows the unequalled courage of the man. Somehow or other, and how, Heaven only knows, he beat off his men from their plunder—a feat, says Mr. Gardiner, 'beyond the power of any other commander in Europe.' Four hundred of his foot he sent on in front, and behind them he kept 200 of his best musketeers as a support to the horse in the case of a stand. Last, as rearguard, went his 150 cavalry. As the Royalists rode out of the east gate of the town Baillie entered at the west gate, and Hurry's van was within a gunshot of Montrose's rear.

Night had now fallen, but the Covenanters were confident of their prey. Hurry followed hard on Montrose as he marched east along the seacoast. A few miles from Dundee he tried to charge, but the picked musketeers among the Royalist horse were too much for him. He was driven back, and halted, while the king's lieutenant pushed on in the direction of Arbroath. Meanwhile Baillie had conceived a better plan. He knew that Montrose must get to the hills as soon as possible, not only for safety, but to pick up the men he had sent to await him at Brechin. He observed too, that he was marching along the arc of a circle, and he resolved himself to take the chord. He had made arrangements for guarding all the hill passes, and hurried north-east towards Arbroath to hem his enemy between his troops and the sea.

It was precisely the strategy that Montrose had anticipated. At midnight he turned sharp in his tracks, marched south-west and then north, and quietly slipped round Baillie's forces in the dark. By daybreak he was at Careston Castle, a Carnegie house on the South Esk, with the friendly hills in sight and at hand. Here he had news from Brechin that the men who were to meet him there had already been given the alarm and had betaken themselves to the mountains. He halted for a little to give his weary troops a breathing space. In the past thirty-six hours they had marched sixty or seventy miles, fought several engagements, and sacked a town. When the halt was sounded nearly every man dropped to the ground and slept like the dead.

Meanwhile Baillie at the first light of dawn had discovered his mistake. Hurry had rejoined him, and Hurry's cavalry were soon hot on the trail of the man who had so befooled them. Montrose had the alarm in time, but his sleepy soldiers would not stir. It looked as if the three miles which still intervened before the hills were gained were to be three miles too many and the labours of that marvellous night rendered vain. But the officers managed to beat up sufficient troops to make some sort of stand, and Hurry's horse were checked. Then with a desperate effort the exhausted Royalists struggled on the last few miles. Hurry fell back, and by midday Montrose was safe among the uplands of the North Esk.

The retreat from Dundee, however we look at it, remains an astonishing feat of arms. Hurry's cavalry were the troops which had done brilliant service under Leven, and Baillie's foot were the finest regular soldiers that Scotland could show. Man for man the Gordon horse, sulky and mutinous as they already were, could not compare with them. The Irish were, of course, tried veterans, and superior to any of the Covenant infantry. But Montrose's men were at the best dog-tired, and at the worst half-drunk and laden with their precious plunder. The general who could stop the sack of a town in a few minutes was a superb leader of men, and he who could execute such a flight was a consummate strategist. 'Which,' writes Wishart, 'whether foreign nations or after times will believe I cannot tell, but I am sure I deliver nothing but what is most certain of my own knowledge. And truly, amongst expert soldiers, and those of eminent note both in England, Germany, and France, I have not seldom heard this expedition of his preferred before Montrose's greatest victories.'[40]

CHAPTER XI

AULDEARN
(APRIL–MAY 1645)

THE letter written by the king in March, promising a troop of horse and holding out hopes of his own coming to Scotland, was carried by a gentleman of the name of Small, and found Montrose somewhere among the Grampians. On his way back to the royal camp the messenger was captured by the Covenanters and shortly afterwards hanged in Edinburgh. From the documents in his possession his captors got their first news of the king's intention, and fell into a panic. They disseminated wild reports of the flight from Dundee, declaring, in order to allay popular fears, that only a few Royalists had escaped to the mountains. But Argyll could not deceive himself, and he knew that the coming north of the king, with Montrose unbeaten in the field, meant that he and his ambitions would be caught between two fires. He communicated his anxiety to the generals, and for the first time Covenanting strategy begins to show some intelligence. The credit probably belongs to Hurry, for Baillie, though a competent enough soldier, never showed any strategic ability. The Covenant army was divided. Instead of pursuing the evasive enemy in one cumbrous whole, it was resolved to try to hold him between two separate forces operating from different bases. Recruiting in the Lowlands was pushed on, and cadets of Lothian and Border families joined the Covenanting standard. It was believed that north of the Grampians also large forces could be raised, and Hurry, borrowing 1,200 foot from Baillie and keeping 160 of his horse, hastened north to pick up these levies and to form the upper millstone for the projected grinding of Montrose. Baillie with 2,000 foot and 500 horse settled himself in the neighbourhood of Perth.

For Montrose there was once more the weary task of finding an army. Lord Gordon was dispatched to Strathbogie to try to raise Gordon troopers in place of those who had gone off with his petulant brother. Alastair departed west into the Macdonald country to whip up those of his clan who had left after Inverlochy. Black Pate of Inchbrakie went into Atholl to organize the Robertsons and Stewarts. Montrose himself had to wait the result of these missions before he could again take the field. But for him waiting was never inaction. He resolved to investigate the state of affairs on the Highland line and to keep Baillie out of mischief. He also wished to gather to his standard one or two gentlemen of his kin who had been hiding in Menteith, and he may have had hopes of pushing south to get some news from the Royalists across the Border. He wrote to the king, and his letter reached Oxford on the 10th of May. In it he spoke no longer of leading an army into England, for he had no army to lead. The most he could do was to keep the Covenant busy in Scotland.

About the 16th of April, with 500 foot and 50 horse, he swept down upon Perth. He halted for the night at the village of Crieff, twelve miles from Baillie's camp. The Covenanting general, as soon as he got the news, set off in the night to surprise him, and at dawn on the 17th found the little army drawn up for battle. A glance convinced Montrose that the odds were too great even for him, so, with his horse fighting a rearguard action, he retreated up the Earn valley past Comrie, and by the evening was safe from pursuit at the head of Loch Earn. Next day he turned south by Balquhidder into the heart of the Trossachs. Here, on the 20th, he fell in with a welcome ally, no less than Aboyne, Huntly's second son, who had escaped from Carlisle and with difficulty made his way across the Lowlands. He found other friends, too, for at Loch Katrine he met his nephew, the Master of Napier, and a son of the Earl of Stirling, who had eluded the Covenant's vigilance.[41] Montrose had more than his share of family affection, and the kinsmen, says Spalding, 'were all joyful of each other.'

Here he had news which put an end to his southern wanderings. Baillie was busy burning in Atholl, and Hurry, now north of the Grampians, was bidding fair to destroy Lord Gordon and his slender force. Montrose retraced his steps by one of those lightning marches which were the despair of his opponents and a confusion to the chroniclers of his day. He could not fight Baillie as he was, and to meet Hurry he must first find his Gordons. He crossed from Loch Earn by Glenogle to Loch Tay, then across the shoulder of Schiehallion into Atholl, and over the mountains to Mar. The Dee was forded near Balmoral, and by the end of the month he was at Skene, on lower Deeside.[42] Somewhere on the road Alastair joined him, and at Skene he found Lord Gordon with a body of Gordon cavalry. His little force was badly off for ammunition, so Aboyne undertook an expedition to Aberdeen for the purpose of supplies. With eighty horse the young soldier seized the town, found twenty barrels of gunpowder in two vessels lying in the harbour, and brought back the loot to headquarters the same evening. Whatever the faults of the Gordon blood it had no lack of fire and speed.

Montrose's force was now a little over two thousand foot and some two hundred and fifty horse. Hurry

meanwhile had not been idle in the north. The Covenanters of Moray and Elgin had risen readily at his call.
Seaforth had recanted his lately-acquired loyalty and
brought the Mackenzies to his side. Sutherland was hastening to his support with his clansmen, and Lord Findlater
was bringing the men of Easter Ross. The local gentry
who hated the Gordon name—Frasers, Forbeses, Roses,
Inneses, Crichtons—brought their swords to his standard.
He had under him two regular regiments, Loudoun's and
Lothian's, seasoned in the English wars, and Campbell of
Lawers led his clan to avenge Inverlochy. Altogether he
had in being or in expectation a force of at least three
thousand four hundred foot, and not less than four hundred horse. While Montrose lay on the Dee, Hurry was
on Speyside with the road to Strathbogie open before
him. It was a vital matter for Montrose to keep the
Gordons in good humour, and for this purpose their
lands must be protected. So he hastened from Skene by
way of the Upper Don to give battle with all speed to
the enemy.

Hurry was a strategist of no mean order, as the campaign was to prove. He fell back for two reasons. First, he
wished to draw Montrose out of the friendly hills and the
Gordon country, and secondly, he had still to receive some
of the promised forces of Seaforth and Sutherland. From
Elgin to Forres he drew the Royalists on, keeping only a
little way ahead, but far enough to prevent Montrose
doing him harm. The ruse succeeded. By the evening of
the 8th of May Montrose had reached the little village of
Auldearn on the ridge of high ground between the valleys of the Findhorn and the Nairn. He believed Hurry to
be retreating on Inverness, and meant to follow him there
the next day. It was a drizzling evening, and the neighbourhood was Covenanting to a man, loving not the
Gordons or the Highlanders, and least of all Alastair's
Irish, whom they remembered after Inverlochy. No news
of the enemy was likely to be got there. Montrose pitched

his camp, posted his pickets carefully, as was his custom, and settled down for the night.

The position needs an exact understanding if we are to appreciate the events that followed. The hamlet of straggling cottages ran north and south along a low ridge. Below the houses to the west were the gardens and pig-styes of the villagers, fenced with rough stone walls, and beyond them lay a flattish piece of ground covered with wildwood which sloped to a marshy burn. North of this bog was firm land, and south stood a bare hillock, now called Deadman's Wood and planted with trees. The burn, which caused the bog in front of the village, curved round to the south and protected the ridge on that side. The position was therefore in the shape of a horse-shoe, if we take the rim for the firmer and higher ground. In the middle of the curve stood the village, and enclosed between the points were the bog and the rough land which sloped from the gardens and pigstyes.

Sometime during the night of the 8th Hurry turned to strike. It was a moonless night with a drenching rain, and the Royalist sentries were not inclined to go too far into the darkness. But Hurry gave notice of his approach, for his men, finding the powder in their muskets damp, fired them off to clear them. They were then five or six miles distant, but the quick ear of Alastair's sentinels caught the sound, and Montrose guessed at once what was afoot. A wet misty dawn was breaking when he drew up his line of battle. He placed Alastair with his Irish at the north end of the ridge beyond the village, and into their charge he gave the royal standard, in order that Hurry might believe the king's lieutenant there in person and deliver there his chief attack. He boldly denied himself a centre, and instead scattered a few men in front of the cottages, with instructions to keep up a continuous firing that the enemy might think the village strongly held. This was the place for his cannon if he had had any, but during the rapid marches of the past eight months he had not had time to recover the guns he had buried after Aberdeen. The rest of his infantry and all his cavalry he kept at the south end of the village, concealed behind the crown of the ridge. It was a brilliant disposition, made at the shortest notice in the half-light of morning. If Hurry attacked Alastair under the impression that he was Montrose, he would have difficulty with his cavalry among the village gardens, while Montrose at the right moment would be free to swing round his horse from their cover behind the ridge and take him unprepared on his right flank.

There was only one mistake in the calculation. Alastair was undermanned. He can have had no more than five hundred men, all infantry, to oppose the attack of 3,400 foot and 400 horse. If we remember that the musketeers of those days were considered to be unable to face cavalry unless drawn up behind hedges or palisades, we get some notion of the desperate odds. They were increased by Alastair's own impetuous conduct. He was never the man to await an onset, and while Hurry's army was struggling through the marshy burn he sacrificed the advantage of his higher ground and rushed to meet them. Eight to one is odds reserved to the champions of fairy tales. 'Why, how the devil,' asks Major Bellenden in *Old Mortality,* 'can you believe that Artamines or what d'ye call him fought single-handed with a whole battalion? One to three is as great odds as ever fought and won, and I never knew any one who cared to take that, except old Corporal Raddlebanes.' But Alastair's deeds were worthy of the Ossianic heroes, and it is not hard to understand how in Highland legend his fame is made to outshine Montrose's. He and his Irish conducted themselves like the fierce warriors of the Sagas. He was forced back, fighting desperately, into the nest of enclosures in front of the village. Like Ajax by the ships he himself was the last to retreat. His targe was full of pikes, but he swung his great broadsword round and cut off their heads like cabbage stalks. He broke his blade, but got another from a dying comrade. Again

and again he rushed out to help his stragglers to enter.
One of his men, Ranald MacKinnon of Mull, fought
swordless against a dozen pikemen with an arrow through
both cheeks and no weapon but his shield. So raged this
Thermopylae among the pigstyes, and every second
Alastair's case grew more desperate.

Montrose, from the crest of the hill, saw what was
happening, and resolved that the time was come for his
master-stroke. The Gordons were still behind the ridge,
and could see nothing of the fight in the village. They
were not seasoned troops, and it was essential that they
should go into action in high heart. So Montrose cried
to Lord Gordon, their leader,—'Macdonald drives all before him. Is his clan to have all the honour this day? Are
there to be no laurels for the house of Huntly?' It was the
word to fire their hearts. Moreover, they had a grim
wrong to avenge. They had not forgotten the death of
Donald Farquharson in Aberdeen, and a few days before young Gordon of Rynie, a mere boy, who had been
wounded and left behind in a cottage, had been brutally
murdered by two of Hurry's lieutenants. With the cry on
their lips, 'Remember Donald Farquharson and James of
Rynie,' the men of Strathbogie wheeled to the charge.

It was the first time that Montrose had used shock tactics. Hitherto his horse had been so few that he had been
compelled to employ them after the old fashion of the
Thirty Years' War, more like mounted infantry, who first
fired their pistols and then charged. But he had not forgotten the new tactics which Rupert had introduced at
Edgehill, and which in Cromwell's hands had given his
Ironsides the victory at Marston Moor.[43] Now was the
time for the *arme blanche*. Montrose had that high gift in
war which can adapt its means not only to its ends but
to its material. He could make his cavalry play a waiting
game, with musketeers interspersed, when he was too
weak to use it otherwise; but when the chance came he
could use it as cavalry should be used, with all the dash

and fury of a Murat, and with more than the skill of a Rupert. He must rank with Cromwell as the greatest cavalry leader of his day.

Hurry, happy in the belief that he was driving Montrose to his death in the village, was suddenly assailed on his right flank by the cry of 'Strathbogie.' His horse, having had a difficult time crossing the bog, were in no mood to stand the assault of fresh cavalry with the impetus of the slope in their favour. The 200 sent the 400 flying with many empty saddles. Lord Gordon with half his force followed in pursuit, and Aboyne with the rest attacked the now defenceless flank of Hurry's infantry. The Covenant regiments went down like ninepins. The 1,200 of Baillie's foot that Hurry had borrowed died almost to a man. Then, following Aboyne, Montrose led the rest of his infantry against the same right wing. Meanwhile among the pigstyes Alastair collected his men for a last effort. He had lost seventeen of his best officers, but the royal standard was safe, and with his blood-stained remnant he charged Hurry's reeling centre. It was the last straw needed to turn the balance. The Covenanting army became a mob, and the mob a shambles. The blood of Ulster and the Isles that day had recovered its ancient berserk fury, and the Gordons were in no mood to spare their foes. Donald Farquharson and James of Rynie did not go unattended to the shades.

For fourteen miles the pursuit continued. Of the Ulstermen who had held the village at least one hundred must have fallen, and almost all the rest were wounded, but otherwise the Royalists had suffered little. It was very different with the Covenanters. The estimates of their dead vary, but the number cannot be less than two thousand. Mungo Campbell of Lawers, whose regiment had fought in the centre against Alastair, perished with all his men. There fell, too, many of the best of the Lowland officers, such as Sir John Murray of Philiphaugh. The northern earls, with the poor fragments of their clans, fled to

Inverness, and Seaforth in the wilds of Kintail had leisure to reflect on the rewards of the forsworn. Hurry himself, with a remnant of one hundred horse, escaped to Baillie.[44]

Auldearn is in its way the most interesting, as it is tactically the most brilliant, of Montrose's battles. It was the first time he had commanded a reasonable force of cavalry, and the first time that he had been the attacked instead of the attacker. Hurry had shown much strategic ability, and attempted with no little skill to meet him with his own methods of surprise. It is rare in the history of war that a man who can devise lightning raids shows an equal coolness and skill in a battle where he stands on the defensive. But the dispositions made within a few minutes on that wet May morning could not have been bettered though they had been the result of days of preparation. Montrose showed a genius for war, which in its way was as sure and undeniable as Napoleon's, and, curiously enough, Auldearn was in miniature an anticipation of the tactics of Austerlitz.

CHAPTER XII

ALFORD
(MAY–JULY 1645)

THE news of Auldearn had its influence on the English war. Leven in Yorkshire, already aware of the king's plan of marching to join Montrose, was summoned by Lord Fairfax to support Brereton at Manchester, who had been driven out of Cheshire by Charles's advance from Droitwich. He announced his coming, but added that he meant to travel by way of Westmorland, as that route was easiest for his guns. His reasons for this circuit are clear. He wished his army to cover the road to Scotland, for he feared that at any moment the king might go north and Montrose come south, and he knew that their meeting in the Lowlands would mean the end of his Covenanting masters. The Estates in Edinburgh were no less concerned, and their first step was revenge. The old Lord Napier, now a man of seventy, whose only offence was that he was Montrose's brother-in-law, was heavily fined and shut up in Edinburgh Castle. The young Master had escaped, and was with his uncle; but his wife, his sister, and his brother-in-law, Stirling of Keir, shared the father's fate. Lord Graham was also imprisoned, and his younger brother, Lord Robert, a boy of seven, was by an order of the Estates committed to the charge of Montrose's wife.

It is one of the few glimpses we get of this lady in history. Apparently she had made her peace with the Covenant through her own family, for Southesk and his son Carnegie were of the type which values property and a quiet life above any barren renown.

Montrose had now won four notable battles, but it was still as difficult as ever—in Bishop Burnet's phrase—to 'fix his conquests.' Hurry's army was gone, but Baillie's remained, and Baillie blocked the way to the Lowlands. He had 2,000 foot and several hundred horse, and, burning his way through Atholl, had by the beginning of May crossed the Dee and entered Strathbogie. As a reserve to his force Montrose's old friend, Lord Lindsay of the Byres, who had been given the earldom of Crawford by the Parliament, was commanding a newly raised army on the borders of Perth and Angus. Lindsay fancied himself a military genius, and, having trenchantly criticized Argyll's performances, had persuaded the Committee to try him in high command. He seems to have had the ear of Parliament, for on their own order Baillie was presently compelled to lend him more than a thousand of his veterans, and accept in exchange four hundred of Lindsay's raw Lowland levies.[45]

After Auldearn Montrose marched first to Elgin, where he halted for a time to rest his weary troops and look after the wounded. As usual, many of the Highlanders went home, but he still kept his Irishry and the Gordon horse. He marched into Strathbogie to draw Baillie, and proceeded to out-manoeuvre him up and down the valley of the Spey. He had no desire to fight until he had recruited his force, for after such a battle as Auldearn there was need of a breathing-space. From Strathbogie he retired to Balvenie, and then to Glenlivat, where Baillie lost all trace of his quarry. He found him again at Abernethy-on-Spey, and presently Montrose was on the outskirts of Badenoch —'a very strait country,' says Baillie, and one by no means pleasant to fight in. Here the two opponents halted and looked at each other. Montrose with his Highlanders could draw supplies from the countryside, but Baillie could only starve. The thing was very soon past bearing, so the Covenanters marched back to Inverness to lay in provisions.

The road was now open to deal with Lindsay, who was waiting in Atholl to prove his boasted generalship. The news of Montrose's coming sent him back in hot haste to Newtyle in Angus to be nearer his base. Montrose sped down the upper glens of Dee, through Glen Muick, and down the headwaters of the South Esk. But when he was within nine miles of Lindsay, and that unfortunate general was already repenting his bold words, a message arrived from the north to spoil all his plans. Huntly had summoned his clan back to Strathbogie. The reason of this conduct we do not know. The natural explanation is that the chief of the Gordons took the opportunity of showing his jealousy of Montrose and paying back old scores. So Lord Gordon interpreted it, and was with difficulty restrained from dealing summarily with those of his clan who proposed to obey his father's commands. But it is at least as probable that Huntly, with Baillie in the neighbourhood, was anxious to protect his own possessions. Montrose saw nothing for it but to turn back and recruit again. He might have fought Lindsay without cavalry and with a much inferior force—he had taken risks as great before; but on this occasion there was a strong reason for retiring. To defeat Lindsay would not advance the main strategy of his campaign one step. He would still have to go back and settle with Baillie, and he would still have to collect an army for the Lowland war. It seemed wiser to do these necessary things first, and to leave Lindsay to be dealt with later—or, more likely, to fall a victim to the endless Covenanting bickerings.

Montrose went back the road he had come by the Spital of Glenshee, crossed the Dee, and settled himself at Corgarff Castle, at the head of Strathdon. Here he was in a strong position—both to retreat, if necessary, to the high hills, or to sweep down on the Aberdeenshire lowlands. He sent off Alastair once more to collect the Clan Donald, while Lord Gordon and Nathaniel Gordon departed to recruit the men of their name. In this way the time passed till the last days of June. Baillie was meanwhile in the receipt of the daily and most vexatious instructions of the warlike Committee of Estates. This body, with tried warriors such as Argyll, Elcho, and Balfour of Burleigh among its members, was resolved to confide nothing to Baillie's unaided judgment. They were represented at the front by a branch committee, who interpreted their resolutions, and must have driven the unfortunate commander to the verge of madness. One of their performances was the transfer of the flower of Baillie's foot to Lindsay, who employed them in futile raiding in Atholl. The Providence which does not suffer fools gladly was preparing for them their reward.

In the last days of June, Baillie, having ravaged the Gordon lands, laid siege to Huntly's castle in the Bog of Gight. The great keep, well defended by Gordon of Buckie, resisted all his efforts, but the position seemed to call for Montrose's aid, more especially as Lord Gordon had now returned with some two hundred and fifty troopers. As he advanced he heard of the transfer which Baillie had been compelled to make to Lindsay, and he may have guessed at the tyranny of the peripatetic Committee. He found the Covenanters at Keith on the Deveron, drawn up on high ground, with a gap in front of them strongly held by horse and commanded by artillery. The Royalists skirmished in front of the gap and endeavoured to draw the enemy, but Baillie was far too wise to move. Next morning Montrose sent him a challenge by a trumpeter, inviting the honour of an encounter in the levels; and Baillie replied that he was not in the habit of taking his marching orders from the enemy. Montrose accordingly broke up his camp and returned southward to Strathdon. He argued that Baillie might be induced to follow if he saw his enemy marching away from the Gordon country in the direction of the Lowlands. It was a ruse which Hurry had tried successfully before Auldearn.

He was right in his guess, for Baillie had heard further news which cheered his spirits. Alastair and most of the Irish were absent from the royal standard. The stand at Auldearn had put the fear of Ulster into the hearts of the Lowland foot, and as the word sped through the ranks that the terrible Alastair was gone the courage of the Covenanters rose. With all speed they marched south after the enemy, and early on the morning of the 2nd of July came up with him at Alford. Montrose had crossed the Don, and drawn up his men in a good position on a hill. But, as at Auldearn, he had stationed a large number of them behind the ridge, so that to an adversary across the river they seemed an inconsiderable force. The upper Don, which in these days of surface drainage is a shallow and easily crossed stream in the month of July, was then a far more formidable river, with long stretches of bog along its banks. There was one good ford at Alford, and it was Montrose's intention that Baillie should cross there. For if he did he had some marshy levels to traverse before he could reach the *glacis* of Montrose's position, and a defeat would put his army in grave jeopardy with a bog and the river behind them.

Baillie walked into the trap; not of his own will, but urged by his precious Committee and by Balcarres, his master of horse, who trusted to the superiority of his cavalry. It is not easy to be certain of the numbers on both sides. Lindsay's drafts had reduced Baillie to 1,200 foot, but that number must have been increased by levies among the northern counties. Montrose's infantry after Alastair's departure must have fallen well below two thousand, so it is probable that in foot the two forces were nearly equal. The Gordon cavalry numbered about two hundred and fifty, and Baillie cannot have had less than from four hundred to five hundred. One advantage Montrose possessed. He had early notice of the enemy's coming, and had time to draw up his men in an advantageous formation. His dispositions were very different from Auldearn. The horse were placed on each wing, and strengthened by divisions of the Irish foot. On the right Lord Gordon commanded, with Nathaniel Gordon in charge of the foot. Aboyne led the horse on the left, with the Irish under Colonel O'Kean. The centre, drawn up in files of six deep, was composed of Badenoch Highlanders, the Farquharsons, and some of Huntly's Lowland tenants, and was under the charge of Drummond of Balloch and Macdonnell of Glengarry. The reserve of foot concealed behind the ridge was commanded by the Master of Napier.

The Covenanting Committee had ordered Baillie, as soon as the Don was crossed, to charge the enemy's position. Montrose, however, anticipated him. Baillie had brought along with him herds of cattle which he had driven from Huntly's lands, and the sight of his father's beasts penned up in an enclosure behind the Covenanting camp infuriated the young Lord Gordon. He swore to drag Baillie by the throat from the centre of his bodyguard. Accordingly, he led his horse to the charge on the Royalist right with the same fury that had avenged James of Rynie at Auldearn. The Covenanting left broke under the onset, but Balcarres was a gallant soldier who did not easily yield. He managed to rally his three squadrons of horse and for a little a fierce and well-matched cavalry battle raged on the edge of the bog. It would appear that during this struggle the remainder of both armies stood still and watched.

It was Nathaniel Gordon who turned the tide. He led the Irish foot on the right wing to the support of the horse, and he conceived a better way of support than by firing into the mass, where they were in grave danger of wounding their own side. He cried to his men to fling down their muskets, draw their swords, and stab and hough Balcarres's horse. The cruel device succeeded. The Covenant troopers broke and fled, and the Gordons turned their swords, as at Auldearn, against the unprotected left flank of Baillie's infantry. Meanwhile Aboyne with his horse had at length charged on the left, and O'Kean's Irish followed. The two Royalist wings closed in on the Covenant centre, and against it also Glengarry led the Gordon foot. The turn of the battle had arrived. Baillie's famous infantry were enclosed and cut down in files. It needed only the advance of the Master of Napier with his reserves to turn the defeat of the Covenant into a rout. The very camp-boys in the Royalist army mounted the baggage-ponies and took their share in the confusion. Baillie and Balcarres with their horse escaped by the skin of their teeth. The Lowland foot remained to die on the field.[46]

The slaughter on the Covenant side fell little short of Auldearn. The Royalists, considering how desperate was the cavalry battle, lost curiously few officers or men. But they sustained one loss which made the victory little better than a defeat. Lord Gordon, determined to avenge the theft of his father's cattle, charged the retreating horse once too often. His aim was to capture Baillie, and he was actually seizing that general by the sword-belt when he was shot dead from behind by a musketeer concealed among the cattle-pens. His death threw the Royalist army, more especially Montrose and the Gordons, into transports of grief. He had been the young Marcellus of the cause, the one hope of the north. Aboyne stopped his pursuit of Balcarres, and—in Wishart's words—'forgetting their victory and the spoil, they fixed their eyes upon the lifeless body, kissed his face and hands, commended the singular beauty of the corpse, compared the nobility of his descent and the plentifulness of his fortune with the hopefulness of his parts, and counted that an unfortunate

victory that had stood them in so much.' It was a sorrowful band that, led by Montrose, took its way slowly
to Aberdeen, where the young lord was laid in the
Gordons' aisle of the old church of St. Machar. He was
only twenty-eight years of age, and had spent his short
span of life cleanly and chivalrously in the service of his
country. To Montrose the loss was irreparable, for Lord
Gordon was the one man who in temper and attainments
was fitted to be his companion. Patrick Gordon, a clansman, describes this noble friendship-in-arms in words
which deserve quotation:—

'Never two of so short acquaintance did ever love more
dearly. There seemed to be a harmonious sympathy in their natural disposition, so much were they delighted in a mutual conversation. And in this the Lord Gordon seemed to go beyond
the limits which nature had allowed for his carriage in civil
conversation. So real was his affection, and so great the estimation he had of the other, that, when they fell into any familiar
discourse, it was often remarked that the ordinary air of his
countenance was changed, from a serious listening to a certain
ravishment or admiration of the other's witty expressions. And
he was often heard in public to speak sincerely, and confirm it
with oaths, that if the fortune of the present war should prove
at any time so dismal that Montrose for safety should be forced
to fly unto the mountains, without any army or any one to
assist him, he would live with him as an outlaw, and would
prove as faithful a consort to drive away his malour, as he was
then a helper to the advancement of his fortune.'

The armies of Baillie and Hurry had ceased to exist. To
be sure there was still Lindsay, but he was hardly to be
taken seriously. The news of Alford roused the drooping
spirits of Charles. 'It is certain,' Digby wrote, 'that the
king's enemies have not any man in the field now in
Scotland.'[47] He had need of heartening, for the king's
cause, whether he realized it or not, had suffered its
death-blow. Shortly after Alford Montrose received
news—perhaps from his friend Thomas Saintserf, who,

disguised as a packman, travelled between his camp and the Border[48]—of a crushing disaster in England. On the 14th of June at Naseby Cromwell's 'company of poor ignorant men'[49] had scattered Rupert's chivalry and annihilated the royal foot. The battle had two vital consequences for Scotland. It was Cromwell's first clear personal triumph, and it enabled him to press on his policy of religious toleration which was sooner or later to destroy the tyranny of the Covenant.[50] On the other hand, it put an end to the danger of Charles's advance to the north, and Leven was able to withdraw his army from Westmorland and march in his leisurely way south to the siege of Hereford, very anxious lest the slaughter of the Irish women after Naseby should be made a precedent by the Malignants for reprisals on the immense female concourse which accompanied the Scots.[51] On the 28th of June Carlisle after a heroic defence capitulated to David Leslie, and thereby released for service elsewhere a veteran force of horse and foot and a general who had none of Leven's timidity. If the royal standard was still to fly in Britain, it was high time that Montrose crossed the Border.

CHAPTER XIII

KILSYTH
(JULY-AUGUST 1645)

THE Covenant made one last effort to ride the storm. The plague had broken out in Edinburgh, so Parliament was compelled to move to Stirling on the 8th of July. Stirling, however, proved no refuge, and the seat of government was transferred to Perth. Orders were issued to call out the nobles and gentry of the Lowlands, and to levy in the same district a force of 8,800 foot and 485 horse. Baillie had brought back no infantry from his campaign, but he had saved a respectable contingent of horse, pro-bably at least 400 strong. The new force was appointed to assemble at Perth on the 24th of July, and was raised mainly in the Perthshire lowlands, Stirling and Fife. Baillie had returned in no very good temper and had resigned his office; but Parliament passed a vote of thanks to him for his serv-ices, and insisted on his taking command of the new army. For his comfort it appointed the usual Committee 'to advise,' a phrase which, as Baillie well knew, meant to dictate. The members were Argyll, Elcho, Tullibardine, Balcarres, Balfour of Burleigh, and Lindsay—experts in their way, for Montrose had beaten all of them except Lindsay, whom, says Mark Napier, he had as yet only scared.

Alford was fought on the Royalist side wanting Alastair and most of his Irish, the western clans, and the Atholl men. For the final assault on the Lowlands it was necessary to collect all available forces. This meant some weeks of waiting at the shortest, and Aboyne was dispatched into Strathbogie to enlist troopers. He made little speed, either because the Gordons were disinclined to fight south of the Highland line, or because he was a poor recruiting sergeant, and Montrose had to send him back to try again. Aboyne is a difficult figure to decipher on the page of history. He was gallant and loyal, and fairly capable; but he had much of the intractable and suspicious temper of his brother Lewis and his father Huntly. The fine flower of the Gordon race had gone with the young lord. Montrose waited for a few days at Craigton[52] on the Dee in the Irvine country, till the news of the muster and the session of Parliament at Perth decided him to go south. It was an excellent chance to strike at the heart of the opposition.

He marched across Don and Dee to Fordoun in the Mearns, where he waited to receive his expected allies. They arrived in good force. Alastair brought the rest of his Irish and a body of Highlanders some fifteen hundred strong. Among them came the ever faithful Macdonalds of Clanranald and Macdonnells of Glengarry, and no less than seven hundred Macleans from Mull, under their chiefs, Lochbuie and Sir Lachlan of Duart. This warrior clan as a fighting force was second only to the Ulstermen. There were also Macphersons from Badenoch, Farquharsons from Braemar, and Macnabs and Macgregors from the southern Highlands. Young Inchbrakie arrived too with a contingent of the Atholl men. Save for the lack of cavalry Montrose had now the strongest force he had yet commanded. He marched by his old route down the Isla to Dunkeld to watch the movements of the Covenant in Perth, and wait for Aboyne and the Gordons.

Parliament met on the 24th of July under the guard of a large force of infantry and 400 horse. If Montrose was to upset their peace of mind, it was necessary to make a show of cavalry to keep the 400 at home. Accordingly he mounted many of his foot on baggage horses; and as the Perth citizens cast their eyes to the north they were amazed to see a cloud of Royalist cavalry on the horizon. It was sufficient to make them shut the gates and keep close within the walls. For a few days from their camp at Methven, eight miles off, the Royalists kept the ancient city in terror. At any moment the assault might be sounded, and Parliament debated with the fear of sudden death in each debater's heart.

The bluff could not be long kept up. Presently it was discovered that the cavalry was a sham, being no more than eighty troopers and a number of amateurs on pack-horses. The courage of the Covenant horse revived, and a sally was ordered. Montrose had no wish to fight a battle till the time was ripe, and he fell back on his camp at Methven. But Methven was too near the plains to be any permanent refuge, and as the Covenanters advanced he was compelled to retire till he had reached the skirts of the hills. The Covenanting horse harried his rear, but his Highland sharpshooters lay in wait for them, and, stalking them through the undergrowth, emptied a saddle with every shot. The retreat, however, had been too hurried to be without disaster. Some of the Irish women, the wives and daughters of Alastair's soldiery, had straggled too far behind in Methven Wood, and were seized and butchered in cold blood by the Covenanters.[53] 'As at Naseby,' says Mr. Gardiner, 'the notion of avenging injured morality probably covered from the eyes of the murderers the in-herent brutality of their act.'[54] But these poor creatures were no painted madams of the court, but the women-folk of humble soldiers, who followed their husbands and fathers for the same motives that had attached Scotswomen in hundreds to the tail of Leven's army in England.

For a week Montrose waited in Dunkeld till Aboyne arrived with 200 Gordon horse and 120 mounted infantry—that is, musketeers who had some skill in riding, mounted on baggage ponies.[55] Not the least welcome was old Airlie, now recovered from his sickness, who rode in with eighty of his mounted Ogilvys. Montrose now commanded a force of at least four thousand four hundred foot and five hundred cavalry;[56] a seasoned force, for all were hard fighting men, and the thousand Irish were probably the best foot in Britain at the time. Most of the troops had, under his leadership, been present at several victories, and all had wrongs to avenge on some section or other of the Covenanters. It was the first time that he had commanded an army comparable in the strength of all arms to its opponents.

Meanwhile Baillie in Perth was in a gloomy frame of mind. He thought little of his new levies, and he was distracted by his Committee of Advice. Once again he resigned, and once again he was induced to withdraw his resignation. Montrose marched upon Methven to have a look at the enemy, and the Covenanters promptly retired to their fortified camp of Kilgraston on the Earn. As Montrose followed at his leisure he had news which determined his strategy. The Covenant was making a desperate bid for success. Eglinton, Cassilis, and Glencairn were raising the Covenanting westlands; Lanark had collected the Hamilton tenantry, and with 1,000 foot and 500 horse was hastening from Clydesdale. Baillie's army was already superior in numbers to his own, and Montrose did not wish the odds to be too great, for he realized as well as the Covenant that on the coming fight must depend the future of the king's cause in Scotland. He resolved, therefore, to fling himself between Baillie and Lanark. Baillie was lying at Kilgraston waiting on his Fife levies. If he fought him now, he would still have the men of Fife to deal with, not to speak of Lanark. If he cut off the Fife men, he would still have Baillie, and during these manoeuvres Lanark would have arrived. The wiser game was to let Baillie get his Fife recruits, and then cut him off from the west. Besides, the further he could draw the Fife levies from their country the less stomach would these home-keeping souls have for fighting. Lanark he knew of old, and he may well have argued that if he scattered Baillie, he could have little to fear from the Hamiltons.

On or about the 10th of August Montrose slipped past Perth and swept down Glenfarg to the neighbourhood of Kinross. Baillie must have guessed that he had gone to cut off the Fife recruits, but the speedy arrival of these levies in his camp convinced him that this was not Montrose's aim. Presently came news that the grim tower of Castle Campbell above Dollar had been sacked and burned. While the Covenanters lay at the north end of the Ochils, Montrose was turning the eastern flank. Further tidings of him came from the lands of Lord Mar, who was the father-in-law of the Master of Napier. In so large a force Montrose could not exercise the personal supervision which is possible in a small army, and the Irish seem to have got out of hand, for they plundered the little town of Alloa, and some of the Mar holdings. Mar, however, bore no ill-will, for, while Alastair led on the foot in advance, he invited Montrose and his staff to dine with him at Alloa House. By this time Baillie had made up his mind. As Montrose was at dinner he received the intelligence that the Covenanters were marching with all speed along the north side of the Ochils to cut him off. It was vital to his strategy that he should keep ahead of them; so, hastily catching up his foot, he led his army that night across the Forth, a mile or two above Stirling. Next day he continued his march in the direction of Glasgow, and by the evening of the 14th of August was encamped in an upland meadow on one of the affluents of the river Kelvin, about a mile north-east of the town of Kilsyth. He argued that it was now Baillie's business to find him and fight him, for the Covenanters must pass beneath him before they could join Lanark, who was marching from Glasgow.

Baillie, making the best speed possible past Dunblane and down the Allan water, was compelled by Argyll to waste time in burning Lord Stirling's castle of Menstrie and the Graham house of Airth. He found, as he expected, that the presence of the Committee made discipline almost impossible, and the Fife levies grew more out of humour and spirit with every mile that increased the distance from their homes. On the evening of the 14th he was encamped at Hollinbush on the road from Stirling, only two and a half miles from where Montrose lay. His scouts had kept him well informed of the enemy's whereabouts, and a great discussion arose in the Committee. Baillie was for taking no risks, and waiting till Lanark, now only twelve miles distant, brought up his reinforcements. But Argyll and his colleagues would brook no delay. They had 6,000 foot, and 800 horse. They were in the Lowlands at last; and Lanark at the latest would be with them in a few hours. Let them strike home at once, and Lanark when he came would help to take order with the fugitives.

The dawn of the 15th was windless and cloudless, giving promise of a scorching August day. With the first light the Covenanters were on the move. They left the road and made straight across country in the direction of Montrose's camp, wading through fields of ripening corn, and scrambling up the steep slopes of the Campsie Hills. Soon they reached the rim of the basin where the Royalists lay, and Baillie, tired of the rough journey, was content to halt in what seemed an impregnable position. He held the high ground, and below him fell the rugged hill to the little burn, beyond which lay Montrose. A quarter of a mile to the right the glen closed in, and the burn descended through a narrow ravine. The military genius of the Committee immediately conceived a plan. They believed that Montrose was doomed to defeat, and their only fear was lest he should escape to the north, for that way lay the road to Menteith and the Highlands. If they could outflank him and take up a position on the ridge due north from his left he would be pinned between them and the Lowlands.

As Montrose watched the enemy's doings he was content with the ground he had chosen. He did not believe that Baillie would charge down the steep; if he did, the use of horse on such ground was impossible, and he could guess the condition in which the Lowland infantry would arrive at the bottom. He believed that the Covenanters would simply wait for Lanark, and he had made up his mind to charge the position above, for the steeps of the Campsies were nothing to men who knew Glencoe and Lochaber. He asked his army whether they chose to retreat or fight, and the fierce cry for battle reassured him of their spirit. Foreseeing the heat of the day, he bade his Highlanders cast their plaids and fight in their shirts, and knot up the long tails of their kilts between their legs to give them freedom of action.[57] His horse he ordered to wear their shirts above their buff jerkins, in order that they might be distinguished from the enemy. It was a necessary precaution in an army of many different levies, where the separate parts were scarcely known to each other. Alastair's men in the heat of battle must have some clear mark by which to distinguish friend from foe, or regrettable incidents would occur. Near the head of the glen, and on the slope of the hill on which the Covenanters stood, were several cottages and little gardens walled with dry-stone dikes. It was a sort of Hougoumont, a place which any prudent commander must seize; so he ordered its occupation by the advance guard of Alastair's centre, which happened to be a body of Macleans under Ewan of Treshnish.

But as Montrose watched the crest of the hill he observed the Covenanters in motion. He could scarcely believe his eyes when he perceived that they were about to attempt a flank march across his front. It is never a safe or easy manoeuvre, more especially when the foe is almost within musket shot, and in mobility and speed is the superior of the side attempting it. Baillie bitterly protested; but the Committee would have their way, and for the rest of the day he was carrying out orders not his own. To reach the hill directly above Montrose's left it was necessary to make the circuit of the glen and cross the burn, which there flowed in a ravine. The movement was led by Balcarres and the horse, and Baillie followed close on him with the foot, accompanied by Lindsay and Balfour of Burleigh.

On one condition alone might such a move have succeeded. If the Covenanters had kept behind the ridge in their march, leaving a small force to occupy the crest of the hill in their old position, they might have safely reached their goal, and once there, with a gradual slope before them on which horse could be used, they would have seriously embarrassed Montrose. But such tactics needed a swiftness and a precision which the Covenanters did not possess. Almost at once they were visible to the Royalists below, owing to a grave breach of discipline. A certain Major Haldane, observing the cottages which Treshnish had occupied, decided on his own authority that he must attack the position. Accordingly with his men he broke off from the main march and started down the hill. He was soon driven back; but it was never the Highland way to repel without a counter-attack. Alastair launched the whole body of Macleans against the assailants, and they were speedily followed by their old rivals, the Macdonalds of Clanranald, who vied with them in the race for the ridge. Young Donald of Moidart won, but Lachlan of Duart was little behind. On surged the billow of Celtic war till it struck the Covenant line in the middle. Colonel Hume, who commanded there, drew off four of his foot regiments behind some dikes on the hilltop, and attempted a stand. But the Highlanders leapt the walls with their targes high and their heads down, and in a few minutes the Covenant centre was in flight.

Macdonald's breach of orders had succeeded beyond its deserts, and Baillie's army was cut in two.

Meanwhile the Covenant van had crossed the burn and rounded the head of the glen. Montrose, who at first can only have guessed at the aim of the flank movement, now saw clearly its motive. It was impossible to let the enemy occupy the height on his left, so he dispatched a body of Gordon foot under their adjutant to forestall them. The bulk of Balcarres's horse must have been behind the ridge, for if Montrose could have seen their full force he would have attempted to hold the hill in greater strength. The Gordons found the task beyond their power.[58] They were driven back, and to the eyes of Aboyne—whom Montrose, remembering Lord Gordon's fate at Alford, had kept at the rear with a strong bodyguard—seemed to be caught in a deathtrap. He broke away with the Gordon horse to the assistance of his kinsmen. But he, too, was surrounded, and Montrose called upon Airlie and his Ogilvys to redeem the day. The gallant old man, for all his seventy years and more, led his troops to the charge, and the tide of battle on the hill began to turn. Then Montrose dispatched Nathaniel Gordon with the remainder of the cavalry, seeing that Alastair was having his own way in the rest of the field. Balcarres's cuirassiers were driven back from the ridge, the advance foot were routed, and the Covenant van shared the fate of the Covenant centre.[59]

Baillie was soon aware that the day was lost. Haldane's escapade brought him racing back from Balcarres's side, but the mischief had been done. He endeavoured in vain to rally the foot, and then in despair galloped to the rear for the Fife reserves. But the men of Fife had early despaired of the issue, and were in full flight for their homes. About the same time Montrose's trumpets sounded the general advance. The whole Royalist army swept up the hill, but no foe awaited them on the crest. The semicircle of the little amphitheatre was empty, and the outside rim was strewn with flying horse and foot. Of the 6,000 men who had set out to fight that morning under the Covenant's banner scarcely a hundred escaped. The murder of their women in Methven Wood had not disposed Ulsterman or Highlander to a mercy which they knew would never be extended to themselves. Many of the horse, too, perished, caught in the mires of Dullatur. The leaders escaped, as always happened in the Covenant's battles. The lairds and nobles had better horses, and they had no scruple of honour in saving their own necks and leaving the plain folk who had trusted them to perish miserably. Well for themselves that the western Covenanters were too late for the fight, and had ample time to escape. Lanark fled to Berwick, Glencairn and Cassilis to Ireland. Baillie sought sanctuary in Stirling Castle, where he was joined by Balcarres and Balfour of Burleigh. Loudoun and Lindsay escaped to England. Argyll galloped twenty miles to Queensferry on the Forth, where he found a boat which landed him at Berwick in the safe keeping of the Scots garrison. As at Inveraray and at Inverlochy he escaped by water from Montrose's swords.

The decisive battle had at last been fought. So far as Scotland was concerned the forces of the Covenant were annihilated, and its leaders were in exile. Scarcely a year had passed since that autumn evening when, with two companions, Montrose had alighted at the door of Tullibelton—without men, money, or prospects, and with no resources for his wild mission save the gallantry of his heart. Since then he had scourged the Covenant from Inveraray to Buchan, and from Lochaber to Angus. With halting allies and few troops, with poor weapons and scanty ammunition, amid broken promises and private sorrows and endless disappointments, he had sought out his enemies and beaten them wherever he found them. He had excelled them in strategy and in tactics, in cavalry and in infantry movements, in the offensive and in the defensive. He had shown himself able to adapt his few resources to any emergency, and to rise superior to any misfortune. His reward had come. For the moment he was the undisputed master of all Scotland.

CHAPTER XIV

THE WAR ON THE BORDER
(AUGUST–SEPTEMBER 1645)

'I PROFESS to you,' wrote Digby to Jermyn on the 21st of September, a month after Kilsyth, 'I never did look upon our business with that assurance that I do now, of God's carrying us through with His own immediate hand, for all this work of Montrose is above what can be attributed to mankind.'[60] Had there been any other Royalist of one-tenth of Montrose's genius the king's crown would never have fallen. But from the south he received nothing but empty praise. What had become of Sir Philip Musgrave's 500 horse, what of the 1,500 which Digby promised? Montrose had been true to his word; he had scattered the Covenant in Scotland, and deprived Leven and Leslie of a base. But to 'fix his conquests' was beyond the power of mortal man unless help came from the south. He himself thought otherwise. He hoped still to lead a great army across the Border, and turn the wavering balance in Charles's favour. But his courage outran the possibilities. Scotland was subdued, not converted, and, unless the king came north as a conqueror, Montrose would have to wrestle daily and ceaselessly to hold her to her unwilling allegiance. Never in history have Highlands dominated Lowlands for long.

At first the prospect looked fair enough. After waiting two days at Kilsyth, during which he sent a message of assurance to the city of Glasgow, the victorious general entered the capital of the west. Glasgow was at this time a thriving and clean little city, clustering around its cathedral and ancient university above the meadows of Clyde. Here seven years before had been held that General Assembly at which Episcopacy in Scotland had been abolished, and Montrose in his Presbyterian zeal had shown himself the foremost in the baiting of Hamilton. The place had never evinced the Covenanting virulence of Edinburgh. Pride in their great church, happily saved from the iconoclasts, had kept its citizens on the side of decency and temperance in religious affairs. A deputation from the town council met the king's lieutenant outside the walls, offering the value of £500 in English money as a largess to the soldiers, and praying that the city might be left unmolested. To this request Montrose readily agreed. He issued stringent orders against theft and violence, and his entry was welcomed with a popular enthusiasm hardly to be looked for in the Lowlands. Unfortunately the sight of the well-stocked booths and prosperous dwellings of the Saltmarket and the Gallowgate was too much for some of his followers, who had not believed that so much wealth existed in the world, and could not readily forget their Highland creed that spoil should follow victory. Looting began, and Montrose, true to his word, promptly hanged several of the malefactors. But he saw that Glasgow was to prove too severe a trial to his army, so two days after his arrival, about the 20th of August, he marched six miles up the river to Bothwell.

Here he took measures for the government of Scotland, which the fortune of war had now entrusted to his hands. The first business was to stamp out the embers of disaffection. Some of Eglinton's levies were still threatening in the west, and Alastair was dispatched to bring them to reason. He met with no opposition, and to his surprise was welcomed cordially at Loudoun Castle by the wife of the Covenanting chancellor. The shires of Renfrew and Ayr sent in their submission and petitioned for favour. Other counties and burghs followed suit, and presently arrived the nobles and gentry to greet the rising sun. The midlands of Scotland were naturally foremost. Linlithgow, Erskine, Seton, Drummond, Maderty—declared Covenanters and passive Loyalists alike—hastened to Bothwell. More important were the recruits from the south, the nobles whom Montrose had solicited in vain at Dumfries the year before. Annandale, Hartfell, and Fleming swore allegiance, as did powerful lairds like Charteris of Amisfield and those Border earls, Roxburgh and Home, who for the past few years had coquetted with both king and Covenant. Traquair, another waverer, sent his son, Lord Linton, with the promise of a troop of horse. Carnwath's brother, Sir John Dalziel, brought the fiercest blood[61] in the Lowlands to the standard. And to crown all came the Marquis of Douglas, who as Lord Angus had been the travelling companion of Montrose's youth. The prestige of the Bloody Heart had not wholly died even in an age which had tried to bolt the door on the past, and the vast Douglas lands in Clydesdale and Dumfries promised a rich recruiting ground.

There were other allies to be gathered. At the earliest opportunity the Master of Napier and Nathaniel Gordon were dispatched Edinburgh-wards on a jail delivery. From the prison at Linlithgow they released Lord Napier and Stirling of Keir, and the ladies of the Stirling and Napier families. Arriving within four miles of Edinburgh they summoned the city in the king's name, and received the humble submission of a deputation from the town council. A money fine was offered, and it was explained that they had been driven into rebellion against their will by the craft of a few seditious men. The plague which was still raging had sapped all civic valour, and the Edinburgh Covenanters were ready to promise anything for peace.

The Tolbooth was full of Royalists, and during the year death and sickness had raged in that noisome place. Crawford, Ogilvy, Reay, the laird of Drum, and Wishart the chaplain were among those set free. Wishart never forgot the experience. It made him, as he said, a 'friend of prisoners for ever,' and he bore the marks of the rats' teeth to his grave. One captive they did not recover. The young Lord Graham was in the Castle, and the Castle was still in Covenant hands. The gallant boy[62] refused an exchange, declaring that it would ill-become one so young and useless to deprive his father of a single prisoner. Napier and Gordon had another mission to execute in the east. They carried a letter from Montrose to Drummond of Hawthornden, begging for a copy of his 'Irene,' the pamphlet written in 1638 during Montrose's Covenanting days, that it might be printed and published 'to the contentment of all His Majesty's good subjects.' The old poet promised to transcribe and send the paper, but before it arrived the curtain had fallen on the new Golden Age which he had thought restored.

By the 1st of September Napier and Gordon with their released prisoners were back in the camp at Bothwell. On that day Sir Robert Spottiswoode, the king's secretary for Scotland, arrived with letters from Charles. He brought with him a patent, dated the 15th of June, creating Montrose lieutenant-governor and captain-general of Scotland. The royal instructions were to join the Border earls and march with all haste to Tweed. As these had been issued before Alford and Kilsyth they seemed to Montrose to have redoubled force now that he was master of Scotland. Besides, Home and Roxburgh had written, pleading with him to come to Tweedside and add their spears to his standard. Every prospect seemed rosy, and Montrose dispatched a post to the king announcing that he hoped speedily to cross the Border with 20,000 men. On the 3rd of September he held a great review of his troops, when the royal commission was presented to the viceroy and handed for proclamation to Sir Archibald Primrose, the founder of the family of Rosebery. Montrose's first act under his new authority was to confer the honour of knighthood on Alastair. He had nobly earned it. The next few months of blundering in Argyll were to show how little of a general he was on his own account. Two years later he was to disappear from history, stabbed in the back in an obscure Irish fray. But as a brigadier under Montrose he was worth an army, and his stand at Auldearn will live as long as feats of valour can stir the hearts of men.

As soon as the king's commission was received Montrose, as viceroy of Scotland, took steps for the administration of the government. He issued proclamations to the chief towns, summoning a Parliament to be held in Glasgow on the 20th of October next 'for settling religion and peace, and freeing the oppressed subjects of those insupportable burdens they have groaned under this time bygone.' He prepared also a statement[63] which he probably intended to present to Parliament when it assembled. It is on the lines of his Dumfries manifesto, but a fuller and clearer confession of faith. He repeats the justification of the National Covenant—the evils of an unnatural and enforced Prelacy, under which ecclesiastics intermeddled with civil government, and, 'the life of the Gospel was stolen away by enforcing on the Kirk a dead Service Book.' To every line of that Covenant he still adhered, but long ago its mission was accomplished. First at Berwick and then at Ripon the king had granted all their demands. Further no true Covenanter could go, for the cause of the Covenant was the cause of king and country. All that had been done since had been alien to the Covenant spirit, and every honest man must needs part company with its perverters. 'We were constrained to suffer them to deviate without us, with the multitude misled by them, whose eyes they seal in what concerns religion, and hearts they steal away in what concerns loyalty.' He expounds his own

difficulties—'wrestling betwixt extremities'—till facts
decided for him. The nobles had tasted 'the sweetness of
government,' and they would not be content till they
had destroyed 'lawful authority and the liberty of the
subject.' The Kirk would have coerced men into blind
obedience, a tyranny worse than Popery. He took up
arms, be says, first, for national religion, 'the restoration of
that which our first reformers had;' second, for the maintenance of the central authority, the king; and, third, for
'the vindication of our nation from the base servitude of
subjects, who, like the Israelites, have their burdens dou-
bled, but are not sensible of them.' He answers his critics,
especially those timorous souls who 'are so stuffed with
infidelity that they can believe nothing but what they see,
and can commit nothing to God.' If he had used the services of Alastair Macdonald, a 'professed Papist,' did not
his opponents employ in Ireland, under Monro, the self-
same people? He repudiates the charge of blood-guilti-
ness. He had never 'shed the blood of any but of such as
were sent forth by them to shed our blood and to take
our lives,' adding, with a touch of the Covenanters' own
manner, 'and what is done in the land it may sensibly seem
to be the Lord's doing, in making a handful to overthrow
multitudes.' Freedom and toleration in religion, a strong
central government, and a lighter taxation for the bur-
dened people of Scotland—for these he had drawn the
sword.

It was the appeal to his countrymen on which he
hoped to build a civil authority to correspond to that
which he had won in war. The merits of the creed as an
ideal of statecraft will be discussed later. At present we
have to consider it as tactics, a step in the game of high
politics. As such it was bound to fail. The appeal was unin-
telligible to all save a few, and the defence would not
convince. The people of the Lowlands had lost friends and
kinsmen in the Highland wars, their ears had been horri-
fied with endless tales of pillage and violence, and at the

back of every Lowland heart lay a jealousy and dislike of the Celt, whether Ulster or Scottish, as of a race they did not understand. To say that Monro had used similar troops in Ireland was no more convincing to most people than to urge that the clans had once fought bravely at Bannockburn for Scottish independence. To point to Argyll's barbarities in the Highlands as worse than any slaughter by Alastair was to miss the point of the grievance. To a Lowlander the victims in the first case were savages and aliens, and in the latter they were 'kindly Scots.' As for the king, there was still some loyal sentiment for him in Scotland, a clannish feeling, for had she not given to England the royal house? But the feeling was only sentimental, while Montrose's royalism was a reasoned appeal for a central authority, whatever name it might be given—an appeal which nobody, except perhaps Napier, understood. As for the Kirk, no doubt its encroachments were becoming a burden, but it had the terrible mastery over its people which is given by the possession of the keys of heaven and hell. Before that tyranny could be broken there were to be long years of struggle and much shedding of innocent blood. Besides, the Lowlands had no other voice than the ministers. They were the sole interpreters, teachers, and guides. No mere proclamation could break through that plate armour of defence to the starved and puzzled souls behind it. The one argument of practical value was the promise to reduce the grievous weight of taxation. But a Lowland peasant or burgher might well have been pardoned for doubting whether Montrose, with an army of hungry kerns to keep, would prove an easier tax-collector. The remonstrance, while of the highest value as a clue to Montrose's philosophy, shows that he wholly misread the immediate political situation. He could look for recruits only to those who were tired of the domineering Kirk, and jealous of the Covenanting leaders. Such were to be found among the nobles and gentry alone, and these, and the tenantry they could command, were all that appeared in the camp at Bothwell.

Meanwhile that army which had fought under him in so many battles was beginning as usual to melt away. The Highlanders wanted to return to their homes. It was their fashion, for the families they left behind them had rarely food for more than a week or two, and would starve if the husbands and fathers did not return often to replenish the pot. Miserably poor, war was a business to them, and they had to deposit their winnings. They had stayed on after Kilsyth, in the hope of the plunder of Glasgow, but Glasgow was inviolate, and one or two of them who had tried to use the rich town as it should be used were now swinging from Glasgow gibbets for their pains. Further, the £500 which the citizens had offered was not to be paid. The town council, fearing lest the meeting of Parliament would cost the city large sums, begged to be let off the contribution, and Montrose had consented. The clans were disgusted, and began to trickle away. There were other reasons. The Macleans must be looking after their homes in Mull, or the Campbells would be avenging Kilsyth. The Macdonalds had still grudges to wreak on Clan Diarmaid which not even Inverlochy had satisfied. There is no reason to blame the Highlanders unduly. Organized Lowland warfare, such as Montrose now proposed, was a thing which they did not understand, and which upset the whole system and tradition of their lives. Sir Alastair alone deserves censure. He was an experienced soldier, and knew something of the difficulties that were before his chief. But his knighthood and his new post of captain-general of the clans under Montrose had turned his head. He proposed to himself a campaign in Argyll which should root the Campbells out of the peninsula. He promised to return, and no doubt honestly meant it, but from the hour when he marched off with half his Irishry and all the Highlanders, Montrose never saw his old lieutenant again. Five hundred Ulstermen—among them the gallant O'Kean—to their eternal honour refused to leave the royal standard.

Douglas and Ogilvy had been already dispatched to the Borders to recruit, and on the 4th of September Montrose broke up his camp at Bothwell and began his march towards Tweed. His plan was to march through the Lothians, and then descend by one of the passes of the Lammermoors to the country of Home and Roxburgh. At the end of the first day, however, he had to face a defection more serious than Alastair's. Aboyne had been rapidly getting out of humour, and his ill-temper was zealously fomented by Huntly, his father. He was insulted because Crawford, instead of himself, had been given the command of the cavalry. The return of Ogilvy had restored to Montrose his oldest comrade, and to the Gordon it seemed that an Ogilvy was preferred before him. The dispatches to the king which he had seen were in his view insufficiently laudatory of his own doings. Last and most important there was old Huntly, whose every letter upbraided his heir for an alliance with an enemy of his house. The untameable perverseness of the Gordon blood triumphed over his loyalty both to his king and his general. In spite of Ogilvy's appeals, he marched off with the Gordon horse and foot. Only Nathaniel Gordon remained; for him the comradeship-in-arms begun after Tippermuir was only to end with death.

Montrose traversed the moorland country of the Lothians, avoiding the plague-stricken Edinburgh, to Cranstoun, south-east of Dalkeith. It was now Saturday, the 6th of September, and on the following day it was intended that Wishart should preach to the army. But news was received from Lord Erskine which changed the situation. David Leslie, the future Lord Newark, and a soldier far abler than Leven or Baillie, had after Carlisle taken his horse to the assistance of Leven at Hereford. But the tidings of Kilsyth altered his plans. His men refused to continue the war in England while Scotland was defenceless, and, though his first intention was only to take half his force, he was soon compelled to take the whole 4,000. The siege of Hereford was raised—it was the one direct result of Kilsyth in the king's favour—while Leslie hastened with all speed to the north. Had the king's army been better led, he would never have reached the Border. There was one moment at Rotherham, as he himself admitted, when, if the adjacent royal forces had struck, he would have been destroyed. But he passed unchallenged, and, collecting reinforcements of foot from the garrisons of Newcastle and Berwick, he had crossed the Border on the 6th of September, with Middleton commanding his advance guard. His aim was to cut off Montrose from the Highlands, so he proposed to take up his position somewhere on the neck of land between Forth and Clyde.

The problem before Montrose was once more the old one of how to raise an army. Cavalry he must find, for Aboyne's defection had left him with scarcely a hundred troopers, most of them probably Lord Airlie's Ogilvys. He could count on some levies as the result of Douglas's recruiting, and for the rest he must depend upon Home and Roxburgh. After that he would go north and test the quality of David Leslie. Accordingly, on the Saturday afternoon, the Royalists turned to their right and marched down Gala water to Tweedside. Next day at Torwoodlee, Douglas and Ogilvy joined them with some 1,200 horse from Nithsdale and Upper Clydesdale and the Borders. The recruits were all lairds or lairds' sons and their immediate retainers, a half-hearted and unstable crew who had none of the old moss-trooping fire. Somewhere, too, on Gala water, Linton joined with his troop of Peeblesshire horse, and his father, Traquair, rode over to visit the viceroy. He came in all likelihood to spy out the nakedness of the land, with results which we shall see.

Marching slowly down Tweed, Montrose reached Kelso on the 8th or 9th. It was the appointed rendezvous, but he found no sign of Home or Roxburgh. He waited for a day, and then he heard ominous news. The Border earls were with Leslie, prisoners, so ran their own story, captured by Middleton and his advance guard. It was a tale which common opinion scouted, and indeed it is intrinsically unlikely that two powerful nobles in their own country-side, twenty miles at least from Leslie's line of march, and with ample knowledge of his coming, should not have been able to escape if they had wished it. It is far more probable that, knowing Leslie's strength and Montrose's predicament, they sought security by putting themselves in the enemy's power.

To tarry at Kelso was mere folly, so Montrose turned wearily up Tweed. Douglas held out hopes of raising the westlands—vain hopes, for in no quarter of Scotland was the power of the ministers so great. He rated the prestige of the Douglas name higher than was warranted by tacts. Montrose accepted the scheme, for in any case it would lead him back to the hills to which he had always turned his eyes for help. He marched to Jedburgh, but there was nothing to be looked for from the Kerrs, whose chief, Lothian, was a Covenanting general. Then he entered the Scott country, but Buccleuch also was a Covenanter of a sort, and the old raiding spirit was dying in his glens. The successors of Wat of Harden and Dickie of Dryhope were a peaceable folk, and brawls at a fair or a clipping were their only form of war. He would have fared better among the Armstrongs and Elliots farther south, who, as Cromwell was to find, were still good men of their hands. During the march Sir Robert Spottiswoode wrote a letter[64]—never posted—to Digby, who was still nursing his vain dreams. He told him of Montrose's desperate plight, and upbraided him for not detaining Leslie in England. He asked what had become of the promised cavalry. Digby at the moment, and for a fortnight later, was full of hope and confidence, which even the disaster of Rowton Heath could not shake. Stories were arriving of a fight in Westmorland, in which Crawford and Ogilvy had annihilated Leslie. Soon he was to hear from Byron that the soldiers in Poyntz's army were celebrating a great victory which had shattered Montrose's power. The first tale was false, the second proved only too true.

On the afternoon of the 12th of September, Montrose had arrived at the gate of the hill country, the flats of Philiphaugh, under the little burgh of Selkirk, where the two glens of Yarrow and Ettrick meet. Just below the junction of the streams, on the left-hand bank of Ettrick, is a level meadow a quarter of a mile wide, with the water on one side, and a steep wooded hill on the other. Here he fixed his camp, and placed his few guns. It was protected on the south and east by the Ettrick and its tributary the Yarrow, on the north by the hill, and on the west by the Yarrow and a steep wood called the Hareheadshaw. The position was a strong one, but as the army did not expect a battle it was probably only loosely occupied. There was no premonition of immediate danger. Leslie was believed to be far away on the Forth, and, in Sir Robert Spottiswoode's letter to Digby, Montrose was said to be re-solute to chase him. He did not know that the pursued had become the pursuer.

At Gladsmuir in East Lothian late on the 11th of September, Leslie had received a letter revealing the weakness of the Royalist force. Popular tradition[65] made Traquair the sender, and there is no reason to disbelieve a tale so consistent with the character of a family which, during the Covenant, as during the later Jacobite, wars, was uniformly treacherous. Traquair had also shown his hand by sending a message to his son, Lord Linton, to withdraw him and his troop from Montrose's camp. Leslie, when he got the news, at once changed his plans. He marched straight down Gala Water, crossed the ridge at Rink, and forded Tweed.[66] Late on the night of the 12th he had reached the hamlet of Sunderland, which stood on the peninsula formed by the junction of Tweed and Ettrick. He was now less than three miles from the

Royalist camp. He had caught his quarry, but only by the skin of his teeth, for another day would have seen Montrose safe in the hills.

The king's captain-general left the posting of the pickets to his officers, and retired himself with the flower of his cavalry across the Ettrick to a lodging in the West Port of Selkirk.[67] Here for most of the night he busied himself with dispatches to the king, and possibly, too, with revising his address to the coming Parliament. It was an inexplicable blunder, only to be accounted for by one of those fits of bodily and mental weariness which come at times upon the greatest commanders. The night was dark as pitch, and though mounted scouts were sent out to patrol all the approaches they saw and heard nothing. Since the scouts were local men and Traquair's tenants, it is possible that they were infected with the treachery of their master. Charteris of Amisfield, indeed, seems to have got in touch with Leslie's pickets at Sunderland, and shots were exchanged, but his account was confused, and the incident was regarded as a drunken brawl among his men and not reported to the general.[68] The morning dawned with one of those thick autumnal fogs which in the valley bottoms in the early hours prevent a man seeing three yards before him. Scouts were sent out again at the first light, and reported to Montrose that the country was clear. So it was, on all sides except the direction of Sunderland, and Amisfield's report from that quarter had been already discounted. Meantime the enemy had divided his force into two parts, and with one marched swiftly up the left bank of Ettrick. The other, 2,000 strong, had crossed that water and by way of Will's Nick had reached the Selkirk road. After cooking a leisurely meal, Montrose's army was assembling for parade, when through the mists came the rush of Leslie's horse.

Montrose was at breakfast when he received the news. He flung himself on a horse, and with Airlie, Crawford, and Napier, galloped back to his army. He found the field in confusion. Douglas's moss-troopers, in spite of their gallant leader, had fled at the first shot. The 500 Ulstermen, however, were fighting a desperate fight, having found or thrown up some shallow defences. Montrose collected his hundred troopers and charged Leslie so madly that for the moment he drove back the whole Covenant horse. But 600 men, taken by surprise, and with no advantages of position, cannot for long do battle with 6,000. Leslie's other division harassed the Royalist right flank with musketry fire from beyond the stream, and presently had forded Ettrick and were attacking them from behind. Again and again the Covenant troopers charged, only to be driven back by the heroic Irish; again and again Montrose's hundred cut their way deep into the enemy's ranks. Philiphaugh was not a battle; it was a surprise and a massacre. Soon only fifty horse were left, and of the Irish more than four hundred were dead. The remnant of the latter under their adjutant Stewart were induced to surrender on a promise of quarter.[69]

Montrose fought with a gallantry and desperation worthy of Alastair, and but for his friends would have died on the field. Lord Douglas and Sir John Dalziel pled with him to take his chance of flight, urging that so long as he lived the king's cause need not go down. He allowed himself to be persuaded. With about thirty others, including the two Napiers, Lord Erskine, and Lord Fleming, as well as Dalziel and Douglas, he cut a road to the west and repulsed a feeble attempt at pursuit. The little party galloped up Yarrow vale, and at Broadmeadows took the drove-road across Minchmoor to Tweeddale. As they disappeared into the green hills, with them disappeared the dream of a new and happier Scotland. Montrose's cycle of victories had proved like the fairy gold which vanishes in a man's hand. The year of miracles was ended.

CHAPTER XV

AFTER PHILIPHAUGH
(SEPTEMBER 1645–SEPTEMBER 1646)

MONTROSE did not draw rein till he reached the old house of Traquair, whose grey and haunted walls still stand among the meadows where the Quair burn flows to Tweed. Its lord shut his door on the fugitives; his welcome was reserved for the conquering Leslie, when with Argyll and Lothian he arrived later in pursuit. At Peebles[70] the company halted for a little, and then pushed on to Biggar, where they spent the night, and long before daybreak were in the saddle and heading for the west. Fugitives were picked up by the way, including an Ulsterman, who had wrapped the colours of the foot round his breast, and, having found a horse, caught up Montrose and restored to him one of the standards. The other, the cavalry colours, was carried by Kinnoul's brother, William Hay, into England, and months afterwards was brought to Montrose in the north. As they forded Clyde they met to their joy old Airlie and Crawford, who had probably taken the route by Meggat and upper Tweed, and had collected on the road a few of Douglas's fleeing troopers. Somehow the party made their way through the midlands, and by the 19th were safe on the confines of Atholl.

Now came the harvest of the triumphant Covenant. It began on the day of Philiphaugh. Three hundred Irish women with their children were butchered on the field. Those who wish to sup deep on horrors can find the details in Patrick Gordon. The cooks and horse-boys also perished to the number of some two hundred. The Irish under Stewart had surrendered on terms, but Argyll and the ministers who accompanied Leslie remonstrated against the Lord's work being hindered by any foolish clemency. They argued that quarter had been granted to Stewart alone and not to his men. Leslie professed himself convinced by this miserable quibble, and the unarmed Irish were cut down as they stood, or shot next morning in the courtyard of Newark Castle.[71] O'Kean and another officer, Lachlan, were spared for the moment, only to be hanged later in Edinburgh without a trial. Stewart was also destined to death, but was fortunate enough to escape to Montrose.

The zeal of the Covenant against the daughters of Heth was not satiated by the butchery at Philiphaugh. Many had escaped, and were slaughtered singly as they wandered among the moors of Tweed and Clyde. In most county histories the slaying is ascribed to the infuriated country people, but for this there is no evidence. The peasantry of the Lowlands have never had a taste for such brutality, and the murders were undoubtedly the work of the soldiers of the Covenant, who beat the hills for Royalists, as Lag's dragoons forty years later were to beat them for Covenanters. One large party of the poor creatures was brought to Leslie's camp at Linlithgow. They were flung over the bridge of Avon, and were either drowned in the river or stabbed with the pikes of the soldiers who lined the banks. The records of the Irish rebellion hold no more horrid cruelties. The inspiration was not Leslie's; it came from the fierce bigots who accompanied him. Sometimes the soldiers sickened of the work, and asked their clerical advisers, as Leslie did at

Dunavertie, 'Mass John, Mass John, have you not gotten your fill of blood?'[72]

The roll of captives was a large one. Ogilvy, Hartfell, Drummond, Sir Robert Spottiswoode, Sir William Rollo, and Nathaniel Gordon were among those who fell into Leslie's hands. He marched slowly through the Lothians towards Glasgow, where a provisional committee dealt with the prisoners. The leaders were all reserved for death, though the laymen as usual were disposed to be merciful. On the 20th of October, on the date and at the place which Montrose had appointed for his Parliament, a committee of the Estates sat in judgment. The first to be dealt with was Sir William Rollo, whose brother had married Argyll's sister. For all his lameness he had never left Montrose's side, and had been one of his most trusted brigadiers. He was beheaded on the 21st. On the following day there died Sir Philip Nisbet, who had fought in the king's army in England, and young Ogilvy of Inverquharity,[73] a handsome boy still in his teens. The lay Covenanters had their scruples over these executions, and recollected that in the English war there had been no such slaying of prisoners. But the ministers were inexorable. 'The work gangs bonnily on,' said Mr. David Dickson, rubbing his hands below the scaffold.[74] Only by blood could the wrath of the strange deity he worshipped be appeased.

Owing to Montrose's threatened raid the rest of the executions were postponed. They began again in St. Andrews before Christmas. The Kirk was in terror lest Parliament should be too merciful, and appeals flowed in from every synod and presbytery. 'We are confident,' wrote the gentle ministers of the Merse, 'that your hearts will not faint nor your hands fail until you have cut off the horns of the wicked.' The delays, according to the Commissioners of the General Assembly, were 'displeasing unto the Supreme Judge of the world, and grievous unto the hearts of the Lord's people.' The Lord's people were soon to be comforted, for the Estates set to work in earnest. But meantime one of their chief victims escaped. Lord Ogilvy could look for no mercy, for his family was the pet aversion of Argyll, and during his short three weeks of liberty he had been the right-hand of the king's captain-general. But he was a cousin of Lindsay and akin on his mother's side to the Hamiltons, so he was allowed the last consolation of a visit from his mother, wife, and sister. He was sick in bed when the ladies were admitted in the dusk of a December evening. Adopting Lady Nithsdale's device of a later day, his sister put on his night-cap and got into bed, while he dressed himself in her clothes. When the guards entered they found three tearful women taking farewell of the doomed prisoner, and conducted them to the prison gates. Horses were waiting close at hand, and Ogilvy galloped across Fife to a shelter in Menteith. Argyll would have visited his wrath upon the heroic lady, but the Hamilton influence was strong enough to save her from his clutches.

There was no such hope for the others. They were tried, not as the law enjoined by their peers or by the whole Parliament, but by a self-appointed committee. Some of the judges voted with qualifications, but the verdict was certain. Hartfell, indeed, was pardoned. He was disliked by the Hamiltons, and Argyll owed them a tit for tat for their clemency towards the Ogilvys. On the 20th of December the 'Maiden,' which had been sent for from Dundee, was set up at the market-cross of St. Andrews, and Nathaniel Gordon, Andrew Guthrie—a son of the Bishop of Moray—and Sir Robert Spottiswoode, paid the last penalty. Two days later died William Murray, a boy of nineteen, whom the half-hearted pleas of his covenanting brother, Tullibardine, could not save.[75] These gentlemen died as they had lived, constant in pride and courage. The night before his death old Sir Robert wrote a letter of farewell to Montrose, which breathes a spirit of Christian forbearance unfortunately lacking in those who had the

name of religion always on their lips. 'One thing I most
humbly recommend to your Excellence that, as you have
done always hitherto, so you will continue by fair and
gentle carriage to gain the people's affection to their
prince, rather than to imitate the barbarous inhumanity of
your adversaries.' The advice was nobly followed. There
were no reprisals on the Covenant prisoners confined in
the castle of Blair. 'Never,' ran Montrose's address to his
troops, 'shall they induce us to rival their crimes or seek to
outdo them except in valour and renown.' In a great civil
struggle no side has a monopoly of the virtues. There were
men in the Covenant ranks in whom the fire of religious
faith had withered up all human fears, and who were to
give an honourable proof to the world of the manhood
that was in them. But in this matter of charity and mercy
there can be little comparison for the candid historian
between the two parties. Montrose's army may have been
guilty of acts of cruelty in hot blood, but never at their
worst did they approach the deadly, cold-hearted malice
of the Kirk and the Estates. Twenty years later, when the
Covenant was the losing side and the fanatics who now
ruled in Edinburgh had been driven to the mosses, there
must have been many old-fashioned quiet folk in the
land who, casting back their memories to the days after
Philiphaugh, saw in the change the slow grinding of the
mills of God. In one respect the later persecution, bad and
indefensible as it was, fell short in grossness of the earlier.
Its perpetrators in their evil work did not profane the
name of the meek Gospel of Christ.

For Montrose, defeat was only a spur to fresh effort.
The flexible steel of his courage could not be bent or bro-
ken. From his refuge in Atholl he sent Erskine to recruit
in Mar, and Douglas and Airlie to raise the Royalists of
Angus. He made a fruitless effort to get into touch with
Alastair, and he wrote again to Digby asking for horse. In
Atholl the folk were busy with the late harvest, but the

name of the viceroy was a spell and 400 followed him. The Gordon cavalry, as ever, was his principal aim. He hastened over the Grampians, and early in October was at Drumminor Castle near Strathbogie, where Aboyne, his late grievances apparently forgotten, joined him with 1,500 foot and 300 horse. A less welcome addition to the force appeared in the person of the unstable Lord Lewis. After Kilsyth Huntly had removed himself from the Strathnaver bogs and was now at his castle of Gight. He sent Montrose a tepid letter of congratulation, and for a moment it looked as if the chief of the Gordons had forgotten his jealousy. Meanwhile Middleton with 800 of Leslie's horse had marched north to the Aberdeenshire lowlands and was now lying at Turriff. Montrose had two alternatives before him. He could attack Middleton with his new army and settle with him before turning to Leslie. Such a course would protect the Gordon lands and might keep Huntly in good humour. On the other hand, his friends were prisoners in Glasgow, and unless he rescued them forthwith they would perish. Again, Leslie was the more formidable foe, and it was always Montrose's habit to meet the greater danger first. Besides, Leslie lay between him and the Border, and on the Border he still cherished vain dreams of meeting the king. Accordingly he gave marching orders for the south.

Lewis Gordon with such of his clan as he could induce to follow him deserted on the second day. Aboyne remained for another day's march, but peremptory letters arrived from his father calling him back. Huntly's insane jealousy had revived, and he would neither fight himself nor permit his men to fight under another leader. Montrose sent Lord Reay and young Irvine of Drum to reason with him, but they were unable to shake his purpose. The precious days were slipping past in this barren diplomacy, and on the 22nd of October Montrose decided to advance without the Gordons. That night he lay at the Castleton of Braemar. Two days later he was on Lochearnside, where he must have heard that the first executions of his friends had already taken place. There also he received news that the king had at last made a desperate attempt to fulfil his promise. On the 14th of October Digby and Langdale had set out from Welbeck with 1,500 horse. Next day they scattered Poyntz's infantry at Sherburn, but were in turn surprised and driven north in confusion to Skipton. Digby, with Nithsdale and Carnwath, resolved to make a wild dash for the Border, and in spite of a defeat at Carlisle, pushed on across Esk with a small party of horse. On the 22nd he was as far north as Dumfries, but he did not stay long. He had no news of Montrose and far too much news of Leslie; his men began to desert, and he himself was compelled to flee to the Isle of Man. On the day that Montrose left Braemar, Digby's raid had come to an inglorious end.

Montrose's object was to prevent further executions, and the appearance of his force of 1,500, including 300 horse, did indeed procure a postponement of the bloody work. He took up his quarters at Buchanan on Lochlomondside—then the seat of the Covenanting Sir John Buchanan, but now the home of Montrose's descendants—and for several weeks threatened Glasgow. Leslie had 3,000 troops in the city, and Montrose with his raw levies did not dare to meet that veteran horse in open battle. It was a hopeless form of war, as he soon realized, and early in November he retired into Menteith. Presently he made a journey into Angus, and was hunted back by Middleton's dragoons. Historians have assumed that he went to attend his wife's funeral; but, since Lady Montrose lived till 1648, that explanation must be abandoned.[76] He returned to Atholl to find that his brother-in-law and closest friend, the old Lord Napier, had died at Fincastle in his absence. Napier was over seventy years of age, and had spent his long and blameless life in the pursuit of humane arts and the service of his fellow-men. He was the wisest head in Scotland of his day, a staunch

Presbyterian, an upholder of popular liberties, an expo-
nent of the unpopular doctrine of toleration, the type of
what the Covenanters might have been in happier circumstances. From his old friend's grave Montrose turned
again to the weary business of chaffering with Huntly. He
sent Sir John Dalziel to him to ask for a conference; but
Huntly, as shy as he was vain, seemed to fear to meet his
rival and declined. Montrose resolved to see him at all
costs, and early in December set off across the hills again.

It was now midwinter, and the weather was bitterly
cold—far colder, says Wishart, than his generation had
ever known. The frost coated everything with ice, but did
not make the streams the easier to cross, and that December passage of the Grampians lived in the memory of
men who were no strangers to hardship. Their feet were
clogged with snow; the horses floundered in half-frozen
bogs or crashed through the ice of mountain pools.
Christmas that year, which saw the deaths of his friends at
St. Andrews, found Montrose pursuing the evasive Huntly
from one refuge to another. He looked for him in Strathbogie, but Huntly fled to the Bog of Gight. Thither
Montrose followed, and the Gordon at bay was obliged
to receive him. Under the spell of the viceroy's grace and
courtesy the cloud of suspicion seemed to vanish.
Huntly was roused to interest. He promised his support
in the northern war, and offered to lead his men through
the lowlands of Moray to the siege of Inverness, while
Montrose marched down Strathspey. The capture of that
town might fix Seaforth's loyalty, which once more was up
for auction. Aboyne and Lewis wished, in Wishart's phrase,
'damnation to themselves' if they failed the king in the
future. They were to do their best to earn it.

The operations of the year 1646 began therefore with
good promise of success. That promise was not fulfilled.
The next few months must have been among the most
wretched in Montrose's life. With a heart still aching from
the loss of his comrades, with a drenched and starving

following, and with no news save the gloomiest from the south, he conducted an ineffective guerilla war up and down Speyside. There were one or two bold deeds, such as Black Pate's repulse of the Argyll men at Callander, and the young Lord Napier's defence of Kincardine Castle; but for the most part these months are a record of forced inactivity and constant disappointments. The viceroy had no more than one thousand men, while Huntly had 2,000, including 600 horse, to do his idle biddings. The splendid fighting force of the Gordons was frittered away. Their chief refused to cooperate with Montrose, or indeed to undertake any serious operation of war except the siege of some little Morayshire castles to gratify private animosities. Montrose's patient letters to him are the only clues we have to the movements of the royal army.[77] It was at Advie and Castle Grant in the end of December, moving about Strathspey in January, at Kyllachy on the Findhorn in February, and at Petty on the coast in March. Without Huntly's help Montrose could do nothing at Inverness, and without some signal victory he could not hope to recruit trimmers like Seaforth, Macleod of Skye, and Sir James Macdonald of Sleat. Middleton had come north again, Leslie having departed to England to look after arrears of pay, and the 1,400 men he brought with him, joined to those he had left, made a formidable army on the Royalist flank. It was the business of the Gordons to watch this force and prevent it crossing the Spey. But Huntly was busy with his private vendettas, and Lord Lewis, who held the castle of Rothes, amused himself by sending false news and playing tricks upon Montrose's officers. The viceroy narrowly escaped being caught at Inverness, and was compelled to flee into the mountains to the south and double back to Speyside.

Matters had now reached a crisis. Huntly was not only no friend, he was becoming an active enemy, and Montrose resolved to treat him as such. But before taking any step he made one more effort to see him. On the

27th of May he rode twenty miles to the Bog of Gight, but Huntly saw him coming and fled. It was the last straw. Montrose decided to write off the Gordons from the royal strength in Scotland, and to let Middleton make of them what he pleased. He would form a light flying squadron and ride through the northern Highlands to beat up recruits for the king. It was a course which his wisest friends advised, and it would be strange if, with Glengarry and Clanranald to help him, he could not bring to the field as stout a force as that which had scattered the Covenant in a year of battles.

But on the 31st of May a fateful message arrived from the king. This is not the place to describe the alternations of hope and despair through which Charles passed, between Digby's fiasco in the north and that day in April when, besieged by Fairfax in Oxford and in fear of falling into the hands of the Independents, he resolved to cast himself upon the mercy of the Scots. Negotiations had been for long in progress with Montreuil, the French ambassador, as intermediary, but Leven and his friends while hinting at much, would commit nothing to writing. On the 5th of May, Charles, having escaped from Oxford in disguise, appeared in Leven' s camp at Southwell. For what happened we have the evidence of an eye-witness, Sir James Turner. Before the king had eaten or drunk he was brought before the Covenanting committee, and Lothian, its president, at once formulated its demands. The Royalist garrison must surrender Newark, the king must sign the Covenant, and must command 'James Graham' to lay down his arms. To this imperious speech Charles replied with the dignity that never failed him: 'He that made thee an earl made James Graham a marquis.'

Then began that pathetic correspondence between the king who had done so little and his captain-general who had done so much. On the 19th of May he wrote to Montrose from Newcastle.

'You must disband your forces and go into France, where you shall receive my further directions. This at first may justly startle you, but I assure you that if for the present I should offer to do more for you, I could not do so much.'

Montrose received this letter on Speyside on the 31st day of May. He called a meeting of his officers, to which he in vain invited Huntly, and laid it before them. In his reply to the king he declared himself at his Majesty's commands, but asked that some protection should be secured for those who had risked all in the royal cause. For himself he was willing 'as well by passion as by action' to serve his master. Then he broke up his camp and marched to Glenshee to await the king's answer. Charles replied on the 15th of June, repeating his commands and promising protection for Montrose's followers. On the 16th of July the king wrote again:—

'The most sensible part of my misfortunes is to see my friends in distress and not to be able to help them, and of this you are the chief. Wherefore, according to that real freedom and friendship which is between us, as I cannot absolutely command you to accept of unhandsome conditions, so I must tell you that I believe your refusal will put you in a far worse state than your compliance will... For if this opportunity be let slip, you must not expect any more treaties. In which case you must either conquer all Scotland or be inevitably ruined. . . . Whereupon, if you find it fit to accept, you may justly say I have commanded you, and if you take another course you cannot expect that I can publicly avow you in it until I shall be able (which God knows how soon that may be) to stand upon my own feet; but on the contrary, seem not to be well satisfied with your refusal, which I find clearly will bring all this army upon you—and then I shall be in a very sad condition, such as I shall rather leave to your judgment than seek to express.'

Towards the end of July Montrose met Middleton on the banks of the Isla to arrange terms. Middleton, who had fought under him long ago on the Covenant side at

Aberdeen, was to stain his later record with many brutalities, but he had some of the instinct of a soldier. He granted better terms than might have been looked for. A free pardon was to be given to all the Royalists except the viceroy, Crawford, and Sir John Hurry, who since Kilsyth had been in Montrose's camp. These three were to leave the country before the first day of September, the Estates providing a vessel. All forfeited lands were to be restored, except to the three exempted, and to Graham of Gorthie, whose estate was already in the hands of Balcarres. Montrose accepted the conditions, and, assembling his army at Rattray near Blairgowrie, he bade his men farewell. He told them that what he did was for the king's sake, and by the king's command. It was a melancholy parting with those Highlanders of Atholl who had never failed him, and with comrades such as Airlie and Ogilvy and the young Napier, who in good and evil report had been true to their salt. For such men 'passion' was a harder service than 'action.'

The Committee of Estates, when they heard of Middleton's terms, were indignant that the 'Lord's work' should be so grievously frustrated. They dared not repudiate their general, for Middleton was not a man to brook insults, and his force added to Montrose's would soon be hammering at the Edinburgh gates. But they resolved to defeat the bargain by chicanery. Montrose had received a private letter from the king bidding him defer his going until the last possible day, and during the month of August he busied himself in organizing the Royalist party that he might not leave Charles unbefriended in Scotland. But as the last days of the month approached he grew suspicious of the Covenant's good faith. There was no sign of the promised vessel, till on the 31st a ship put into Montrose harbour with a sullen master and a more sullen crew. English men-of-war, too, began to appear off the coast. When Montrose proposed to embark at once, the skipper declared that he must have a few days to caulk his vessel and attend to the rigging. This meant that the days of grace would be exceeded and the viceroy left stranded—an outlaw at the mercy of his enemies. Happily a small Norwegian sloop was on the same day in the harbour of Stonehaven, and its master, one Jens Gunnersen, announced his willingness to sail with the exiles. Hurry, Wishart, and Drummond of Balloch; Harry Graham, Montrose's half-brother; John Spottiswoode, one of the nephews whom old Sir Robert had entrusted to the viceroy's charge; three of Montrose's captains, Lisle or Lillie, whom we shall meet afterwards at Carbisdale, Melvin, and Guthrie; a Frenchman, Lasound, who had been Lord Gordon's valet; and a German servant called Rudolf made up the little party. The sloop sailed down to Montrose Roads, and that evening Mr. James Wood, a minister, and his servant put off from the shore and were taken aboard. The servant was Montrose. 'This,' says Wishart, 'was in the year of our Lord 1646, and the thirty-fourth of his age.'

CHAPTER XVI

THE YEARS OF EXILE
(SEPTEMBER 1646–MARCH 1650)

I

AFTER a week's tossing in the North Sea Montrose reached the Norwegian port of Bergen, where he found a Scot, one Thomas Gray, in command of the castle. His aim was to visit Denmark to meet Christian the Fifth, with whom, as the uncle of Charles, he might confer on his next step. He had sheathed his sword at his master's bidding, but his life was still dedicated to the cause, and from that devotion there could be no release but death. From Bergen the exiles made their way overland to Christiania, probably sailing up the Sognefjord to Leardalsören, and then crossing the backbone of mountains by the Leardal valley and Valders. When he reached Copenhagen he found that King Christian was in Germany, so he crossed to Hamburg and waited there some months. Before he left Scotland he had sent Crawford to Henrietta Maria in Paris with a proposal to raise the clans and save the king from his captors. He was also awaiting those credentials as ambassador to

151

France which Charles had promised him. But the circle of parasites and adventurers who surrounded the queen were very resolute that Montrose should not break in upon their follies with his untimely zeal. At Jermyn's instigation Ashburnham was sent to meet him in Germany with a vague proposal that he should return to Scotland and renew the war. As no reference was made to his own proposals sent through Crawford, Montrose naturally refused to engage in an enterprise for which he had no resources and no warrant from his master. Ashburnham then suggested that he should make his peace with the Covenanters, following the royal precedent. The proposal was indignantly repudiated. 'Not even the king,' he said, 'should command his obedience in what was dishonourable, unjust, and destructive to his Majesty himself.'

Early in the year 1647, tired of waiting on instructions that never came, he set out for Paris. The queen received him graciously, but made it very clear that his counsels were not those most grateful to the royal ears. Jermyn and the rest gave him tepid smiles and the cold shoulder. To one of his temper the mingled silliness and vice of Henrietta's court must have been repulsive in the extreme. The king was a captive, the flower of English and Scottish chivalry had died for his sake, and these mountebanks were turning life into a thing of backstairs gossip and idle laughter. It was suggested that his niece Lilias Napier should become a maid of honour, but Montrose sternly forbade it. 'There is neither Scots man nor woman welcome that way; neither would any of honour or virtue, chiefly a woman, suffer themselves to live in so lewd and worthless a place.' But if the tawdry court-in-exile had little to say to him, Paris made amends. His fame had gone abroad throughout Europe, and the most distinguished men in France came to pay him their respects. He was given precedence before the regular ambassadors. Cardinal de Retz, who had followed his campaigns with admiration, welcomed him as a Roman hero reborn in a degenerate world. The great Mazarin offered him the command of the Scots in France and a lieutenant-generalship in the French army; then the captaincy of the gendarmes, with a large pension; and last, the captaincy of the king's own guard and the rank of marshal of France. The young Napier, who had now joined him, was eager that he should accept. A dazzling career opened before him, for with his talents in the field he might look to be a second Condé, the rich and idolized head of a great army, and not the discredited captain of a few ragged exiles. But to enter the French service meant in common decency to give up all thoughts of any other, and his sword had been dedicated and was not his own to sell.

Meanwhile in Scotland strange things were happening. Early in the year the Scots army, as Montrose had anticipated, had handed over the king to the English Parliament, and the carts laden with the deferred pay of Leven's soldiers and subsidies for Covenanting nobles were soon rumbling across the Border. In June the king passed from the Parliament to the control of Cromwell's army. The event alarmed the more moderate of the Covenanters, and that party began to reveal the characteristic of all factions, and split in two. Hamilton had returned to Scotland, and was busy making a party of those who favoured the Covenant but did not favour Cromwell, and professed devotion to the principle of monarchy. On December 27, 1647, in Charles's prison at Carisbrooke a secret engagement was entered into, with Lanark, Loudoun, and Lauderdale as signatories. When the Estates assembled in March of 1648 the Engagers had a large majority, and Argyll and the more fanatical leaders of the Kirk found themselves isolated. The Estates ordered the raising of an army to rescue the king; the extreme Covenanters went into open rebellion, and in May inspired a riot in the westlands at Mauchline which was quelled with difficulty by Middleton. The Covenant was finding enemies within its own borders, and it looked as if out of the strife of sects a moderate royalism might yet come by its own.

One of the first steps taken by the Engagers was to communicate with Henrietta and the Prince of Wales. The queen did not inform Montrose of their proposals till she had made up her mind to accept them and had already committed herself. He knew too much of Hamilton to look for great things in that quarter, but he offered to do all in his power to save the situation by enlisting under his own banner those Royalists who would enlist under no other, and by supporting the Engagers in the field. Hamilton's envoys, however, had warned the queen that Montrose must have no share in the business, and his offer was coldly declined. In despair he looked elsewhere for a man's work, and forgot his former scruples about entering foreign service. If his master would not have him—if, indeed, as the queen seemed to hint, he was a positive hindrance to the Royalist cause—then the way was clear to look elsewhere. He had doubts about the French service. Mazarin and his friends were half-hearted in Charles's cause, and too cordial in their treatment of the English Parliament. So in the early spring of 1648 he slipped away from Paris with some of his friends, and travelled by Geneva and Tyrol to the Emperor's court at Vienna.

Wishart's Latin account of the *annus mirabilis* of 1644-5 had been published, probably in Holland, towards the close of 1647, and had leaped at once into a wide popularity. The doings of the Scottish soldier were the talk of every court and camp in Europe, and at the Imperial Court Montrose found himself welcomed as a hero. The Emperor Ferdinand, whom he found at Prague, gave him the crimson baton of a marshal of the Empire, and empowered him to levy troops in any quarter of his dominions. Europe at the time was filled with the debris of great armies, and with the magic of his name there was likely to be little dearth of recruits. The Emperor's brother, the Archduke Leopold, was governor of the Spanish

Netherlands, and Montrose was advised that the western border of the Empire was the place for his purpose. It had the further merit of being nearer Britain in case of a summons from home. Germany was too much harassed with wars to make easy travelling, so Montrose returned by Cracow and Dantzig to Denmark, and thence by way of Groningen to Brussels. He found the Archduke at Tournay, but it was his fortune to look for help from those who at the moment had none to offer. As he had met Rupert on the morrow of Marston Moor, so he found Leopold on the morrow of Lens, where on the 20th of August the genius of Condé had scattered the imperial forces. He accordingly returned to Brussels, where he received startling news from Scotland. Hamilton and the Engagers had marched into England on the 8th of July with more than ten thousand men, including the veterans of Baillie and Monro—the largest force which had yet crossed the Scottish Border. His campaign had been one long series of blunders, and on the 17th of August Cromwell, having in Montrose's fashion made a rapid flank march over the Lancashire hills, had fallen upon him at Preston. His army was in flight or in captivity, and he himself was a prisoner, while Cromwell was marching north to settle with Lanark and receive the welcome of the extreme Covenanters. Argyll had begun that alliance with Oliver which was to bring him in the end to the scaffold.

The tidings revived in Montrose the old eagerness to strike another blow for the king. He was now at Brussels, and during the winter of 1648 was in constant corre-spondence with Rupert. There was no word, however, from the queen and the Prince of Wales: they had still hopes of the Engagers, and feared to offend them by any intercourse with their deadly enemy. Presently the young Charles emancipated himself from his mother and her set, and took up his residence with Hyde at the Hague. Montrose had friends who had the young prince's ear, and early in the new year he received a message from him, bidding him arrange to meet Hyde for a secret interview. The prince had entered upon the policy of keeping two strings to his bow. While holding the Engagers in play, he wished to have Montrose as a last resort; but, as the insistence on secrecy shows, he was desperately anxious to make the former believe that he looked only to them. Montrose replied that he would joyfully obey the summons, but implored the prince to distinguish true loyalty from false. 'If your highness shall but vouchsafe a little faith unto your loyal servants, and stand at guard with others, your affairs can soon be whole.' This was on the 28th of January. Two days later, on a snowy afternoon, in Whitehall, the king's head fell on the scaffold.

II

From the day when he heard from Hyde the news of the tragedy almost to the close of his life a strange oppression settled upon Montrose. He became 'fey,' with a sense of dark fate hovering ever about him. He had been no sentimental cavalier; he did not believe in Divine Right; and to him the Lord's Anointed had none of the sanctity which he possessed for many Royalists. But out of his inner consciousness he had created the figure of an ideal monarch, wise with a wisdom to which no earthly king ever attained, a personification of those dreams which had always haunted his soul. He had, too, the devotion of a loyal soldier to the master for whom he had risked so much. But, more than all, he saw in the tragedy the darkening of the skies over his unhappy land. The savage and stupid barbarism of the Covenant, which had revelled in blood in the Lord's name, now seemed at last to have reached omnipotence, for it had destroyed the centre of all civil order. Henceforth there could be no compromise. He knew nothing of the folly and duplicity which

preceded Charles's final heroism; his rejection of compromises which would have secured to him all that was most
worthy in his cause; his futile search for allies who were
alike perjured and impotent; and his double-dealing to-
ward those who had on their side both honesty and
power. He saw only the shedding of innocent blood,
which must make a breach for all time between those
who loved righteousness and those who pursued iniquity.
When he heard the news he fainted among his friends.
For two days he kept his chamber, and when Wishart
entered he found on the table these lines:—

> 'Great, good, and just, could I but rate
> My grief, and thy too rigid fate,
> I'd weep the world in such a strain
> As it should deluge once again.
> But since thy loud-tongued blood demands supplies
> More from Briareus' hands than Argus' eyes,
> I'll sing thine obsequies with trumpet sounds
> And write thine epitaph in blood and wounds.'

Henceforth there is an uncanniness about him, as of
one who lived half his time in another world. He has
himself painted in coal-black armour; his eyes have a fire
which changes their cool greyness into something wilder
and fiercer; all youthful weaknesses seem purged away,
for his patience becomes unearthly and his gentleness
unhuman. He has the air of a 'fey' man, one for whom
the barriers between the seen and the unseen are breaking down.

In the middle of February he met Hyde at Seven-
bergen. Hyde never liked him as Nicholas and Hopton
did, and in the writings of the future Lord Clarendon
admiration is always tinged with acid; but he was a loyal
servant of the new king, and he recognized capacity when
he saw it. A little later Montrose was at the Hague, where
the young Charles was already in the midst of Scottish
intrigues. The result of the king's death had been to send

THE MARQUIS OF MONTROSE

a wave of loyalty over Scotland. On the 4th of February Charles the Second was proclaimed at the market cross of Edinburgh by the Covenanting chancellor. There had always been an odd Royalism flickering through the nation, often in the most unlikely places. The king was a poor thing, but their own, like the misguided Covenant. It might be well for his own people, the Scots, to take order with him, but it was high treason in those who hated Scotland as much as they hated Charles. The feeling was on a level with the later Jacobitism, an assertion of nationality on the part of a small, proud, bitterly poor country, jealous of its rich neighbour, not yet confident in itself. It was sentimental, not reasoned, and was found even among the extreme Covenanters. Mr. Blair of St. Andrews was anxious to attend Charles on the scaffold. 'He made his account to die with the king, and would as willingly have laid down his head to the hatchet as ever he laid his head to a pillow.'[78] In 1660 we find Mr. Robert Baillie writing to Mr. David Dickson:—'If my lord Argyll at this strait should desert the king . . . I think, and many more with me of the best I speak with, that it would be a fearful sin in him, which God will revenge.'[79] No doubt in ministerial breasts loyalty was intertwined with the Covenant, but it was loyalty of a kind. Hamilton's death on the scaffold early in 1649 intensified the feeling of national exasperation which Preston had kindled. The luckless duke was not a brilliant figure. His epitaph has been spoken by Mistress Alison Wilson in *Old Mortality*— 'That was him that lost his head at London. Folks said that it wasna a very gude ane, but it was aye a sair loss to him, puir gentleman.' It had been prophesied—and the prophecy had hag-ridden his mind—that he would succeed the king; but he fell heir not to a throne, but to a scaffold. Montrose, watching Scotland from a distance, must have believed that the aspect of affairs was more promising than ever before. There were, indeed, no Gordons to appeal to. Huntly had at last fallen into Argyll's hands and had suffered death, lamenting pathetically at the end that he had done so little in life for the cause he died for. Aboyne was in exile, dying of a broken heart, and the Gordon lands were in the power of Lord Lewis, who was soon to make his peace with his uncle. But the great northern clan of Mackenzie was hopeful. Its chief, Seaforth, had arrived at the exiled court, and his brother, Mackenzie of Pluscardine, had raised his men in March, and along with Reay and Ogilvy had taken Inverness and given much trouble to David Leslie. They were soon to be scattered, but the hope of the Mackenzies remained. Most important of all, the young king had turned a cold shoulder to Argyll's emissary, Sir Joseph Douglas, who arrived at the Hague on the 20th of February, and had confirmed Montrose in his old commission of lieutenant-governor and captain-general of Scotland.

But the royal favour was to prove a fickle thing. During the next few months the Hague was the battleground of contending factions. There were three parties in Scottish politics: the rigid Covenanters, with Argyll at their head; the Engagers, whose emissaries to Holland were Lanark and Lauderdale; and the Royalists, *sans phrase,* who looked to Montrose. In March the envoys of the Estates arrived, Cassilis and Mr. Robert Baillie, who with many protestations of loyalty demanded as the price of kingship the signature of the Solemn League and Covenant and the repudiation of 'James Graham.' The Engagers thought these terms unreasonable, but the second figured also in their own modest demands. Lanark, indeed—now Duke of Hamilton in his brother's stead—was willing to serve under the greatest commander of the day; but Lauderdale's pure soul had been shocked (so he said) by Montrose's barbarities, though on cross-examination he was unable to give any instances. The man whose filthy table-talk was the byword of the Restoration court, and whose brutalities were to make his name a scandal in his own land, had some cause to dislike a character so immeasurably beyond his comprehension. Charles demanded an opinion from both the Royalists and the Engagers as to the conditions of the Estates. Montrose's reply is still extant, and differs in no way from the other remonstrances and declarations through which he had already published his faith to the world. It traced the whole history of the Covenant movement, from its justifiable beginnings to its impossible end; it pointed out that the Covenanters demanded from the king a renunciation of his own private form of worship, 'and yet they made it a ground of rebellion against your royal father that they but imagined he intended to meddle with them after the like kind.' The document was read in Charles's council on the 21st of May, the terms of the Estates were rejected, and Montrose was appointed admiral of the Scottish Seas.

Apparently the king had made up his mind. He had rejected Argyll, and, having accepted Montrose, had also rejected the Engagers. He stood committed now to some such bold attempt as his captain-general had always urged. Montrose and the Royalists in general wished Charles to join Ormonde in Ireland, but the king favoured an invasion of Scotland, desiring, as we now know, to have another asset in bargaining with the Covenanters. In the wars of the Middle Ages both sides on the eve of peace endeavoured to take as many fortresses as possible in order to have something to give up when the day of renunciation came. So it was with Charles now. The intrigues still went on, though their venue was removed to Paris and the court of Henrietta. Jermyn seems to have patched up a friendship with the new Hamilton, and attempted to get Montrose's commission of viceroyalty annulled in his favour. 'They are all mad, or worse,' wrote Elisabeth of Bohemia; and the judgment is not too severe for that nest of futile and selfish schemers. Montrose during these months, with his heart still burning with the memory of the scene in Whitehall, must have found the times sorely out of joint for an honest man. Some loyal friends he had, such as Napier and Kinnoul, and he was much in the company of Elisabeth herself. We are fortunate in possessing many letters written to him by that 'Queen of Hearts'—and sorrows.[80] It is a curiously intimate correspondence. She rallies the grave cavalier, invites him to archery meetings at her country home, and gives him the news of the court from the standpoint of an assiduous well-wisher. It was at her request that he sat for the splendid Honthorst portrait, which she hung in her cabinet that it might 'frighten away the Brethren.' The lady whom Sir Henry Wotton had sung in imperishable verse had lost little of her beauty and none of her wit with the passage of years. There is small likelihood. that Montrose, as was rumoured, fell in love with one of her daughters, the Princess Louise.[81] That chapter in his life had been closed long ago. But in the mother of Rupert and Maurice he found one who was a perpetual stimulus to honour and great deeds, and it was a joy to him in that rabble of half-hearted casuists to meet a clear and dauntless spirit.

III

The preparations for the last campaign began early in June. Charles had promised that he would do nothing in any of his negotiations to prejudice Montrose's commission as viceroy of Scotland, and he had further nominated him his ambassador to the northern courts. Recruits there were in plenty—mercenary Scots who had fought in the German wars and were only too anxious to sell their swords; patriotic Scots such as Gustavus's old colonel, John Gordon, who longed to strike a blow for their country. But foreign troops and foreign money were necessary, and to secure these Montrose sent his emissaries far and wide. His half-brother, Harry Graham, was dispatched to the Elector of Brandenburg, and got the promise of a large sum. In August Kinnoul, with 80 officers and 100 Danish recruits, set sail for the Orkneys. The reason for the choice of such a base is clear. The islanders were strangers to the religious strife of the mainland, and Lord Morton, the feudal superior, was Kinnoul's uncle and well-disposed to the Royalist cause. The Commonwealth navy, occupied with preventing Rupert's escape from Ireland, was less likely to interfere with the transports if their route lay so far to the north. Further, the adjacent mainland was not far from the Mackay and Mackenzie country, and Montrose looked for support from both clans. If he could command the northern apex of Scotland, then Leslie to meet him would have to march through the hostile hill country, and in the event of a Royalist victory the whole Highlands would rise as one man.

After bidding the Queen of Bohemia farewell at her castle of Rhenen, Montrose himself arrived at Hamburg early in September. Here he negotiated for supplies with the Duke of Courland, and presently set off to Schleswig to meet Frederick, the new king of Denmark. He lingered some time at Copenhagen, for his diplomacy was a slow business, and there he had news of Kinnoul's successful landing. Morton had welcomed him with open arms, and all was going well for the cause. The common people of Scotland, so Kinnoul reported, were on the brink of revolt against their masters. 'Your Lordship is gaped after with that expectation that the Jews look for the Messiah, and certainly your presence will restore your groaning country to its liberties and the king to his rights.' But he had other news less pleasing. Charles wrote from St. Germain instructing him to go on with the work of his commission, and 'not to be startled with any reports you may hear, as if I were otherwise inclined to the Presbyterians than when I left you.' Henrietta was at St. Germain, and Montrose knew too well her notions of policy. He feared that reports of a treaty with the Covenanters would utterly dishearten the Scottish loyalists, and to counteract such a danger he prepared the last and most famous of his

declarations. It is well worth reading, if only for the spirit
of unclouded courage that inspires it. He is as confident of
the sacredness of his mission as any Covenant minister. He
summons all true Scottish hearts to make a last effort to
break their bonds, 'resolving with Joab to play the man for
their people and the cities of their God.' The declaration
was circulated in Edinburgh in December, and Johnston
of Wariston published a reply.[82] His chief argument is to
describe Montrose as 'that viperous brood of Satan whom
the Church hath delivered into the hands of the devil, and
the nation doth generally detest and abhor.' For the Kirk's
ban Montrose cared little, but the suspicion and dislike of
the Lowlands were to prove his undoing.

In November he was at the court of Queen Christina
of Sweden, Gustavus's daughter, and Descartes's erratic
disciple. He took up his quarters at Gothenburg, where a
Scottish merchant, one John Maclear, put his wealth and
influence at his disposal. Early in December a ship arrived
from the Orkneys with melancholy news. David Leslie
had marched north to Caithness in the end of October,
and had written to Kinnoul advising him to depart while
there was yet time. The letter was ordered to be burned by
the hangman, and Leslie went south without crossing the
Pentland Firth. But on the 12th of November the loyal
Morton died, and a few days later Kinnoul followed him
to the grave. The loss of his brave friend and 'passionate
servant' was a heavy blow to Montrose, but Sir James
Douglas, who arrived in the Orkney ship, brought good
news of the general feeling in Scotland. He implored
Montrose to sail at once, for 'his own presence was able to
do the business, and would undoubtedly bring 20,000
men together for the king's service, all men being weary
and impatient to live any longer under that bondage,
pressing down their estates, their persons, and their consciences.' The viceroy may well have believed a report so
consonant with his desires. His ardour was always prone to
minimize difficulties, and he had no wise old Napier to

tell him that the feelings of Sir James Douglas and the gentry were scarcely an index to the temper of the burgesses and the peasantry, wearied out with poverty and the terrors of an Old Testament God.

In December he made an effort to leave. Transports were indeed dispatched with Danish troops and Scottish officers, as well as ammunition and stands of arms, and the wild weather they encountered gave rise to tales of shipwreck which gladdened the heart of the Estates. He wrote to Seaforth on the 1st of December, saying that he meant to sail for Scotland next day. But the winds were contrary and ice blocked the harbour, and it was not till January 10, 1650, that he actually embarked in the *Herderinnan,* a frigate which Maclear had bought for him. Still he did not start, and on the 18th we find him living in Maclear's house on shore. We know now the reason of that delay which so puzzled the Swedish statesmen and the spies of the Commonwealth. He had received word that a dispatch was on its way to him from the king in Jersey. For such a message he could not choose but wait.

He sailed eventually in the middle of March. Whether he received the king's letter before he left or on his arrival in the Orkneys is a disputed point,[83] but the odds are that he got it in Gothenburg, though his reply is dated from Kirkwall. It was dispatched on the 12th of January, and with it came the George and the blue riband of the Garter. There were two letters, one to be shown to his friends and the other a private note for Montrose's own eyes, and copies of the correspondence with the Commissioners of the Estates were enclosed. As to the first letter, it had already been published in French in Paris, and a fortnight earlier a précis had been in the hands of the Commonwealth Government. In it the king informed his viceroy of the negotiations with the Estates and the chance of a treaty. Montrose, however, is assured that 'we will not, before or during the Treaty, do anything contrary to that power and authority which we

have given you by our commission, nor consent to anything that may bring in the least degree of diminution to
it; and if the said Treaty should produce an agreement, we
will, with our uttermost care, so provide for the honour
and interest of yourself, and of all that shall engage with
you, as shall let the whole world see the high esteem we
have of you. It ends with an exhortation 'to proceed vig-
orously and effectively in your undertaking;' and then the
reason is made clear: 'We doubt not but all our loyal and
well-affected subjects of Scotland will cordially and effec-
tually join with you, and by that addition of strength
either *dispose those who are otherwise minded to make reasonable demands to Us in a Treaty,* or be able to force them to
it by arms, in case of their obstinate refusal.' He wanted an
asset to bargain with, a second string to his bow. The private note merely assured the recipient that Charles would
never consent to anything to his prejudice, and bade him
not to take alarm at 'any reports or messages from others.'

It was a clear instruction to proceed with the invasion
of Scotland, but it had an ugly look of double-dealing.
The warning against reports argued that something had
been done or said to give good cause for reports. But
Montrose, singularly regardless of self, thought only of the
danger to the king—the risk that by trusting his enemies
he might walk into the same trap as his father. In his reply
from Kirkwall, on the 26th of March,[84] he besought his
master 'to have a serious eye (now at last) upon the too
open crafts are used against you, chiefly in this conjunc-
ture, and that it would please your Majesty to be so just to
yourself, as ere you make a resolve upon your affairs or
your person, your Majesty may be wisely pleased to hear
the zealous opinions of your faithful servants, who have
nothing in their hearts, nor before their eyes, but the joy
of your Majesty's prosperity and greatness, which shall be
ever the only passion and study of your most sacred
Majesty's most humble, faithful, and most passionate subject and servant.' What Montrose did not know was that

the king's letter had been published, and was now sown broadcast over Scotland. It is one thing to fight in a crusade; it is another to conduct a campaign whose avowed purpose is no more than to create an asset to bargain with. On such mercantile terms you cannot conjure the spirit that wins battles. Well might Mr. Secretary Nicholas write to Ormonde: 'Some (not without reason) apprehend that the report of the now approaching Treaty will make those of the better sort forbear to appear for him, until they shall see the issue of this Treaty.'[85] The dice had been loaded against the venture before it was begun. The king had sent Montrose to his death.

CHAPTER XVII

THE LAST CAMPAIGN
(MARCH–MAY 1650)

IT has been the fashion among historians to describe the last campaign as doomed from the start. So in a sense it was, but its hopelessness did not lie in the actual military and political situation in Scotland at the moment. That had never been more favourable. Montrose was, indeed, as far off as ever from commending himself and his faith to that Covenanting *bourgeoisie,* which he never lost the hope of converting. But the arm of the Covenant was growing slack. Hamilton's march to Preston had depleted the fighting strength of the Lowlands, and had driven a wedge into the Estates. Many nobles who had once obeyed Argyll were now prepared to follow him only in so far as he allied himself with the king. The incredible folly of Covenanting government, as seen in such performances as the Acts of Classes, had disgusted all moderate men. A real bitterness against England had surged up in the nation, and this meant popularity for Charles, and a fall in esteem for those who had meddled with Charles's enemies. The Estates had no money to pay troops; every burgh in the south had been bled white with taxation and was furious with the Edinburgh junta. Of the former Covenant generals, Baillie had been an Engager, and

Hurry was now one of Montrose's companions. Only Leslie remained, with his lieutenants Holbourn and Strachan, and he had at the most three thousand foot and fourteen hundred horse strung out over a wide front in the northern Highlands. When Montrose sent Crawford to Henrietta in the autumn of 1646 he sent with him an estimate[86] of what forces might be raised for the king in Scotland. Leaving out 2,000 from Antrim, it reached the large total of 21,400 men. He counted on 2,000 Macleans, 1,300 from Clanranald, 3,000 from Atholl. There were uncertain items, it is true, like the 1,000 who were credited to Lord Nithsdale, the 2,000 to Macdonald of Sleat, the 1,500 to Huntly, and the 2,000 to Seaforth; but, putting all doubtful elements aside, it looked as if in the Highlands alone he could count on 10,000 men. Things had improved since the date of that estimate. The clan of Mackenzie had risen with Pluscardine, and might rise again, for though their chief was not in the venture yet he was not hostile. Again, if Montrose got one quarter of the levies and supplies promised him on the Continent, if he got one-eighth of the help hinted at from Ireland, he would put in the field from four thousand to five thousand regular troops as well. Leslie was in a miserable position both for attack and defence, and defeat to him would mean annihilation. For Montrose to succeed it was essential that he should have sufficient troops in the far north to win the first round. If that happened, he might count on the Macleods and the Mackenzies; probably, too, on the Gordons; and then the safety of his route to the south would be assured. Once in Badenoch he had all the loyal levies of the west and of Atholl to draw upon, and with the Lowlands divided it was hard to see what could prevent him from dominating Scotland. Then let Cromwell return from Ireland with his weary troops and meet him. We know today, what was then not understood, how little hold the army of the Commonwealth had upon the affections of the English people. Of the two leaders

Montrose was the greater military genius, and if with 20,000 Highland and foreign foot and Lowland horse he had met Cromwell somewhere in Yorkshire, the odds are that the Restoration would have been antedated by ten years.

As it chanced, every condition of success was to fail. He had far too few foreign troops, the local clans did not rise in his support, and there was no sign of movement in the Lowlands. Scotland stood idly by and looked on. The king's letter and the personal jealousy of the nobles had done their work. Men were weary of fighting and half-hearted in any cause. The satiety which attended the Restoration was beginning. Let them be shown a way of peace and they would acclaim it; but meantime it was the duty of cautious folk to stay at home.

The king might handicap and betray him, but Montrose was true to himself. For him there could be no turning back on this side the grave, for he had been to the end of the world and looked over the other side. The 'waft of death' had gone out against him, and all his doings have a touch of wildness. He devised strange standards. His foot bore on a black ground the bleeding head of the dead king with the motto *Deo et victricibus Armis*. The cavalry colours, too, were black, with three pairs of clasped hands holding three drawn swords, and the motto *Quos pietas virtus et honor fecit amicos*. His own flag was of white damask, with two steep rocks and a river between, and a lion about to leap from one to the other. His motto was *Nil medium*. He was about to put it to the touch, as he had sung, 'to win or lose it all.' There was an air of doom and desperation in everything, as of some dark Saga of the North.

The early days of April were spent in marshalling his little force. There were four or five hundred Danish troops already in the Orkneys.[87] The Orcadians, then very far from being a warlike people, raised 1,000 men, for the king's cause was welcomed gladly by all classes in the islands. With Montrose were a number of cavaliers and soldiers of fortune—Lord Frendraught, his old opponent at Aberdeen; a brother of Charteris of Amisfield; Sir William Johnston; Colonel Thomas Gray, a mercenary of the German wars; his half-brother, Harry Graham; Hurry, now threefold a turn-coat; Hay of Dalgetty; Drummond of Balloch; the new Kinnoul; Ogilvy of Powrie; Menzies of Pitfoddels; Douglas, a brother of Lord Morton's; and one or two English Royalists such as Major Lisle. These gentlemen were mounted and made up the whole cavalry of the force, probably some forty or fifty in all. Hurry was dispatched in advance with a picked body of 500 men to look into the chances of a landing on the mainland. He found no difficulty, and, hastening on, secured the Ord of Caithness, the narrow pass on the shore through which ran the road to the south.

Montrose with the rest of his army followed about the 12th of April. It was his business, seeing that his forces were so inadequate, to push on with the greatest possible speed, so as to pass the low coastlands and reach the shelter of the hills, where the Covenant horse could do him no harm and reinforcements could be awaited. Leslie held the castles of Brahan, Chanonry, Eilandonan, and Cromarty; and the Earl of Sutherland, who was hot for the Covenant, garrisoned Dunrobin, Skibo, and Dornoch. If Montrose marched with his old speed, another week would find him in Badenoch. At first his movements were rapid enough. Landing at John o'Groats he dashed upon Thurso, and the local gentry, except the Sinclairs, took the oath of allegiance. Leaving Harry Graham with 200 men to keep them to their word, be marched south through Caithness to Sir John Sinclair's castle of Dunbeath, took it after a few days' siege, and left a garrison. He had about eight hundred men left when he joined Hurry at the Ord of Caithness. He summoned Sutherland's castle of Dunrobin, but admission was denied, and the place was too strong to take. Now began his fatal delay. He did not dare to face the garrisons of the Dornoch lowlands, so he turned inland up the glen of the Fleet, past Rhaoine to Lairg at the foot of Loch Shin. He was hoping for recruits from the Monroes and the Rosses, and above all from the great clan of Mackenzie. In the last days of April, or the beginning of May in the new style,[88] he began his march from the valley of the Shin to Strath Oykell. There the Mackenzies must be awaiting him, and in any case to go south he must turn the long inlet known as the Kyle of Sutherland.

Meantime Leslie was hurrying north to a rendezvous at Brechin which he had appointed for the 25th of April. He instructed Strachan and Halkett, who commanded the Covenant troops in Moray, to do their best to check Montrose's advance, so Strachan with the garrisons of Brahan and Chanonry came north to Tain, where he was joined by other Covenant garrisons. He had 220 horse, all veterans, 36 musketeers of Lawers' regiment, and a reserve of 400 Monroes and Rosses whom Montrose had vainly hoped to attach to his standard. Sutherland was sent north of the Kyle to oppose Harry Graham, and cut off the way of retreat in that direction.

On Saturday, the 27th of April, Strachan marched west from Tain to a place called Wester Fearn on the southern shore of the Kyle, some few miles south-east of Bonar Bridge and the mouth of the river Carron. Leslie only left Brechin on the same day. Montrose had marched down Strath Oykell to a spot near the head of the Kyle on its south side under the lee of a steep hill called Craigcaoinichean. It was covered with a light scrog of wood, and in front was a piece of more or less level ground with the tarn of Carbisdale at the north end, and to the south-east the deep channel of the Culrain burn. Two miles farther down the Kyle lay the lowlands around the Carron mouth. He had been encamped there apparently for several days, waiting on the Mackenzies. It was a strong position if he had stayed by it, for no cavalry could have forced the pass of Craigcaoinichean. His scouts could

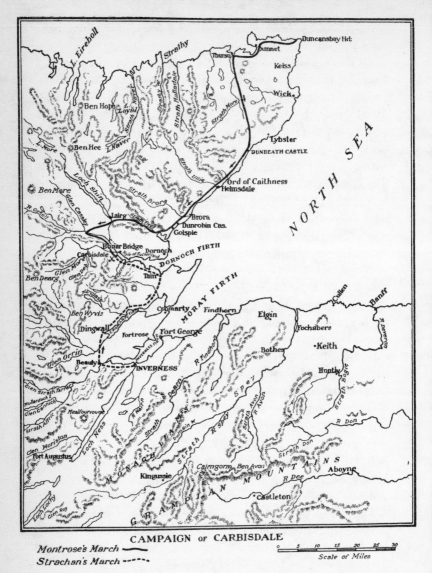

CAMPAIGN of CARBISDALE

Montrose's March ———
Strachan's March - - - - - -

Scale of Miles
0   5   10   15   20   25   30

command the shore road down the Kyle and bring him early intelligence of any foe.

Strachan reached Wester Fearn about three in the afternoon of the 27th. He knew the position of the enemy, and he knew their weakness. It was his business to draw them down from the hill to the flat ground where his cavalry could act. Accordingly he concealed most of his horse among the long broom which covered the slopes above Wester Fearn. The Monroes and Rosses went up the Carron to a point on the heights above Carbisdale where they awaited the issue. Their heart was not in the fight, and they wanted to see how the day went before sharing in it. Strachan then advanced a single troop up the valley till he had passed the Carron.

Major Lisle, who commanded Montrose's forty horse, was sent to reconnoitre, and returned with information of the single troop. One of his gentlemen-volunteers, Monro of Achnes, assured the viceroy that there was but one troop of horse in all the shire, and that he saw it before him. Montrose ordered Lisle to halt, and gave the word to his foot to advance. Meantime Strachan was bringing up the rest of his troops from Wester Fearn. As soon as the Royalists were on the low ground they would see nothing of his movements, and in the cover of the broom and wildwood the whole Covenant cavalry crossed the Carron and advanced to meet Montrose.

Suddenly upon Lisle's forty horse Strachan dashed with a hundred of his dragoons. The little force was driven backward upon the foot, who were not deployed for battle and were easily cast into confusion. There cannot have been more than twelve hundred of them—four hundred Danes and Germans, and the rest the raw Orkney levies. The foreigners were not accustomed to receive a cavalry charge unsupported, and the Orcadians had probably never seen a dragoon in their lives before. They fell back in disorder, and Montrose saw that his one chance was to regain the safety of the Craigcaoinichean entrenchments. He had done the same thing under greater difficulties once before at Dundee. But then his force had been of a different quality. Had he had his 500 gallant Irish the day would have been saved, but they had long been below the turf of Slain-Man's-Lee. The mercenaries retreated in some order, but the hapless islanders, decent farmers and fisher-folk utterly unused to war, fled without a blow. Upon the fugitives came Strachan's reserves, Halkett's and Hutchison's troops, and Lawers' musketeers. Montrose's standard-bearer, Menzies of Pitfoddels, was shot dead at his side. Soon the scattered remnant of the Royalists, a few hundred at the most, was making its last stand on the wooded slopes of Craigcaoinichean.

Down from the hills came the Monroes and Rosses, convinced at last, to take their share of the victory. The Orkney men were drowned in hundreds trying to cross the Kyle, or were cut down in the haugh. Not a family in the islands but lost a son or a brother. The fire from the woods slackened, and the Royalists making for the higher slopes were shot or stabbed by the horse. Hurry was captured, and with him fifty-eight officers and nearly four hundred soldiers. Montrose was wounded several times, and his horse shot under him. It was Philiphaugh over again, and once more he was prevented from finding in battle the death which he desired. Young Frendraught, himself spent with wounds, forced him upon his own horse, and bade him remember his duty to the king's cause. In the late spring gloaming the viceroy of Scotland, with Kinnoul and two of the Sinclair gentry, turned his face from the stricken field towards the trackless wildernesses of the west.[89]

He flung away his sword-belt and coat with the star of the Garter that he might escape recognition, and managed to buy or borrow some rough Highland clothes. Strath Oykell was no place to ride, so he soon abandoned his horse, whereby his enemies found the clue they sought.

His first object seems to have been to go north to Strathnaver, and so reach Harry Graham at Thurso, and finally pass into Orkney. But he had no knowledge of the country, and during the first night the fugitives lost their way and wandered due west up the Oykell. For two days and two nights they were without food or shelter. There were few houses in the land and no roads; it had been a backward year and the snow was probably still on the high hills; the bogs, too, would be full and the streams swollen. Somehow they struggled over the watershed, where the burns began to flow to the Atlantic. They were now in a desperate case, and it was resolved to separate. Kinnoul and one of the Sinclairs were never heard of again. They died of famine somewhere in the wilderness, and 'the foxes and the eagles alone could tell the tale' of their end.[90] On the third day Montrose was given bread and milk at a herd's shieling, and hid below a trough when a party arrived in pursuit. On departing he regretted that he had put his host in danger, and 'determined never to do the like again to avoid death, of which, he thanked God, he was not afraid.[91] He was now some thirty miles from the scene of the battle.'

But the hue and cry was out against him. The laird of Assynt was a certain Neil Macleod, a member of a sept with a dark record for deeds of blood. He had married a daughter of Monro of Lemlair,[92] whom Montrose had looked upon as an ally, and he himself had been protected by Seaforth, and seems to have passed for something of a Royalist. His brother-in-law sent him a letter bidding him search his country for fugitives, and 'chiefly James Graham,' and Neil was no laggard in the business. One of his men found the famished wanderer on the confines of the Assynt country, and when Montrose heard his master's name he probably asked to be taken to him. He thought he had much to hope for from a Macleod and a son-in-law of Lemlair. On the evening of the 30th of April he was brought to the castle of Ardvreck, whose shell still stands on the northern shore of Loch Assynt. There he found Neil, and there he met, too, the surviving Sinclair, who had been brought in by Neil's scouts. But from Assynt he got no kindness. The head of the viceroy was worth sufficient gold to set up his impoverished family for good. Montrose besought him to take him to Orkney, and offered him money, but Neil was resolute, knowing well that the Estates could outbid the fugitive. He sent off an express with the happy news to Leslie, who had now arrived at Tain, and confined the prisoners in the cellars of his castle. A few days later, on the 4th of May, Holbourn arrived at Ardvreck, and Montrose was committed to his hands.

Carbisdale, like Philiphaugh, was a surprise and a rout rather than a battle. It was the first fight which Montrose ever fought with a superiority in numbers, for he had 1,200 men as against Strachan's 660; but the only contest was between the 220 Covenant troopers and Montrose's forty horse and 400 foreigners. Further, infantry in those days, unless magnificently posted, had no chance against even a weak body of cavalry, so for the purpose of the battle we may rule out all the foot who were straggling in the flats, and say that the struggle lay between Lisle's forty gentlemen-volunteers and Strachan's horse. There could never have been any doubt as to the issue, and though Strachan deserves all credit for a bold feat of arms, yet his task was easy. Montrose was doomed when he left the heights of Craigcaoinichean, and he left the heights, as we have seen, because of the defective information of his local scoutmaster. But indeed he was lost long before, during the days he waited for the Mackenzies who never came. He failed because, instead of pushing on with all speed to Badenoch, he wasted time on a half-hearted clan. If Neil Macleod was the immediate cause of Montrose's fate, his patron, Seaforth, was the ruin of the campaign; and Seaforth's indecision in turn was due beyond a doubt to the two-faced tactics of Charles. On the 1st of May, the day Montrose was taken, the king signed with the Covenanters the draft of the Treaty of Breda.

The name of the laird of Assynt lives in Scottish history with that of Sir John Menteith, who betrayed Wallace. Ian Lom, the bard of Keppoch, has left bitter verses on the 'stripped tree of the false apples, Neil's son of woeful Assynt.' He made little of his infamy. After the Restoration he was frequently in jail, and was twice tried for his life. His castle was burned, and his family, as if under a curse, soon withered out of existence. He was awarded twenty-five thousand pounds Scots* for his services, of which twenty thousand were to be paid in coin and the rest in oatmeal. It does not appear that he ever got the money, but the receipts for the meal exist, and Highland tradition is positive that two-thirds of it was sour.[93]

* About £1,360.

CHAPTER XVIII

THE CURTAIN FALLS
(MAY 1650)

I

NOW that the last blow had been struck, and only death remained, the oppression seems to have lifted from Montrose's soul. The 'fey' mood had passed and his spirit was enlarged. Once more he is the clear-sighted and constant patriot, the great gentleman who in the hour of deepest degradation can meet the taunts of his enemies with a smiling face, the Christian who has compassion upon the frailty of mankind. For six years his name had terrified the Covenanters, and as their hold upon the nation declined so also did their nerve and courage. The news of his landing in the north had shaken the Estates to their foundation. The crowning mercy of Carbisdale was at first scarcely believed, and when Strachan himself arrived post-haste to claim his reward their exaltation knew no bounds. Mixed with it was the zest of coming revenge. Their tormentor had been marvellously delivered into their hands, and we can judge of their past anxiety by the punishment they devised.

The measure of their vengeance is the measure of their fear.

It is difficult to judge Charles fairly. He was a young man, undisciplined, ill-advised, and without a trace of serious purpose. His one good quality, his courage, need not imply any nice sense of honour. But it is probable that before signing the Treaty of Breda he had convinced himself that he had made provision for the safety of his captain-general. On the 5th of May he wrote to Montrose, bidding him lay down his arms and disband his men. He seems to have received assurances from the Scottish Commissioners of an indemnity for the Royalist army. On the 8th of May he wrote to the Estates asking that Montrose and his forces should be allowed to leave the country in safety. A private letter was also written to the viceroy, telling him that 10,000 rix-dollars were at his call in Sir Patrick Drummond's hands. Sir William Fleming, a cousin of Montrose's, had further orders dated the 12th of May, written apparently after some rumour of Carbisdale had reached the king. These latest instructions were not to deliver the letter of the 8th of May to Parliament unless Montrose was still unbeaten and at the head of a reasonable army; if he had been defeated, the letter was to be concealed. Apparently Charles did not wish to ask grace for his captain-general from the Estates if he was a fugitive; he trusted to his private arrangement with the Scottish Commissioners. It is a tangled business, but it is inconceivable that the king hoped to conceal or disavow his complicity in the invasion. This was already clear from the public letter of the 12th of January, which every one in Scotland knew of; and from his personal letter of the 5th of May to Montrose, which was delivered and read to the Estates. A further letter, dated the 12th of May, was also read to Parliament, in which Charles disclaimed all responsibility for Montrose's doings. But it is impossible to believe that the king, who was no fool, and had the rest of the correspondence in his memory, could have been guilty of so futile and purposeless a piece of treachery, by which no one could be deceived. It is more likely that this was a fabrication of Will Murray, Argyll's emissary, with a view of alienating from the now Covenanting king the last remnants of Royalist respect in Scotland and Cavalier support in England. Base and heartless as was Charles's conduct, it is incredible that it reached the height of perfidy which Argyll and Lothian would have had the world believe.[94]

To Montrose royal duplicity and Covenanting intrigues had become matters of little moment. For him the long day's task was nearly done, and the hour of unarming had struck. He was led in triumphant progress by his captors through the length of Scotland, but the triumph was not theirs. On the 5th of May Holbourn hurried him from Ardvreck by way of Inveran to Skibo on the north side of the Kyle. A night was spent there, and the lady of the castle, finding that the rank of the prisoner was not sufficiently recognized, beat Holbourn about the head with a leg of mutton and had Montrose given the place of honour.[95] He was ferried over the Kyle, and on the 8th delivered to Leslie at Tain. Thence next day he was carried by way of Dingwall to Brahan Castle. On the following day he was at Beauly, and we have the record of Mr. James Fraser,[96] then a boy of sixteen, and afterwards Lovat's chaplain, who now joined the march. The viceroy 'sat upon a little shelty horse, without a saddle, but a quilt of rags and straw, and pieces of ropes for stirrups ; his feet fastened under the horse's belly with a tether ; a bit halter for a bridle.' It was the mode of progress which was later suffered by many saints of the Covenant, notably Mr. Donald Cargill. He still wore peasant's clothes, on his head was a montero cap, and around his shoulders a ragged old reddish plaid. His neglected wounds pained him greatly, and he was in a high fever. At Muirtown, near Inverness, he begged for water, and there the crowd from the town came out to gaze on him. The two ministers of Inverness also appeared, and seem to have been more decent in their behaviour than the run of the brethren. At the bridge-end an old woman railed at him and reminded him of the houses he had burned when he besieged the town. 'Yet he never altered his countenance, but with a majesty and state beseeming him kept his countenance high.'

The magistrates met him at the cross, where they had set up a table of refreshments. He was offered wine and mixed it with water. Fraser saw the other prisoners drinking heartily under a forestair, and remarked among them Sir John Hurry, 'a robust, tall, stately fellow, with a long cut in his cheek.' Hurry was a true soldier of fortune, own brother to Dugald Dalgetty, and in his varied career and many changes of side he kept a certain soldierly honour. As was said of a more famous Sir John, the world could have better spared a better man. The provost, Duncan Forbes of Culloden, a courteous member of an honourable house, said on taking leave, 'My lord, I am sorry for your circumstances.' That night the prisoners lodged at Castle Stewart on the road to Nairn.

On the way through Moray many friends came to greet him, college companions at St. Andrews and loyalists such as Pluscardine, whose clan had so grievously failed him. At Elgin he was greatly cheered by the sight of an old college friend, the minister of Duffus. His well-wishers convoyed him over Spey, and on the 11th he halted at Keith, where he lay on straw in a tent set up in the fields. The next day was the Sabbath, and he attended the ministrations of Mr. William Kinethmont, who preached on the favourite Covenanting text of the hewing of Agag and the Amalekites. He violently abused the prisoner, till he disgusted even his Covenanting hearers. 'Rail on, Rabshakeh,' was the victim's only reply. On the 13th the procession reached Pitcaple Castle,[97] the home of an Engager. The quicker road to the south through Mar was not taken, probably through fear of a rescue by the Farquharsons, and the route chosen was the one by which Montrose had so often led his swift armies. Now he traversed the scene of his victories with a herald pacing before him, proclaiming, 'Here comes James Graham, a traitor to his country.' He was probably at Fordoun on the 14th, and on the 15th he reached Southesk's castle of Kinnaird. There he saw his two younger sons, Robert and David, boys of fourteen and twelve. When he left them he left behind the last slender ties which still bound him to earth. His wife and his eldest son were dead; his best friends had perished on the scaffold; his cause, the clean and sane ideals he had fought for, was undone. Death could have few terrors to one who had nothing to live for, and who had faced it so often with the gaiety of a lover. Like Kent in *King Lear* he might have said:—

> 'I have a journey, sir, shortly to go;
> My master calls me, I must not say no.'

On the night of the 15th he halted at the house of Grange, a property of the Durhams, five miles from Dundee. Here, if we are to believe the author of the *Memoir of the Somervilles*,[98] there was an attempt, as at Pitcaple, to assist him to escape. The lady of the house plied the guards with strong ale and brandy, and they, being Highlanders of Lawers' regiment, willingly succumbed. But the outer guards had not been tampered with, and the fugitive was discovered by a trooper of Strachan's horse. There is only one authority for the story, but we have no reason to discredit it. Next day he entered Dundee, and to the eternal credit of that staunchly Covenanting town, which moreover had suffered more than most at Montrose's hands, he was received with decency and respect. 'The whole town expressed a good deal of sorrow for his condition; and furnished him with clothes and all other things suitable to his place, birth, and person.' We have no record of the two days' march across Fife. No doubt the ministers flocked to upbraid him, and the few heroes who had returned from

Tippermuir and Kilsyth came to stare at one who had given them little cause to love him. From Dysart or Kirkcaldy the company took ship for Leith, and reached it about four o'clock on the afternoon of Saturday the 18th. On the same day and at the same port arrived Sir William Fleming with the king's letters of disbandment.

The Covenanters had made ample preparation to receive the prisoner. They knew that what they had to do must be done quickly. The viceroy must be dead before the king's coming to Scotland, or trouble would follow. Further, the Commonwealth had never shown any bitterness against the great captain, and might interdict those of the Estates who favoured Cromwell from the kind of vengeance which Cromwell as a rule preferred to leave to the Lord. There were magnanimous men, too, in Scotland in all parties who resented the unsoldierly treatment of a soldier, and there were his friends in foreign courts, notably in the court of France, who would be certain to plead for him if time were allowed. Such an appeal[99] was actually sent, signed by the young king Louis the Fourteenth, in which it was eloquently urged that Montrose had always acted within the terms of his royal commission, and therefore could not be condemned by those who now acknowledged the royal authority. But the appeal arrived after the deed had been done. Argyll was not the man to waste time when it was a matter of getting rid of a dreaded and hated rival.

Immediately after the news of Carbisdale the Estates had sat to consider the question of punishment. In a time of civil strife nice questions of legality are out of place, and the condemnation of Montrose was as legal as anything else that was done by the Scots Parliament. He had been attainted and outlawed in 1644, and there had been no reversal of the sentence. A commission was appointed to decide on the details of the penalty, and on the 17th of May had made its report. The captive was to be met at the gates by the magistrates and the hangman, and conducted with every circumstance of ignominy to the Tolbooth. Thereafter he was to be hanged on a gibbet—not beheaded as was the custom with state prisoners—with Wishart's book and a copy of his own last Declaration tied around his neck. Thus would be fulfilled the words of the prophet Rothes, and he would be 'lifted up above the rest in three fathoms of a rope. After death the head was to be struck off, the body dismembered, and the limbs fixed in public places in Stirling, Glasgow, Perth, and Aberdeen. If he repented of his misdeeds, the ban of excommunication would be removed and the body buried in Greyfriars' Churchyard; if not, it would go to the felons' pit on the Boroughmuir. It was piously hoped that the common folk of Edinburgh, who had lost kith and kin in his wars, would await his entrance and show their hatred with filth and stones. For this purpose his hands were to be pinioned behind his back.

The afternoon was clear and chilly, such as is common on the shores of the Forth in late May. The magistrates of Edinburgh met him at Leith, and the procession was formed, the other prisoners on foot and Montrose himself mounted on a cart-horse. His face was drawn and wasted with fever, and his grey eyes burned with an unnatural brilliancy. The good folk of Dundee had given him clothes more suited to his condition than those he had worn when captured, and he bore himself among the hostile crowd with a gentle dignity. A smile, it is said, flickered about his mouth, not of scorn, but of peace. When he entered the Nethergate of the city, where the *faubourg* of the Canongate began, in which stood the houses of the nobility, he found awaiting him the officers of justice, the hangman, and a hangman's cart drawn by four horses. He was shown the sentence of the Estates and read it carefully, saying that he was sorry that the king, whose commission he bore, should be so dishonoured. Then he entered the cart, and was tied to a high seat with cords across his breast and arms. The hangman exchanged hats with him, and Montrose was compelled to wear the red bonnet of the outcast trade.

Slowly in the bright evening the procession moved up the ancient *via dolorosa* of Scottish history.[100] The street was blocked with people—the dregs of the Edinburgh slums, black-gowned ministers, the retainers of the Covenanting lords, all the elements most bitterly hostile to the prisoner. But to the amazement of the organizers there was no sign of popular wrath. Rather there was silence, a tense air of sympathy and pity and startled admiration. The high pale face set up in that place of public scorn awed the mob into stillness. 'In all the way, there appeared in him such majesty, courage, modesty, and even somewhat more than natural, that those common women who had lost their husbands and children in his wars, and who were hired to stone him, were, upon the sight of him, so astonished and moved that their intended curse turned into tears and prayers.'[101] In the strained quiet, broken only by excited sobs, there was one jarring note. Lady Haddington, Argyll's niece and the sister of Lord Gordon, by reputation the most abandoned woman in Scotland, laughed shrilly and shouted a word of insult from the balcony where she sat. A voice cried out of the crowd that the right place for her was in the hangman's cart to expiate her sins.

In the lodgings along the Canongate the Covenanting nobles were assembled to feast their eyes upon the degradation of their old enemy. In the balcony of Lord Moray's house Lord Lorn sat with his young bride, the same man who thirty-five years later was himself to go to a not inglorious scaffold. Inside the house, with the shutters half-closed, stood Argyll with Loudoun and Wariston. Montrose as he passed caught a glimpse of the sour, anxious, unhappy face which he knew so well, and for the first time for long the two men looked into each other's eyes. The shutters were closed and the faces disappeared. There was an English soldier in the crowd who observed the incident, and cried, 'It was no wonder they started aside at his look, for they durst not look him in the face these seven years bygone.'

As he passed the cross he saw the new gallows standing ready to receive him. About seven o'clock he reached the Tolbooth. His bonds were cut, and as he descended he gave the hangman gold, and thanked him 'for driving his triumphal chariot so well.' Scarcely was he within the prison when a deputation from the Estates with its retinue of ministers arrived to interrogate him. He refused to answer, for indeed he was very weary with travel and neglected wounds, and his tormentors withdrew. His parting words to them were a jest. 'The compliments they put upon him that day,' he said, 'had proved something tedious.' He was still young, only thirty-eight.

II

Next day being the Sabbath there was a great preaching. From every pulpit in the city the clergy thundered against the excommunicate James Graham and no less against the mob who had refused to stone him. The prisoner was visited by the usual deputation of ministers, but they got no satisfaction. He told them, in the words of the Wigton manuscript, that 'if they thought they had affronted him the day before by carrying him in a cart they were much mistaken, for he thought it the most honourable and joyful journey ever he made; God having all the while most comfortably manifested Himself to him, and furnished him with resolution to overlook the re-proaches of men, and to behold Him for whose cause he suffered.'

He was given no peace. At eight o'clock on the Monday morning his persecutors returned to the attack. Mr. James Guthrie, Mr. Mungo Law, Mr. Robert Traill, and others, hoped to extract some confession from him which could be used to undo the profound impression which his appearance had made on the people of Edinburgh. They charged him at a venture with imaginary personal vices of which he had none. Then they accused him of taking up arms against his country, of using Irish troops, and of shedding Scottish blood. He replied, as Wodrow's informant told him,[102] in a manner 'too airy and volage, not so much suiting the gravity of a nobleman.' Using their own favourite argument, he reminded them that David in the Cave of Adullam had gathered an odd fighting force; and as for bloodshed he declared 'if it could have been thereby prevented, he would rather it had all come out of his own veins.' Lastly they charged him with a breach of the Covenant, and his answer was ready. 'The Covenant which I took I own it and adhere to it. Bishops, I care not for them. I never intended to advance their interests. But when the king had granted you all your desires, and you were every one sitting under his vine and under his fig tree—that then you should have taken a party in England by the hand, and entered into a League and Covenant with them against the king, was the thing I judged my duty to oppose to the yondmost.' One of the ministers lost patience and told him that he was a faggot of hell which already he saw in torment. Mr. James Guthrie then touched on the excommunication, and said that since the prisoner showed himself obdurate it must remain. With the strange arrogance of his creed he had the 'fearful apprehension that what is bound on earth God will bind in heaven.' Montrose replied gently that he would gladly be reconciled to the Church of Scotland, but he could not call that his sin which he accounted to have been his duty.

When the ministers left him he was given a little bread dipped in ale for his breakfast, but he was not allowed a barber to shave him. At ten o'clock he was taken before the bar of Parliament to hear his sentence. It was common knowledge that he had acted under the king's credentials, and therefore nothing in the nature of a trial could be allowed, for it was difficult for Loudoun and Argyll to deny a mandate for which they had the royal evidence. Loudoun seems to have harped on the incidents of the Highland wars, mingled with violent denunciations of the viceroy's person. Since his arrival in Edinburgh, Montrose had been furnished, probably by the Napier ladies, with clothes worthy of his rank. When he stood up before his accusers in Parliament he wore a suit of fine black cloth, with a richly laced scarlet cloak to the knee; on his head was a black beaver hat with a silver band; and on his legs stockings of carnation silk.[103] He replied to his accusers in a speech, happily preserved,[104] in which he repeated the substance of his many declarations—his loyalty to the true Covenant, his abhorrence of the Solemn League. 'How far religion has been advanced by it these poor distressed kingdoms can witness.' War could not be waged without the shedding of blood, but he had repressed all disorders as soon as known. 'Never was any man's blood spilt but in battle; and even then, many thousand lives have I preserved. And I dare here avow, in the presence of God, that never a hair of Scotsman's head that I could save fell to the ground.' He asked to be judged 'by the laws of God, the laws of nature and nations, and the laws of this land.' But he knew that the plea was vain, so he appealed to a higher tribunal—to the 'righteous Judge of the world, who one day must be your Judge and mine, and who always gives out righteous judgments.' He had said his say; he had fulfilled the proud boast which he had made to Parliament nine years before: 'My resolution is to carry along fidelity and honour to the grave.' His judges had no answer. Loudoun, the chancellor, replied with a torrent of abuse, and Johnston of Wariston read the sentence, which Montrose heard on his knees. We are told that he lifted up his head as the grim words were uttered and looked Wariston calmly in the face.

He was taken back to the Tolbooth where all day he was tormented by ministers. The captain of the town guard was the famous Major Weir[105], the warlock of Edinburgh legend, who afterwards expiated his many crimes at the stake. By his orders the guard were always in the prisoner's room, and filled it with tobacco smoke, which Montrose, unlike his father, could not abide. None of his friends were allowed to come near him. Neverthe-less, we are told, in spite of fever and wounds and the imminence of death, he continued his devotions unperturbed, and slept as peacefully as a child. That last night, like Sir Walter Raleigh and much in the same strain, he, who had for so long forsaken the Muse, returned to his old love. These lines were written amid the smoke and wrangling of the guards:—

> 'Let them bestow on every airth a limb,
> Then open all my veins, that I may swim
> To Thee, my Maker, in that crimson lake,—
> Then place my parboiled head upon a stake,
> Scatter my ashes—strew them in the air.—
> Lord! Since Thou knowest where all these atoms are,
> I'm hopeful Thou'lt recover once my dust,
> And confident Thou'lt raise me with the just.'

On Tuesday morning the 21st of May he rose for the last time. Like the Spartans before Thermopylæ, he combed his long locks for death. Probably they were matted with the blood of his untended wounds. The usual concourse of ministers and politicians was in his cell, and Wariston sneered at him for his care of the body. 'My head is still my own' was his answer. 'Tonight, when it will be yours, treat it as you please.' Presently he heard the drums beating to arms, and was told that the troops were assembling to prevent any attempt at a rescue. He laughed and cried, 'What, am I still a terror to them? Let them look to themselves; my ghost will haunt them.'

He was taken about two in the afternoon by the bailies down the High Street to the cross, which stood halfway between the Tolbooth and the Tron Kirk. He still wore the brave clothes in which he had confronted Parliament. James Fraser who saw him wrote:

'He stept along the streets with so great state, and there appeared in his countenance so much beauty, majesty, and gravity as amazed the beholders. And many of his enemies did acknowledge him to be the bravest subject in the world.'

The scaffold was a great four-square platform, breast-high, and on it a thirty-foot gallows had been erected. On the platform stood the ministers, Mr. Robert Traill and Mr. Mungo Law, still bent on getting a word of confession. They were disappointed. Montrose did not look at them, but, after speaking apart with the magistrates, addressed the mob, which surged up against the edge of the scaffold. A boy called Robert Gordon sat by and took down his words in some kind of shorthand,[106] and the crowd, with that decency which belongs to all common folk, kept a reverent silence. The Estates were afraid lest he should attack the king and spoil their game, but he spoke no word of bitterness or reproach. It was the testament of a man conscious of his mortal frailty but confident in the purity of his purpose and the mercy of his God.

'I am sorry if this manner of my end be scandalous to any good Christian here. Doth it not often happen to the righteous according to the way of the unrighteous? Doth not sometimes a just man perish in his righteousness, and a wicked man prosper in his wickedness and malice? They who know me should not disesteem me for this. Many greater than I have been dealt with in this kind. But I must not say but that all God's judgments are just. And this measure, for my private sins, I acknowledge to be just with God. I wholly submit myself to Him. But, in regard of man, I may say they are but instruments. God forgive them; and I forgive them. They have oppressed the poor, and violently perverted judgment and justice. But He that is higher than they will reward them. What I did in this kingdom was in obedience to the most just commands of my sovereign, and in his defence, in the day of his distress, against those who rose up against him. I acknowledge nothing, but fear God and honour the king, according to the commandments of God, and the just laws of nature and nations. And I have not sinned against man, but against God; and with Him there is mercy, which is the ground of my drawing near unto Him. It is objected against me by many, even good people, that I am under the censure of the Church. This is not my fault, seeing it is only for doing my duty, by obeying my Prince's most just commands, for religion, his sacred person, and authority. Yet I am sorry they did excommunicate me; and in that which is according to God's laws, without wronging my conscience or allegiance I desire to be relaxed. If they will not do it I appeal to God, who is the Righteous Judge of the world, and who must, and will, I hope, be my Judge and Saviour. It is spoken of me that I would blame the king. God forbid. For the late king, he lived a saint, and died a martyr. I pray God I may end as he did. If ever I would wish my soul in another man's stead, it should be in his. For his Majesty now living, never any people, I believe, might be more happy in a king. His commandments to me were most just; and I obeyed them. He deals justly with all men. I pray God he be so dealt withal that he be not betrayed under trust as his father was. I desire not to be mistaken; as if my carriage at this time, in relation to your ways, were stubborn. I do but follow the light of my conscience, my rule; which is seconded by the working of the Spirit of God that is within me. I thank Him I go to heaven with joy the way He paved for me. If He enable me against the fear of death, and furnish me with courage and confidence to embrace it even in its most ugly shape, let God be glorified in my end, though it were in my damnation. Yet I say not this out of any fear or mistrust, but out of my duty to God, and love to His people. I have no more to say, but that I desire your charity and prayers. And I shall pray for you all. I leave my soul to God, my service to my prince, my goodwill to my friends, my love and charity to you all. And thus briefly I have exonerated my conscience.'[107]

There is a tradition that during the morning there had been lowering thunder-clouds and flashes of lightning, but that as Montrose stood on the scaffold a burst of sunlight flooded the street. When he had finished speaking he gave money to the executioner, and prayed silently for a little. His arms were pinioned, and he walked up the ladder with that stately carriage which had always marked him. His last words were, 'God have mercy on this afflicted land.' Tears ran down the hangman's face as he pushed him off, and we are told that a great sob broke from the crowd. They had cause to sob, for that day there was done to death such a man as his country has not seen again.

According to the sentence, the body was dismembered and the limbs distributed among the chief towns. The remains in Aberdeen must have caught the eye of Charles when he arrived a few weeks later. The trunk was buried beside the public gallows on the Boroughmuir. The head was placed on a spike in front of the Tolbooth, and eleven years later was taken down to make room for the head of Argyll.

III

There was to be another funeral besides that melancholy scene by lantern light among the marshes of the Boroughmuir. After the Restoration one of Charles's first acts was to give public burial to the remains of his great captain. On January 4, 1661, the Scots Parliament resolved on 'an honourable reparation for that horrid and monstrous barbarity in the person of the great Marquis of Montrose.'[108] The trunk was taken up and the limbs gathered from the several towns, a ceremony attended by 'the honest people's loud and joyful acclamation.' The remains, wrapped in fine linen, in a noble coffin, lay in state in the Abbey Kirk from the 7th of January to the 11th of May. On the last date took place the great procession to St. Giles's.[109] First rode Sir Harry Graham, Montrose's half-brother, carrying the arms of his house. Then followed the Graham gentry with their different standards—Duntroon, Morphie, Monzie, Balgowan, Gorthie; and Black Pate of

Inchbrakie, who had been with Montrose on that August afternoon in Atholl when the curtain rose upon his campaigns, bore his Order of the Garter. The body was carried by fourteen earls, including the men or the sons of the men who had betrayed him, such as Seaforth and Home and Roxburgh, as well as old opponents such as Eglinton and Callander. Twelve viscounts and barons bore the pall, among them Strathnaver, the son of the Sutherland who had locked the gates of the north after Carbisdale. The young Montrose and his brother Lord Robert followed the coffin, and in the procession were the representatives of almost every Scottish house. Argyll's friend and Montrose's brother-in-law, Rollo, was there, and Marischal, who had held Dunnottar against him, and Tweeddale and Forrester who had voted for his death. There, too, were the faithful friends who had not failed him, Maderty, and Frendraught, and the Marquis of Douglas, and old Napier's grandson. The morning had been stormy, but we are told that as the procession moved from Holyrood the sun shone out brightly, as it had done at his end. The streets were lined with the trainbands, who fired their volleys, while in reply the cannon thundered from the castle, wherein lay Argyll under sentence of death. The nobles of Scotland according to their wont had moved over to the winning side. The pageant was an act of tardy justice, and it attracts by its dramatic contrasts, but it had little relevance to Montrose's true achievement. He was as little kin to the rabble of the Restoration as to the rabble of the Covenant. The noble monument which now marks his grave in the ancient High Kirk of Scotland is a more fitting testimony, for it has been left to modern days to recognize the greatness of one who had no place in his generation.

The heart was not carried from Holyrood on that Saturday in May. Its story is the most romantic of all.[110] Shortly after his death young Lady Napier sent her servants by night to the grave on the Boroughmuir, and had the heart taken from the body. It was skilfully embalmed, and placed in a little egg-shaped case of steel made from the blade of his sword. This in turn was enclosed in a gold filigree box which had been given to her husband's grandfather by a Doge of Venice. She sent the box to the young Marquis of Montrose on the Continent, where it remained for many years, passing somehow out of the possession of the family. It was recognized in a Dutch collection by a friend of the fifth Lord Napier, who procured it for him. Napier bequeathed it on his death to his daughter, who had married a Johnston of Carnsalloch, an official of the East India Company. It was carried to India, and on the way was struck by a shot in a battle with a French squadron off Cape Verd Islands, and the gold filigree box was shattered. But the adventures of the heart were not ended. It remained for some time in the Johnstons' house at Madura, where the natives came to reverence it as a talisman. It was stolen and purchased by the Nabob of Arcot, in whose treasury it long lay. The young Johnston in a hunting expedition happened to save his life, and the Nabob in gratitude restored the relic to his family. It was brought home to Europe by the elder Johnstons in 1792, and as they travelled overland through France they heard of the edict of the Revolution government requiring the surrender of all gold and silver trinkets. Mrs. Johnston entrusted it to an Englishwoman at Boulogne till it could be sent to England, but the lady died soon afterwards, and in the troubled days that followed the relic disappeared. Since then it has been lost to the world. Some day, perhaps, an antiquary, rummaging in the old shops on the quays, may come on a casket of Indian work, and opening it find the little egg-shaped case. It would be a precious discovery, for it holds the dust of the bravest of Scottish hearts.

CHAPTER XIX

'A CANDIDATE FOR IMMORTALITY'*

I

MONTROSE founded no school and left no successor. He was a lonely figure in his day, and for two centuries almost his bequest remained unnoted and unshared. Cromwell, indeed, came north into Scotland the same year and enforced one part of his message. Dunbar was the avenging of Philiphaugh and Carbisdale, and the heavy hand of the greatest of Englishmen was laid on the strange edifice which plotters and fanatics had built out of the rubbish of the Middle Ages. The nine years of the English occupation saw the plain man raising his head once more. Sir Alexander Irvine of Drum was moved to tell the ministers that their wild charges were 'but undigested rhapsodies of confused nonsense,' and none could gainsay him. Cromwell enforced his views on religious toleration, and did his best to curb the appetite of the Kirk for witch-finding. He made an attempt at uniting Scotland with England, reduced taxation, established free trade

*The phrase is Wishart's, and is used in the last sentence of his *Life*.

with the south, took the sting out of excommunication by preventing any civil penalties attending it, and finally, to the infinite comfort of the lieges, suppressed the General Assembly. For the first time for a generation even-handed justice was done between all classes. And, as we know from Mr. Robert Law, the spiritual life of the country, long bound under the desolate frosts of faction, began to put forth hopeful shoots.

Cromwell passed, and the king who had so cheerfully betrayed his servant came to his own again. The old strife was renewed of nobles and king and Kirk, and again the common folk of Scotland were the victims. One thing had indeed been gained—the impossible theocracy had perished. The Kirk, as always happens, having asked too much was to get less than her due, and the spiritual liberty which she had forbidden to others in her heyday was now to be denied to herself. The later Covenanters, whose sufferings have left so dark a memory among their countrymen, fought for a cause similar only in name to that of their predecessors before 1660. They resisted a despotic 'bond' imposed on them by the Government to the outraging of their consciences, as Montrose had resisted the 'bond' of Guthrie and Wariston. The men who suffered on the western moorlands, though his name was an anathema to them and they revered his executioners, yet stood for the very cause for which he died. They asked for the spiritual liberty he had pled for, and resisted that constraining of men's consciences which he had warred against. But the evil had been wrought. Fanaticism had raised a counter-fanaticism, and the struggle had to continue till both were dead of their wounds. The way was prepared for the long lacklustre régime of eighteenth-century Scotland, when the Kirk was ossified into a thing of dogmas and forms and civil government sunk to a dull and corrupt servitude to the powers of the moment. The spiritual fires of the Covenant had burned too murkily to be allowed to last, and the clear flame of Montrose had gone from a world that was not worthy of it. Scotsmen can now look back upon that tangled era and judge both parties without bitterness. Argyll's monument stands close to Montrose's in St. Giles's, and the most fervent admirer of the great marquis can see the value of the tradition which the Covenant has bequeathed to us. But it should not be forgotten that that tradition, which has at once educated and ennobled the Scottish people, was a by-product, and was never the chief aim of the pre-1660 Covenanters. For their enduring work, the liberty of the Kirk of Scotland and the elevation of the lowliest citizen to the dignity of an immortal soul, Montrose laboured as zealously as they. In their declared objects, which were the establishment of a theocracy above any civil power and an inquisition over every man's conscience, they failed utterly and disastrously, and in their failure brought their country to the last misery and degradation.

The history of Scotland was written first by the Divines and then by the Whigs, so it is small wonder that Montrose has fared badly. A kind of literary convention arose, according to which the most pagan of Edinburgh lawyers, when he took pen in hand, thought it his duty to pay tribute to the Solemn League and its abettors. It is only within the last two generations that the balance has been redressed, and the rarity and majesty of Montrose's character understood. But popular tradition has been more just. The fear of the great marquis in the Lowlands seems always to have been attended with a kind of respect. Stories of his humanity, his beauty, and his tragic fate were handed down, a curious interlude in a memory of blood and suffering. Lowland legend never gave him the name of 'persecutor,' and he never sat at that grim tavern-board in hell with 'the fierce Middleton, and the dissolute Rothes, and the crafty Lauderdale.' It would be strange if he had, for these were the men who had brought him to his death. As for Celtic Scotland she has long taken him to her heart. He is her chosen hero, the only Lowlander who has ever entered the sacred circle of Gaelic folk-tale and song. Under him the Celt reached his apotheosis, and for one short year held the Saxon in the hollow of his hand. Clan rivalries have been forgotten in the homage to a racial hero. As the old gillie on the Beauly said, 'My name is Campbell, but my heart is with the great Montrose.'[111]

On the political side Montrose was a modern man, as modern as Burke or Canning, and speaking a language far more intelligible to our ears than that of the Butes and Dundases of a later Scotland. The seventeenth-century, in most ways an epoch of reaction, produced two curiously premature characters in the great marquis and Sir George Mackenzie;[112] but Mackenzie, being a lawyer, made a sharp distinction between theory and practice, and while his theory was modern his practice was of the Dark Ages; whereas Montrose knew no cleavage between thoughts and deeds. It is not enough to say that he was in advance of his day. Most great men have been that. They saw several stages ahead, and tried to expedite the slow process of time. Some, again, such as Bolingbroke and Shelburne and in a fashion Disraeli, half from a sense of paradox and half from insight, threw out ideas which were to fructify afterwards in a form of which they had not dreamed. But Montrose was before his time, not from paradox or from hurry, but because almost alone in his age he looked clearly at the conditions of all government, and, having formed his conclusions, was not deterred by prudence or self-interest from acting upon them. He saw behind the sanctions of religion to the crazy reaction of the Kirk; he saw behind the catchwords of democracy to an oligarchical purpose; he saw behind an outward cloak of law to the ultimate certainty of anarchy. He realized that there must be one central authority, incontestable and inviolate so long as it fulfilled the conditions of its being. As has been already pointed out, he had none of the contemporary belief in Divine Right, and he was willing to accept any form of government, provided it fulfilled the requirements

which are indispensable in all governments. He had no
excessive reverence for a king as such, and very little
for a nobility; he would not have shrunk from the views
of Cromwell's Ironsides as to the historical origin of
the peerage, which so scandalized worthy Mr. Richard
Baxter.[113] But like Burke he had a natural preference for
monarchy, because it happened to be the form in existence in his land. The central power, however constituted,
springs from the free people and is limited by the law
of God, the law of nations, and the law of the land.
Parliaments are the guardians of popular rights, the watch-
dogs of liberty, and they must be free and frequent; but
they are not in themselves the central authority, but only
part of it. Their powers of change are limited by the law
fundamental and by the right of veto in the monarch.
It should be noted that the legislative supremacy of
Parliament is an eighteenth-century doctrine, and one by
no means rooted in our constitutional history. It was an
innovation which cost us the American colonies; and it
would appear that today we are moving away from it
again, and returning to that direct appeal to the people
which is at the bottom of the old talk about the 'law
fundamental.'

This central authority, whatever form it takes, is the
people's creation, and therefore it is foolish to consider
that it and the people are 'two contraries, like the two
scales of a balance, when the one goes up the other goes
down,' and that 'what power is taken from the king is
added to the estates of the people.'[114] The central authority is the nation: if they weaken it they weaken themselves;
and what power is taken from it goes not to the citizens
at large but to sects and factions of subjects, the nobles
who are always lying in wait to encroach upon the people and the people's king. Montrose saw clearly that a
direct plebiscitary government was impossible in the
Scotland of his day. The authority must be delegated to
safe and competent hands, and those who favoured

plebiscitary government sought power not for the people but for themselves—'as a cunning tennis player lets a ball go to the wall where it cannot stay, that he may take it at the bound with more ease.' We must be on our guard against reading more into this philosophy of politics than Montrose meant. He was not a democrat in our modern sense, for the common people in his day were scarcely conscious of political rights, and needed rather to be wisely protected than to be endowed with ill-understood duties. But, in contrast to his generation, he saw that with the whole community rests the sanction of government, and that any disturbance of the equipoise in the distribution of public duties would not add to popular liberty, but by increasing anarchy augment the power of this or that oligarchical faction. The law is the only safeguard of the plain man; it is the true monarch, of which the king is but the creature. He is altogether free from any mediaeval political ideas either as to monarchy or religion. The Kirk must be free in spiritual matters, which are her province, but if she meddle in civil government there will only be confusion. He saw government not as a ready-made thing sprung full-grown from some divine ordinance, but as a slow growth, an organism perfected by degrees with checks and balances. In his *Discourse on Sovereignty* and his many declarations there is scarcely an idea which is not modern; and, what is far rarer, the application is modern too.

Open Burke anywhere. 'I see no other way for the preservation of a decent attention to public interest in the representatives, but the interposition of the body of the people itself, whenever it shall appear, by some flagrant and notorious act, by some capital innovation, that the representatives are going to overleap the fences of the law, and to introduce an arbitrary power. It is Montrose's defence first for signing the Covenant, and then for taking up arms against it. 'Here it says to an encroaching prerogative, 'Your sceptre has its length, you cannot add a hair to

your head or a gem to your crown but what an eternal law
has given to it.' Here it says to an overweening peerage,
'Your pride finds banks that it cannot overflow.' Here to a
tumultuous and giddy people, 'There is a bed to the raging sea.' It is Montrose's conception of constitutional law.
Or again: 'If civil society be the offspring of convention,
that convention must be its law. That convention must
limit and modify all the descriptions of constitutions
which are formed under it. Every sort of legislative, judicial, or executive powers are its creatures. They can have
no being in any other state of things; and how can any
man claim, under the convention of civil society, rights
which do not so much as suppose its existence—rights
which are absolutely repugnant to it?'[115] It is Montrose's
case against the encroachments of the Kirk. He took the
historical as opposed to the metaphysical view of human
institutions, and, moreover, in his practical interpretation
he has curiously anticipated the modern attitude. He
could have little part in an age when men believed that
kings and aristocracies and Kirks were mystically ordained
of God. It has been the fashion, even among his warmest
admirers, to represent him as no statesman, and to exalt
Argyll by contrast. If for 'statesman' we read 'politician'
there is truth in the comment. Montrose, in the game of
parliamentary intrigues, was easily surpassed by his rival.
Nor did he read the temper of the people with the accu-
racy of Argyll, or the possibilities of the moment with the
practical acumen of Cromwell. He was an optimist about
his dream; he saw the Lowland peasantry looking for a
deliverer, when they regarded him as a destroyer; he did
not understand the depth of the antipathy of Saxon to
Celt, or how utterly the use of Alastair's men prejudiced
his cause; he looked for loyalty in quarters where he found
only self-interest, and courage among those who had it
not. As a politician Argyll was far wiser in his generation;
he cut his cloak according to his cloth, and, at any rate, he
completed it. The trouble was that the cloak turned out to

be no shelter against the storm. If Montrose failed, so did Argyll, and with a far more hopeless failure. Of all that he had built nothing remained. The theocracy on which, not from fanaticism, but from cold prudence, he had founded his power, crumbled beneath him. He was to live to call his associates 'madmen,' and to confess to his son that he was a distracted man living in a distracted time. His conduct towards Charles the Second in the matter of the signing of the Covenant and the offer of his daughter's hand, his intrigues with Cromwell, and his behaviour at the Restoration deprive him of the defence which can be put forward for an honest fanatic. His parliamentary reforms of 1640[116] are usually quoted to his credit, for he is said to have liberalized the basis of representation. Yet the power remained with the nobles and the Kirk, and the Scottish people were as far off as ever from a voice in their government. Argyll played patiently and adroitly for his own hand, and failed; as he in no way thought of posterity, posterity has little motive to think of him.

Montrose was a most fallible politician; did he also fail as a statesman? Statesmanship requires two qualities—the conception of wise ends, and the perception of adequate means. Essentially it works by compromises, accepting the second and third best as an instalment, and by slow degrees leading the people to acquiesce in an ideal which they have come to regard as their own invention. It must judge shrewdly the situation of the moment, and know precisely what elements therein are capable of providing the first stage in the great advance. It must have infinite patience and infinite confidence in the slow processes of time. Such a gift Montrose did not possess; indeed it may be questioned whether the nature of the problem before his age permitted of such evolutionary methods. There was no material to his hand in the shape of a nation at least partially instructed and a band of like-minded colleagues. Seventeenth-century Britain produced no statesman in this full sense, no Cavour or Alexander

Hamilton. But one of its two constituents he possessed, if it be part of statesmanship to see far ahead and to stand, in Mr. Gardiner's phrase, for 'the hope of the future.' He stood for the Scottish democracy both against those who would crush it and those who betrayed it with a kiss. Here, as in his defence of toleration, lies his kinship with Cromwell. The Lord Protector fought for 'the poor godly people;' Montrose for the plain folk without any qualification. Both were idealists, striving for something which their age could not give them. Montrose had one obstacle in his way above all others, and that was Scotland. Her jealous nationalism was not ripe, even had the century been ripe, for his far-sighted good sense. She was still hugging to her heart her own fantastic creations, her covenants, her barren survivals, her peculiar royalism; still jealous of the south, and prepared to sacrifice reason and prosperity to her pride. If Cromwell shipwrecked upon the gross and genial materialism of England, Montrose no less split upon the rock of the mediaeval conservatism of his own land. Scotland was not ready for civic ideals or luminous reason. She had not found the self-confidence which was to give her a far truer and deeper national pride. She had still to tread for long years the path of coarse and earthy compromises, lit by flashes of crazy quixotry, till through suffering and poverty she came at last to find her own soul. Montrose was too far in advance of his age, he was too far in advance of England at her best, but he was utterly and eternally beyond the ken of seventeenth-century Scotland. Yet of the two great idealists he has had the happier destiny. Cromwell, brilliantly successful for the moment, built nothing which lasted. Except for his doctrine of toleration, he left no heritage of political thought which the world has used. The ideals of Montrose, on the other hand, are in the very warp and woof of the constitutional fabric of today.

The moderate man rarely appeals to arms. He sees too clearly the values on both sides to commit himself to a desperate hazard. But there is a moderation which is in itself a fire, where enthusiasm burns as fiercely for the whole truth as it commonly does for half-truths, where toleration becomes not merely a policy, but in itself an act of religion. Such inspired moderation is usually found in an age of violent contraries. Henri the Fourth of France possessed it, as did William the Silent. Montrose, like Henri, was the one moderate man of his age; and, like Henri too, he realized that it needs a fierce man to enforce moderation in a rabble of fanatics and debauchees. Therefore he drew the sword.

No revolution has ever been effected or suppressed except by force of arms. If men's passions are deeply stirred, there must be an appeal to the last and sternest arbitrament. It is the soldier who turns the scale, whether it be Cæsar's army of Gaul, or the Puritan New Model, or Washington's militia, or Napoleon's Grand Armée, or Garibaldi's Thousand, or Lincoln's citizen levies. A Holles or a Vane may dream his dreams, but it is Cromwell who brings his into being. Montrose both courted and warred against a revolution. He desired to preserve the monarchy as against its anarchical assailants, but he was as ardent a revolutionist as Lilburne in his crusade against the existing régime in Scotland, with its stupid tyranny of Kirk and nobles. In such a strife the soldier must speak the ultimate word.

II

As a soldier Montrose ranks by common consent with the greatest of his age, with Cromwell and Condé. He has been described by Mr. J. W. Fortescue in his classic *History of the British Army* as 'perhaps the most brilliant natural military genius disclosed by the civil war.'[117] Like Cromwell, he seems to have learned his art rather by intuition than by experience, for till his great campaign his only training was the inglorious First Bishops'War. He had never, like Leven and Leslie, served under a great foreign general; he was as unprofessional as Rupert, and, like him, he had that natural eye for country and dispositions, that power of quick resolution, and that magnetism of leadership which discomfited the more prosaic commanders who found themselves opposed to him. He had learned the lesson of which his friend, the Cardinal de Retz, has given a famous epitome:'Il n'y a rien dans le monde qui n'ait son moment décisif; et le chef d'œuvre de la bonne conduite est de connaître et de prendre ce moment.' It has been sometimes urged that it is easy to over-praise Montrose's military capacity, since he usually fought against inferior troops and incompetent generals, and that on the only occasions on which he met a commander of ability and a seasoned army he was defeated. But the argument does not bear examination. The men he scattered at Tippermuir and Aberdeen were, it is true, raw levies, though present in great numerical superiority; but they were precisely the men with whom he had been victorious in his first war, and his conquering Highlanders were of the race which he had routed when they fought under Aboyne in 1639. At Inverlochy he had against him the best disciplined of the Highland clans, and Auchinbreck had ten times his own experience of war. At Dundee and Auldearn and Alford he faced regular cavalry and foot, the pick of the men who had won renown under Leven in England; and Hurry and Baillie were among the most skilled commanders of the day. Philiphaugh and Carbisdale are too much unlike normal battles to be made the basis for any judgment of one side or the other. No doubt Montrose's Highland and Irish levies, nourished on beef and game, were of a more stalwart physical type than the bannock-fed Lowlanders. But the regular Covenant foot were stout fellows, and they had the priceless advantage of a high discipline and freedom from the endless clan jealousies. So far as equipment goes, Montrose won his victories in the face of crushing odds.

As a strategist he showed an extraordinary eye for country. The tangled passes of the Grampians, little known except in patches to the different clans, were grasped by him as a geographical whole, and he arranged his marches accordingly. He had a boldness, too, which staggered even those inured to mountain warfare, and his flank march before Inverlochy seemed both to friends and foes beyond the limits of human possibility. His incredible speed was a strategical advantage, for he could march over twenty miles in a single night among snowy mountains as in his pursuit of Argyll in December 1644, or in thirty-six hours cover seventy miles with fighting between, as at Dundee. This swiftness, indeed, was apt to be a snare to him. He despised his slower enemies, and was twice almost caught, at Fyvie and Dundee, before the final surprise came at Philiphaugh. For strategy in the widest sense he was given no scope. He could not plan a campaign to correspond with the king's in England, for his hands were tied by the composition of his army. His Highlanders would not fight south of the Highland line, and they deserted in troops after each victory. Under such conditions there could be no continuity of purpose, and the marvel is that Kilsyth was ever fought. We can say at any rate that Montrose was fully alive to the need of the larger strategical intention, and it was only the lack of response from the English side that confined him to mountain warfare. With such a force as Charles repeatedly frittered away he would have swept these islands from Sutherland to Devon.

In tactics he had the supreme gift of suiting his scheme of battle to his material, using his horse now as mounted infantry and now as cavalry, and getting full value from the impetuous Highland charge. His power of rapid decision never failed him, and in the stress of fight he could keep his head and alter his arrangements at the shortest notice. As proofs we have the sudden strengthening of the left wing at Aberdeen, and his rapid dispositions in the hurry of the surprise before Auldearn, as well as the marvellous retreat from Dundee. At leisure he could dispose a battle with great skill, as at Alford, and could defy the ordinary rules of war with success, as at Kilsyth. Kilsyth is, indeed, an interesting case, for there is every reason to believe that Montrose deliberately chose what seemed to be the worse position. He was probably convinced that the Covenanters, finding themselves with the hill in their favour, would take some foolish risk, and he counted on the power of his Highlanders to charge up a slope and arrive unwearied at the top. He knew, too, the value of the sudden word in the stress of battle to turn the tide; and his insight into the hearts of fighting men was at least as great a factor in his success as his tactical skill.

More notable than his gifts of strategy and tactics, was his unique power of leadership. He welded into an army the most heterogeneous materials on earth. He discovered the fighting value of the clans, of which his kinsman, Claverhouse, was to offer a further proof. Hitherto it had seemed impossible to band two minor septs together for one purpose for more than a week; Montrose united the whole central Highlands in a campaign of a year's duration. Nor did he win this strange authority by any pandering to the vices of savage warfare. Except for the sack of Aberdeen, there is no stain on his record. He refused to turn the captured cannon on the fugitives at Tippermuir; he tried to check the slaughter after Inverlochy; he punished looting severely, as at Glasgow; unlike his opponents he observed scrupulously the etiquette of war; he never put a prisoner to death, not even when his dearest friends were being murdered by the Estates. He did not stoop like his opponents to the methods of the dirk and the ambuscade. Remember, he was no fire-eating giant like Alastair, but a slim young man of middle height, somewhat grave and courtly in his manner, and fonder of a book than a drinking-bout. Yet no iron-fisted Hercules ever kept a wilder force in a sterner discipline. The man who at Dundee could draw off half-tipsy troops in the middle of a sack in the face of a superior enemy, and lead them, weary as they were, for thirty miles in the thick of night to the safety of the hills, had miraculous gifts as a leader. We may search for long in the records of war to find an equal achievement.

Cromwell also had that moral authority which fused the forces under him into a single weapon for his hand to direct. But Cromwell, except at Dunbar, fought with numbers on his side, and he had the supreme advantage that his men were largely bound already by the tie of a strong religious faith. For Montrose there was no such assistance. It was personal authority and personal authority alone that kept Gordon and Macdonald in the same firing line. The two great captains were never fated to meet, and their relative prowess must remain in the realm of hypothetics. Mr. Gardiner rates Montrose the higher. 'On the battlefield,' he says, 'Montrose had all Cromwell's promptness in seizing the chances of the strife, together with a versatility in varying his tactics according to the varying resources of the enemy, to which Cromwell could lay no claim, whilst his skill as a strategist was certainly superior to that of his English contemporary.'[118] Probably the judgment is just. At any rate we can say that Montrose performed feats not inferior to Cromwell's best, against far greater odds, and with far inferior resources.

In virtue of his achievements he is probably the greatest Scottish man of action, and it may be argued with some force that he is the greatest of Scottish generals. From a modern standpoint we cannot judge fairly the exploits of Bruce and Wallace, and among modern Scottish soldiers it is hard to see who is to be put above him. Not Frederick the Great's Marshal Keith, nor Napoleon's Marshal Macdonald; they were skilful brigadiers, but they never revealed that originality and mastery in a campaign which

Montrose showed in 1644-5. Possibly Sir John Moore, if he had lived, and if he can be ranked as a Scot, would have come nearest to him. If we leave him out, it is difficult to find a rival among the many brilliant commanders that Scotland has given to the British army. He is the only Scot who approaches that small and charmed inner circle of the profession of arms, which contains no other British names than Marlborough and Wellington.

III

Few careers have more romantic unity than his. In one aspect he is the complete paladin, full of grace and courtesy, winning fights against odds, and scribbling immortal songs in his leisure, and in the end dying like some antique hero with the lights burning low in the skies and the stage darkened. But there have been other paladins before who have done the same. What gives Montrose his historical, his deep philosophical importance is that aspect we have already discussed—the fact that he read as no one else did the riddle of his times, that he preached a doctrine of government that had to wait nearly two hundred years till it could be restated with some hope of acceptance. His merit is that in that fierce seventeenth century, when men died for half-truths and less, when the great forces of the State were apt to be selfish competitors for material gain, and the idealists were driven into the wilds or over-seas— in that gross and turbid time he lit the lamp of pure duty and pure reason. There were those who did their duty, but it was too often blindly. There were those who loved reason, but they either fled from the struggle or, like Falkland, fought with an air of martyrs rather than soldiers. Montrose was armed and mailed Reason, Philosophy with its sword unsheathed. In truth he is a far rarer and stranger type than the quietist who has fascinated historians, or even than the grim Ironside—'the most formidable of combinations, the practical mystic.' He had all the calm lucidity of a Falkland, but he had none of his melancholy and despair. He went out joyfully to do battle for his creed, with the unquenchable faith of a strong soul. He was as passionate and stubborn in his cause as any Ironside, but he was no fanatic; he was not even any kind of mystic. He saw life very clearly and calmly, and his daemonic force did not come, as it so often comes, from a hectic imagination or a fevered brain. The springs of his being were a pellucid reasonableness of soul, joined to a power of absorption in duty which is commonly found only in the ranks of fanaticism.

It is a figure that must always haunt those who travel the rough roads of Scottish history. We see him in the gorgeous clothes which still dazzle us in his portraits, the long, north-country face, the broad brow, the inscrutable grey eyes. He is thinking, wondering, puzzling out the needs of his land, while others are preying on them. Then he reaches his conclusion, and, with something between the certainty of the thinker and the gaiety of the boy, he sets out on his hopeless errand. He is happy, boyishly happy, for he has no misgivings, and he cares little for what befalls him. He fights all the more fiercely because his cause is pure, and has nothing selfish in it. But he is always very human, very much the man, for Alastair and his kerns would never have followed an ordinary dreamer. And then, when his last blow is struck, he has neither fears nor reproaches. Clearly and reasonably he states his defence, and when it is flouted and he is condemned to a shameful death, he takes it meekly, knowing something of the fallibility of mankind. He awes the Edinburgh mob into a hush by his appearance; his enemies said that it was his fine clothes and noble looks; but we read it otherwise as that inward light, that vision splendid, which is the beatitude of the pure in heart. The Cardinal de Retz judged truly: Montrose is the eternal type of the heroic.

'A Candidate For Immortality'

'This is the happy Warrior; this is he
What every man in arms should wish to be.'

NOTES

BIBLIOGRAPHY

Contemporary Sources.—The chief MS. authorities for Montrose's career were collected and published by Mark Napier in his exhaustive *Memorials of Montrose* (Maitland Club, 2 vols. 1850). They contain the result of his researches among the charter chests of the Huntly, Napier, Wigton, Southesk, Hamilton, and Montrose families, as well as among the Wodrow MS. in the Advocates' Library, and the state papers in the Scottish Register House. Mr. S. R. Gardiner's *Charles II and Scotland in 1650* (Scottish History Society, 1894) contains some further documents that escaped Napier's eye.

Of contemporary biographies Wishart's great *Life* stands first. The first edition in Latin was published, probably at the Hague or Amsterdam, in 1647. A second edition was issued in Paris in 1648, a third in the same year, and a fourth in 1649. An English translation appeared, probably in 1647, at the Hague, and was re-printed in 1648 and 1649. In 1652 the same translation, with additions consisting of a continuation of Wishart's Part I. by a different hand, and an account of Montrose's trial and death, was issued in London under the title of *Montrose Redivivus*. A new translation with various letters and additional notes appeared in 1720, and a revised version was published by

Ruddiman in Edinburgh in 1756. This was reprinted with some further notes by Constable in 1819. Finally, in 1893, Canon Murdoch and Dr. Morland Simpson issued, under the title *Deeds of Montrose*, a complete edition of both parts of Wishart's Latin narrative, with a new English version, and three new chapters on Montrose's years of exile, largely based on the Danish and Swedish archives. This will probably rank as the definitive edition, and the editors' learned and ample notes cannot be over-praised. [In the succeeding notes, Wishart's text is referred to by its chapters, and when a page is indicated the reference is to the Latin text in this edition. The editor's own contributions are quoted as 'M. & S., p.-.']

Wishart was in prison till after the battle of Kilsyth, and his account of the earlier campaigns is based upon hearsay, and, since he was no soldier, is sometimes confusing; but from the period after Kilsyth till the last return to Scotland, his authority is excellent. Other contemporary, or nearly contemporary, narratives are *Britane's Distemper* by Patrick Gordon (Spalding Club, 1852), which is useful for the campaigns, and provides a defence of the House of Huntly; Gordon of Sallagh's continuation of the *History of the Earls of Sutherland* (Edinburgh, 1813), and Gwynne's *Military Memoirs* (Edinburgh, 1822)—both useful for the final campaign; Spalding's *Memorials of the Troubles* (Spalding Club, 1851); the Rev. Robert Baillie's Letters and Journals (Edinburgh, 1841); Bishop Guthrie's *Memoirs* (Glasgow, 1747); Sir James Turner's *Memoirs* (Maitland Club, 1829); Carte's *Ormonde Papers* (1739); and Johnston of Wariston's *Diary* (Scottish History Society, 1911). There are also the Scottish Acts of Parliament, the Records of the Commission of the General Assembly, and a large literature of pamphlets, some of which are referred to in subsequent notes.

Modern Biographies.—First must rank Mark Napier's three books, *Montrose and the Covenanters* (Edinburgh, 2 Vols., 1838), *Life and Times of Montrose* (1840), and *Memoirs of Montrose* (2 Vols., 1856)—the last being the final form of the work. Napier is a keen partisan, and writes in the heroic manner, but he is acute and laborious, and it is his honourable distinction to have placed Montrose's reputation on a new basis. He is the quarry from which all succeeding biographers must draw. [In the following notes 'Napier' means the *Memoirs of Montrose*. The *Memorials of Montrose* are cited as *Memorials of M.*]. Other monographs on the subject are scarce. The only two known to me are Mowbray Morris's *Montrose* (London, 1892; 'English Men of Action' Series), a brilliant and judicial sketch, and Mrs. Hugh Pryce's *The Great Marquis of Montrose* (London, 1912), a careful and most enthusiastic appreciation. I should also mention the fine study of Montrose's politics and his relation to the two Covenants contributed by Lord President Inglis to *Blackwood's Magazine* of November 1887.

General Histories.—Till recent years Montrose has not fared well with the historians of the period. Bishop Burnet, as the Hamilton champion, is naturally hostile, and even Clarendon, a fellow loyalist, is inclined to be grudging. More recent writers, such as Laing and Brodie and Hill Burton, have been uniformly unfavourable, and even the great Hallam repeats without examination certain baseless charges. Our modern Scottish historian, Mr. Hume Brown, in his admirable History of Scotland, is, for so just a writer, curiously carping in his references. Mr. Gardiner, however, has made amends both in his great History and in an article in the *Edinburgh Review* for January 1894. His estimate remains the fairest and most complete that we possess. Mr. Andrew Lang in his *History of Scotland* (Edinburgh, 1900–6) has done full justice, as we should expect, to the 'most sympathetic figure in Scottish history.' An admirable picture of Montrose and a penetrating study of the whole ethos of the religious wars will be found in Mr. W. L. Mathieson's *Politics and Religion: a Study in Scottish History from the Reformation to the Revolution* (Glasgow, 1902).

Poetry and Romance.—It is strange that a career so full of romance as Montrose's has been so little used for the purposes of imaginative literature. In poetry, apart from Wishart's Latin verses, we have only the Gaelic songs of Ian Lom Macdonald, and W. E. Aytoun's 'The Execution of Montrose'—the best of his *Lays of the Scottish Cavaliers.* In fiction there is, of course, the *Legend of Montrose*, in which, however, the great marquis is a minor character, and, let it be said, something of a lay figure. Scott never carried out his intention of making Montrose the hero of a full-length novel. Hogg deals with the battle of Philiphaugh in his spirited tale, *Wat Pringle o' the Yair.* Two other romances may be mentioned: Mr. J. A. Steuart's *The Red Reaper* (1895), a vigorous story of the campaigns, and Mr. Neil Munro's *John Splendid* (1898), which contains a brilliant picture of the raid into Lorn and the fight at Inverlochy.

★★★

NOTE 1.—A full description of Montrose's person by Thomas Saintserf, the son of the Bishop of Galloway and a companion of his early travels, will be found attached to the *Relation of the True Funerals*, 1661. See Napier I. 92. Another description, probably by Saintserf, is found in the *Montrose Redivivus.* One of the best is by Patrick Gordon in *Britane's Distemper*, 76. See also Burnet's *History of his own Time*, I., 53. An account of Montrose's undergraduate tastes is given by Saintserf in his dedicatory epistle to the second Marquis of Montrose appended to his translation of M. de Marmet's *Entertainments of the Course*, 1658. For a mass of personal details of his boyhood and youth see Napier, I. *passim.* There are three portraits which may be regarded as authentic: (1.) The portrait by Jameson in the collection of the Earl of Southesk at Kinnaird Castle. It was painted in 1629 as a wedding present (see p. 18). (2) The portrait by Dobson (probably about 1644) in the collection of the Duke of Montrose at Buchanan Castle. It has been attributed to Vandyke, who died at the end of 1641, but it is hard to see how he could have had a sitting from Montrose. (3.) The splendid portrait by Honthorst (Gherardo dalle Notte), painted in 1649 for Elisabeth of Bohemia, and now in the collection of the Earl of Dalhousie at Brechin Castle. There are various engravings, none of them contemporary.

NOTE 2.—Napier, I. 104.

NOTE 3.—Marischal had an odd career. He was a signatory to the Cumbernauld Bond, but afterwards became a Covenanter and was at Fyvie with Argyll, where his brother was killed. He opposed Montrose after Inverlochy, but later became an Engager, and was out in Pluscardine's rising.

NOTE 4.—Clarendon.

NOTE 5.—As the Bond was burned the world was left to guess its nature from hostile descriptions, till Mark Napier discovered a copy in the handwriting of the Lord Lyon, Sir James Balfour. See Napier, I. 269-70.

NOTE 6.—Act of 1584, cap. 134, and 1585, cap. 10. The punishment was reduced by 6 Geo. IV. cap. 47 and abolished by 7 Will. IV. cap. 5. According to Baillie it had never been put in force before (I. 381-2). It was the Act under which Mr. Oldbuck in *The Antiquary* threatened vengeance upon Mrs. Macleuchar, the proprietrix of the Queensferry diligence.

NOTE 7.—In the first edition of Clarendon's *History of the Rebellion* (Oxford 1702-4) Montrose is accused of offering to the king, at a private interview, to make away with Hamilton and Argyll. This story was repeated by most historians, though discredited by Hume on general grounds. In 1826, however, a new edition of Clarendon was published, collated with the original MS. in the Bodleian, and containing many suppressed passages. In this the original version of the incident was restored, a version which I have followed and which is now generally accepted.

NOTE 8.—This was the code of law to which Montrose appealed at his trial in 1650. It sheds an interesting light on seventeenth-century legal views. Till after the Resto-ration the 'law fundamental,' or the 'law of the land,' was regarded as something beyond the reach of legislative change. Magna Charta was a solemn embodiment of one portion of this law. In 1604 the Speaker of the House of Commons divided the laws into (1) the Common Law, not mutable, (2) the Positive Law, to be altered by the occasion of the times, and (3) customs and usages which have time's approbation. This distinction appears in Sir Walter Raleigh's *Prerogative of Parliaments* and was repeatedly made by Cromwell. Sir Edward Coke maintained that the function of the king and Parliament was not 'jus dare' but 'jus dicere'—to 'declare the law.' The doctrine of the legislative sovereignty of Parliament was first put forward by the Long Parliament and acquiesced in by the statesmen of the Restoration.

NOTE 9.—See the letter of an English soldier in Scotland (Sept. 1650), quoted by Lang, III. 204.

NOTE 10.—*Memorials* (Edited by C. Kirkpatrick Sharpe, 1819).

NOTE 11.—Cromwell's *Letters and Speeches* (Ed. by Lomas), II. 78-79.

NOTE 12.—The texts of this famous song vary considerably. Napier (I. App.), prints a large number of verses. Montrose's poems are printed in an appendix to Napier's *Montrose and the Covenanters*, and have lately been edited by Mr. R. S. Rait of New College (London, 1901).

NOTE 13.—Sir James Rollo or Rollock was the eldest son of the Laird of Duncrub, who was made a peer by Charles II in 1651. He married first Montrose's sister Dorothea, and secondly Argyll's half-sister, Lady Mary Campbell. He was present at Inverlochy, and fled in Argyll's boat. He was among the company at Montrose's funeral in 1661. His brother, Sir William, was Montrose's faithful companion till he was executed at Glasgow after Philiphaugh.

NOTE 14.—This was the second earl, who died at Whitehall, October 5, 1644. His son George, the third earl, joined Montrose after Tippermuir, and was a loyal adherent of the Royalist cause till his death in Orkney in the autumn of 1649. His brother became fourth earl, and died of starvation during Montrose's flight to Assynt. A younger brother, who saved the royal standard after Philiphaugh, became fifth earl, and made a sensational escape from Edinburgh Castle in 1654. See, however, on the fourth and fifth earls, Note 90.

NOTE 15.—See Montrose's 'Instructions to Lord Ogilvy,' Napier, II. 406-9.

NOTE 16.—*Memorials of M*, II. 146.

NOTE 17.—*Great Civil War,* II.132.

NOTE 18.—Lang, III. 116; Napier, II.399-402; Spalding, II. 379; *Memoir of the Somervilles* (Edin. 1815).

NOTE 19.—Wishart anticipates and calls him 'Earl of Tullibardine.' He succeeded his father as fourth earl four days after the battle. *Military History of Perthshire*, I. 252.

NOTE 20.—The narrative of the battle is based on *Memorials of M*, II. 149, Wishart, Spalding, and Patrick Gordon. Mr. Gardiner provides an admirable account, *Great Civil War*, II. 139-42. The story of an Irish officer who was present is to be found in Carte's *Ormonde Papers,* I. 73. See also *Military History of Perthshire*, I. 251

NOTE 21.—See Note 14.

NOTE 22.—Mr. Gardiner assumes that Montrose left Perth with the intention of meeting Balfour at Aberdeen; but Wishart (ch. vi.) says clearly that he did not get news of Balfour's army till he was in Angus. Probably he went there merely to recruit, for news from Aberdeen would be slow to travel south.

NOTE 23.—*Great Civil War*, II. 143.

NOTE 24.—Frendraught was the son of the grim hero of the 'The Fire of Frendraught,' and was born about

1620. He was with Montrose in his last campaign, and assisted him to escape after Carbisdale. The story of his suicide after the battle, given by the old peerage writers, and accepted by the *Dictionary of National Biography,* is without foundation. He lived till 1664 or 1665. See Napier, II. App. vi., and Balfour Paul's *The Scots Peerage,* IV. 129-30.

NOTE 25.—Wishart's account of the battle is confused, and Mr. Gardiner in his reconstruction depends chiefly upon Partick Gordon.

NOTE 26.—The only authority for the atrocities is Spalding (II. 406, etc.), who, however, enumerates no women in his list of victims. Patrick Gordon, whom Mr. Gardiner cites, does not mention them, nor is there any reference to them in the Burgh Records of Aberdeen. Spalding gives 118 as the total number slain in the battle and afterwards, which scarcely suggests a massacre. Baillie, writing as a Covenanter, merely says that 'the town was well plundered.' Alexander Jaffray in his *Diary* (London 1834) mentions the slaying of women and children, but, since he fled as fast as his horse would carry him, he cannot be taken as an authority on what happened after the fight. Still the evidence of the Royalist Spalding is hard to get over.

NOTE 27.—'Montrose hasted into the town to save it from being plundered, whereby it had little loss save by those who were killed in the battle.' *A True Relation,* etc. 1644—a pamphlet in the Bodleian, cited by M. and S., liii.

NOTE 28.—Gardiner says that the guns were buried at Rothiemurchus (II. 149). Wishart says simply *in palustri quodam loco'* (ch. vi. 374). Patrick Gordon gives the locality as between Strathdon and Strathavon. According to Wishart, Huntly dug them up and appropriated them after Philiphaugh. So the *caché* was probably nearer the Gordon centre than Rothiemurchus.

NOTE 29.—His name is spelt variously O'Kean,

O'Cahan, O'Kyan, and MacGahan. He was captured at Philiphaugh and hanged at Edinburgh without a trial.

NOTE 30.—On this point Mr. Gardiner's map (II. 151) is wrong. He makes Montrose go up Glen Lochay from Loch Tay, which would have meant a considerable circuit and the crossing of a high and difficult pass. Patrick Gordon (96-97) clearly describes Loch Dochart and the Macnab country.

NOTE 31.—Wishart says that Montrose left Lorn on the 28th or 29th of January. But he was at Kilcumin on Loch Ness on the 31st of January, and as a bond was signed there, he must have arrived by at least the 30th. From Lorn to Kilcumin was three or four days' march even for Montrose. Further, we know from Balfour's *Annales of Scotland* (III. 256), that the Estates heard by the 18th of January, that Montrose had left Lorn and was in Glen Urquhart. This may have been a false report, but it is probable that the Royalists began to leave about the middle of the month, and that the rearguard had gone by the 26th at latest.

NOTE 32.—The ordinary route given by Napier and others is by the Pass of Corrieyairack, down the sources of the Spey, and thence into Glen Roy. But such a road would have taken Montrose far too much to the east and over unnecessarily high ground. Dr. Morland Simpson, basing his view on the Clanranald MSS. (*Reliquiæ Celtic* II. 185), has suggested a much more probable way-namely, up the Tarff, crossing above Cullachy; then parallel to the Canal till the Calder burn was struck above Aberchalder Lodge; then ascending the burn and turning due south up the Alt-na-Larach till the headwaters of the Turritt were reached; then south-west into Glen Roy along the 'Parallel Roads.' See Pryce's *The Great Marquis of Montrose*, 240 *n*.

NOTE 33.—Highland tradition in general credits Montrose with descending upon Argyll by way of Glen Nevis. To do this it would be necessary to march to the head of Loch Treig, and then up Glen Treig, and so into Glen Nevis. This would mean a very long journey for very tired men, accompanied by several horses, and, in my view, an unnecessary toil, for Argyll would expect Montrose by the main road which descended the Lochy, and would be equally taken by surprise by a flank march along the northern skirts of Ben Nevis. Montrose would have good guides in the Camerons and Macdonalds to explain to him the configuration of the country. Mr. Hugh T. Munro, of Lindertis, whose topographical knowledge of the Highlands is unrivalled, kindly informs me that he accepts the traditional view, but suggests as an alternative route that Montrose may have ascended the Alt-nan-Leacan, and crossed the Learg-nan-Leacan to half a mile west of the head of Loch Treig-the easiest pass over the range. I am inclined myself to think that the suffering from snowdrifts and ice was experienced on the first day's march to Glen Roy, and that on the 1st of February Montrose contented himself with keeping to the skirts of Ben Nevis. This would seem to be also the view of Mr. Gardiner, Mr. Lang, and Messrs. Murdoch and Simpson.

NOTE 34.—Patrick Gordon, 102. See also Wishart, and Carte's *Ormonde Papers,* I. 76.

NOTE 35.—Ian Lom's wild poem is worth quoting in Mark Napier's spirited translation:—

'Heard ye not! heard ye not! how the whirlwind, the Gael,
To Lochaber swept down from Loch Ness to Loch Eil—
And the Campbells to meet them in battle array,
Like the billow came on-and were broke like its spray?
Long, long shall our war-song exult in that day.

'Twas the Sabbath that rose, 'twas the Feast of St. Bride,
When the rush of the clans shook Ben Nevis's side;
I, the Bard of their battles, ascended the height
Where dark Inverlochy o'ershadowed the fight,
And I saw the Clan Donnell resistless in might.

'Through the land of my fathers the Campbells have come,
The flames of their foray enveloped my home;
Broad Keppoch in ruin is left to deplore,
And my country is waste from the hill to the shore—
Be it so! by St. Mary, there's comfort in store!

'Though the braes of Lochaber a desert be made,
And Glen Roy may be lost to the plough and the spade,
Though the bones of my kindred, unhonoured, unurned,
Mark the desolate path where the Campbells have burned—
Be it so! *From that foray they never returned.*

'Fallen race of Diarmaid! disloyal, untrue,
No harp in the Highlands will sorrow for you;
But the birds of Loch Eil are wheeling on high,
And the Badenoch wolves hear the Camerons' cry—
'Come feast ye! come feast, where the false-hearted lie."

NOTE 36.—Napier, II 484–88.

NOTE 37.—Wishart implies that Lord Lewis Gordon deserted before Dundee. Patrick Gordon (113) denies this, and in W. Gordon's *History of the Illustrious Family of Gordon* (II. 453), Lord Lewis's presence at Dundee is asserted on the authority of an eye-witness. Mr. Gardiner also agrees with this view, which is indeed inherently probable, for the Gordons would take the easiest road home, which lay through Angus, and would not miss the chance of a sack.

NOTE 38.—Wishart makes it clear that Montrose left Dunkeld shortly before midnight on the 3rd of April. Mr. Gardiner (II. 219) says he left before dawn on the 3rd. The march was twenty-four miles, and the speed was evidently considered remarkable. But if Mr. Gardiner is right there would be nothing remarkable in doing twenty-four miles in thirty hours.

NOTE 39.—Wishart, ch. ix. 185.

NOTE 40.—Wishart, ch. ix. 387. In Mr. Gardiner's map (II. 217) the position of Careston Castle is not quite accurate, and the route up Glen Esk is wrongly given.

NOTE 41—Spalding, who is followed by Napier, makes a younger Stirling of Keir join Montrose in Menteith, but there does not appear to have been any such person.

NOTE 42.—There seems to be no contemporary authority for the details of Montrose's march after fording the Dee at Balmoral. Mr. Gardiner's map takes him into Speyside; Napier, probably following some tradition, takes him to Skene, about ten miles from Aberdeen. Aboyne's raid on Aberdeen, of which there is no reason to doubt, would have been possible only from such a base as Skene.

NOTE 43.—The tactics were those of Gustavus Adolphus, and their first use in Britain has been generally ascribed to Cromwell. See, however, as to Rupert's claim, Bulstrode's *Memoirs,* 81 (cited by Gardiner, *Great Civil War*, II. 146) and Fortescue's *History of the British Army*, I. 200.

NOTE 44.—The battle of Auldearn has been brilliantly reconstructed by Mr. Gardiner (II. 223-27). The contemporary accounts by Wishart (ch. x.) and Patrick Gordon (123, etc.) are far from clear. The details of Alastair's exploits are from the Clanranald MSS. quoted by Napier, II. 303-4.

NOTE 45.—Wishart says that Baillie gave up 1,000 men and got only 'tirones et rudes' (ch. xi. 393). Baillie, the general, says he gave up 1,500 and got 400. Baillie's *Letters and Journals*, II. 409.

NOTE 46.—The reconstruction of the battle is Mr. Gardiner's, (II. 280-3). Wishart's account is impossible to understand, and is obviously a collection of half-remembered stories from those who had been present. The figures of the numbers engaged are mainly taken from Wishart, whom Mr. Gardiner follows, though I think the number of foot on both sides is put too high. Baillie in his own account greatly exaggerates the Royalist forces. See Baillie's *Letters,* II.409, and Patrick Gordon, 128-35.

NOTE 47.—Digby to Rupert, the 28th of July, cited by Gardiner, II. 283.

NOTE 48.—Napier, II.516. Saintserf seems to have travelled as a theological colporteur.

NOTE 49.—*Letters and Speeches* (Ed. Lomas), III. 247.

NOTE 50.—Cromwell to Lenthall. *Letters and Speeches* (Ed. Lomas), I. 205.

NOTE 51.—He was said to have a following of 4,000 women and children. See Nicholas to Rupert, cited by Gardiner, II. 264 *n.*

NOTE 52.—Wishart (ch. xii.) gives 'Craigston,' and Napier, who is followed by Mr. Gardiner, assumes that he marched north to Craigston Castle in Buchan, a detour of thirty miles which would have been impossible in the time. Montrose in his letter of the 6th spells it 'Craigton.' Craigton-on-Dee is only seven miles from Aberdeen, where Lord Gordon was buried, and in the midst of friendly country.

NOTE 53.—Wishart (ch. xii.) is our only authority for this massacre, but he must have had an account of it from the Irish after Kilsyth, and, as Murdoch and Simpson point out, they showed great exasperation afterwards in the march past the Ochils.

NOTE 54.—*Great Civil War*, II. 292-3.

NOTE 55.—They corresponded to the 'dragoons' of the New Model Army and represented the light cavalry of the day. See Fortescue's *History of the British Army*, I. 216.

NOTE 56.—Wishart makes the Gordon contingent 200 horse and 120 musketeers on baggage ponies. Patrick Gordon, who generally overstates the Gordon forces, gives them 400 horse. Montrose had nearly a hundred horse before they joined (Wishart), and Ogilvy brought eighty. Gordon probably included the musketeers among the Gordon cavalry. Five hundred seems a reasonable estimate for the total Royalist cavalry.

NOTE 57.—For a discussion of Highland costume in battle, see Gardiner, II. 296 *n.* and M. and S., 213 *n.*

NOTE 58.—Wishart seems to imply some hesitation in the Gordon cavalry, but he is not an unprejudiced witness. There is no such reference in any other authority.

NOTE 59.—The contemporary authorities for the battle are Wishart (ch. xiii.), Patrick Gordon (137, etc.), the Clanranald MSS., and Baillie's own account (Baillie's *Letters,* II. 420, etc.). Mr. Gardiner, from a careful inspection of the ground, has produced what must be taken as the final account of the tactics (II. 295-300). Napier's narrative is far from clear.

NOTE 60.—Digby to Jermyn, *Bankes MSS.,* cited by Gardiner, II. 344.

NOTE 61.—There was a curious wildness in the Carnwath family, conspicuous even in a wild age. Montrose on his way north from Oxford found in Newcastle's army, where Carnwath was present, a reputed daughter of his, a Mrs. Pierson, commanding a troop of horse under the name of Captain Francis Dalziel. She displayed a black banner with the device of a naked man hanging from a gibbet and the motto, 'I dare.' See Napier, II. 393.

NOTE 62.—Thomas Saintserf in his dedication to the second marquis of his translation of the *Entertainments of the Course,* (London, 1658). See Napier, II. 563.

NOTE 63.—The document is printed in *Memorials of M.,* I. 215, and in Napier, I. App. iii. It is in the elder Lord Napier's handwriting. Mr. Gardiner agrees with Napier in assigning it to this period.

NOTE 64.—See the letter in Napier, II. 572-3, and *Memorials of M.,* II. 233-4.

NOTE 65.—For the conduct of the Jacobite Traquair, see *Memorials of John Murray of Broughton* (Scottish History Society, 1898). Patrick Gordon says that Traquair recalled his son four days before the battle; Wishart, with whom Guthrie agrees, says 'on the very night.'

NOTE 66.—Philiphaugh is the most confusing of all Montrose's battles, and the most difficult point is the exact route of Leslie's march. Sir Walter Scott, apparently following local tradition, in his *Minstrelsy of the Scottish Border*, makes Leslie encamp on the night of the 12th at Melrose, and he is followed by Mr. Mowbray Morris. For several reasons I find it difficult to accept this view. (1.) Leslie was at Gladsmuir when he received the news from Traquair, or whoever sent it. He knew his enemy, and his object was to cut off his retreat into the hills. Therefore he must have chosen the shortest route to the opening of the hills at Selkirk. He left Gladsmuir the day Montrose left Jedburgh, so he had no time to lose. If he had crossed by Soutra, and marched down Leader Water, he would have passed Melrose; but we know that he came by Gala (Wishart, ch. xvi.). To follow Gala to its foot below Galashiels and then ford Tweed and encamp at Melrose would have been a perfectly aimless detour. Further, it seems certain that Montrose arrived at Selkirk early in the afternoon of the 12th, and his presence there would be known in Galashiels—for he must have passed within a mile of it on the opposite bank of Tweed—and communicated to Leslie on his arrival. The easiest way was to march from Galashiels by the old Edinburgh-Selkirk road over the hill to Rink, and thence by the ford in Tweed below the Rae Weil to Sunderland. (2.) Patrick Gordon says definitely that Leslie was at Sunderland on the night of the 12th, and if so he could not have been at Melrose unless he had left Melrose in the afternoon and forded Ettrick. But in that case Montrose would have got word of him. Wishart does not mention Sunderland, but he says that the Covenanters spent the night four miles from Selkirk, which indicates Sunderland rather than Melrose. Further, in describing the turning movement executed by Leslie's 2,000, he writes *'quos adversa amnis ripa hostes transmiserant.'* But they would not have crossed Ettrick if they had been coming from Melrose till just at the battlefield, and Wishart's words indicate a crossing at the beginning of the morning's march. The Covenanters' account (*A More Perfect and Particular Relation,* etc., Haddington, Sept. 16,

1649) says that Leslie encamped within three miles of the enemy. (3.) Local tradition seems also to point to the Galashiels-Sunderland route. In the preposterous ballad of the 'Battle of Philiphaugh' Leslie is said to have sent his right wing round Linglie Hill, the height between Yair and Ettrick. Such a movement would have been impossible to a force coming from Melrose. It is not a very likely story, but it shows the popular idea of the Covenanting movements.

NOTE 67.—Craig Brown's *History of Selkirkshire,* I. 185, etc. As a proof of the attitude of the Lowland peasantry towards Montrose, it is said that the woman of the house was busy putting a sheep's head into a pot when the general passed the kitchen door, and that she declared she wished it was Montrose's head, for in that case she would be careful to hold down the lid. See Russell's *Reminiscences of Yarrow.*

NOTE 68.—Patrick Gordon, 158. Wishart does not mention the incident, though he was probably present at the battle. It seems to me probable that Amisfield's adventure was supposed at headquarters to be merely a brush with the country people, who were notoriously hostile to Montrose—Pringle of Blindlee being almost the only recorded Royalist in the shire.

NOTE 69.—The authorities for the fight are Wishart (ch. xvi.), who was an eyewitness, Patrick Gordon (156, etc.), and Bishop Guthrie's *Memoirs* (201, etc.). The Covenanting newsletter issued at Haddington three days later (cit. by Lang, III. 158 *n.*) exaggerates the numbers engaged, especially on the Royalist side; these were probably as stated in the text, except that it is difficult to believe that Douglas had the 1,200 with whom Patrick Gordon credits him. Leslie's own account puts the Royalist force at 2,000, adding, 'I never fought with better horsemen and against more resolute foot.' See *The Great Victories,* 1645, a paper in the Bodleian, cited by M. and S., lvi. He says that the foot were 'drawn up amongst the closes,' which looks as if the Irish had occupied some folds, the buchts of Philiphaugh farm. Bishop Guthrie also mentions 'a little fold.' Leslie in after life always referred to Philiphaugh as an easy victory. For some of the country stories about it, see Russell's *Reminiscences of Yarrow* and Craig Brown's *History of Selkirkshire*. The ballad on the subject, printed in Scott's *Minstrelsy*, is probably an eighteenth–century production, and of little use as evidence. The ancient father who guided Leslie must have been at least 116 at the time, for he boasted of having been at Solway Moss, which was fought a century before. He was a prophet as well as an ancient, for he added that he had been at 'curst Dunbar,' which was not fought till five years later.

It was not till this book was in type that my attention was called to the admirable study of the battle contained in *The Trustworthiness of Border Ballads*, by Lieutenant-Colonel the Hon. Fitzwilliam Elliot (1906). Colonel Fitzwilliam Elliot reconstructs the fight after a careful study of the authorities, and with the aid of his military experience and wide local knowledge. I am glad to find that he agrees with my view of Leslie's route. In my narrative I have adopted his suggestion as to the reasons why Montrose's scouts on the morning of the 13th reported no enemy, and as to the details of the flanking march of Leslie's 2,000. As to the incidents of the battle his reconstruction is probably as near the truth as we are likely to get. I differ from him only—if a civilian may, with all deference, differ from a soldier—in the estimate of the relative military capacity of Montrose and Leslie.

NOTE 70.—Wishart makes him halt for the night at Peebles, but as that ancient burgh is only sixteen miles from the battlefield, and as the fighting was over by twelve o'clock, it is difficult to believe that the fugitives stayed more than a short space to rest. On contemporary maps their place of encampment is marked as the parks between Neidpath Castle and the town. They probably rode on fifteen miles to Biggar before halting for the night. Tweeddale as a shire was more royalist than Selkirk. Tait of the Pirn and the laird of Hawkshaw did penance for their loyalty, and the county furnished the prototype of Sir William Worthy in Allan Ramsay's *Gentle Shepherd* (Pennicuik's *Tweeddale*, 99).

NOTE 71.—The authorities for the slaughter of the Irish are Wishart (ch. xvi.), Patrick Gordon (160), Bishop Guthrie (203) and the evidence of Sir George Mackenzie given by Napier (II. 584, etc.) These, of course, are hostile sources, but we find the same story given in a Covenanting tract quoted by M. and S., lvi. The reader will find the little that can be said in extenuation in Dr. Mitchell's introduction to the *Commission of the General Assembly Records,* I. (Scottish History Society). It is difficult to understand the view taken by some historians that the Irish were nameless savages, who by their crimes had forfeited all consideration from mankind. Patrick Gordon (161) gives us the most hostile account of them: 'The Irishes in particular were too cruel; for it was everywhere observed they did ordinarily kill all they could be master of, without any motion of pity or consideration of humanity; nay, it seemed to them there was no distinction between a man and a beast; for they killed men ordinarily with no more feeling of compassion and with the same careless neglect that they kill a hen or capon for their supper.' No doubt it was brutal warfare, but we must remember that Patrick Gordon, as a decent Aberdonian, disliked the ruder western clans. The Irish, who were mainly Scottish Macdonalds, slew fiercely, but so did the Covenant troops at Philiphaugh and Carbisdale, so did the Campbells when Argyll carried fire and sword through the north, and so would have the Covenanters in the First Bishops' War if Montrose had not restrained them. They observed, however, the etiquette of war, and they did not murder prisoners as the Covenanters did. Even Baillie protested against that practice; 'to this day no man in England has been executed for bearing arms against the Parliament' (*Letters*, II. 322). Nor is there any record, with the doubtful exception of the sack of Aberdeen, of that slaughter of women which stains the fair fame of the other side. Our evidence shows that they were cheery fellows, who cracked jokes in the thick of a battle. As for the women, no doubt they stole, but so did Leven's Scottish female following (see Nicholas to Digby, cited by Gardiner, II. 263 *n*.). Many of them seem to have been of Scottish and even Lowland blood, for among the names of the female prisoners in Selkirk jail after Philiphaugh are Dunbar, Anderson, Forbes, Lamond, Young, Simson, Tait, Watson, Walker, Park, and Stuart: Acts of Parliament, vi. (I) 492. It is sometimes argued that the two sets of outrages stand in different moral categories, because the Covenanters were inspired by a religious creed. But it makes very little difference to the guilt of murder whether the murderer slays because his blood is hot in battle and he likes doing it, or whether he calmly massacres because he is playing at being an early Israelite.

NOTE 72.—Guthrie's *Memoirs*, 243. He is confirmed by Sir James Turner, who was present.

NOTE 73.—See Patrick Gordon, Wishart, Guthrie, and the account of an eyewitness, Robert Burns, a Glasgow bailie (cited by Napier, II. 589).

NOTE 74.—Guthrie's *Memoirs*, 208.

NOTE 75.—Murray's death seems to have been justified on the ground that he had killed a minister. See Acts of Parliament, vi. (I) 526.

NOTE 76.—Napier took the story from Burns's diary in Maidment's *Historical Fragments*, and it has been generally accepted. But in the disposition of the Montrose lands by the Committee of Estates to Sir William Graham of Claverhouse on February 21, 1648, provision is made for her liferent. She seems to have died shortly afterwards.

See Balfour Paul's *The Scots Peerage,* vi. 253. Her life was so retired that a story like Burns's passed without contradiction.

NOTE 77.—See the letters in Napier, II. 619, etc., and the itinerary in M. and S., 165 *n.*

NOTE 78.—*Life of Robert Blair,* 215. (Wodrow Society 1848.)

NOTE 79.—Quoted by Napier, II., App. viii. For other examples of clerical loyalists see Baillie's *Letters and Journals,* III. 35, etc., and *Commission of the General Assembly Records,* I 427.

NOTE 80.—The letters are printed in Napier, II. 711, etc.

NOTE 81.—*Memoirs of the Electress Sophia of Hanover.*

NOTE 82.—The Declaration is printed in M. and S., 267. The reply of the General Assembly was published on January 2, 1650, and the reply of the Estates, written by Wariston, on the 24th. They are set forth in full in the 1819 edition of Wishart.

NOTE 83.—Murdoch and Simpson think he received the king's letter in Gothenburg, Lang and Gardiner think at Kirkwall. The first place seems to me the more likely, for Harry May, the king's messenger, would have some difficulty in finding a ship to sail from Gothenburg to the Orkneys after Montrose had gone, and if Montrose got the letter at Kirkwall he must have got it immediately on his arrival, for he answered it on the 26th of March.

NOTE 84.—This tragic letter was printed for the first time by Mr. Gardiner in his *Charles II. and Scotland in 1660* (Scottish History Society, 1894).

NOTE 85.—Nicholas to Ormonde. *Ormonde Papers,* I. 375.

NOTE 86.—Napier, II. 654 *n.*

NOTE 87.—Almost our only authority for the Orkney part of the campaign is Gwynne's *Military Memoirs* (Edinburgh, 1822), See M. and S., 293. Gwynne was left stranded in Orkney, and finally escaped in a herring-boat to Amsterdam, where he was found fainting in the streets from starvation.

NOTE 88.—The chronology of the period is confused owing to the overlapping of the Old and New Styles. The Old Style, which I have followed, was about ten days behind the sun.

NOTE 89.—By far the best account of the Carbisdale campaign is that given by Murdoch and Simpson, 289-321. It is based on various contemporary authorities, of which the chief are Gordon of Sallagh, an eye-witness (*History of the Earls of Sutherland*, Edinburgh, 1813), Balfour's Annales, IV., Monteith's *Hist. des Troubles de la Grande Bretagne* (Paris, 1661), and Taylor's *Dunrobin MSS.* They have also used local tradition—as, for example, in the account of the flanking movement of the Monroes and Rosses.

NOTE 90.—The only evidence for Kinnoul's death is Gordon of Sallagh—a contemporary of the event he chronicles. It seems to me unlikely that he would have made a mistake about the Kinnoul who fought at Carbisdale, for if he is wrong, then William Hay must have been there, and that Kinnoul, famous for his escape from Edinburgh Castle in 1654, was a noted personage whose doings were public property. If we reject Gordon's story, then William is the fourth, not the fifth earl. It is possible that Gordon did not know about the death of George, the third earl, in Orkney; and seeing that, after Carbisdale, William received the title, assumed that his predecessor had died in the flight to Assynt.

NOTE 91.—*Miscellany* (Scottish History Society), I. 223, cited by Lang, III. 216.

NOTE 92.—Monro had been out in Pluscardine's rising.

NOTE 93.—The question of Assynt's guilt is exhaustively examined by Murdoch and Simpson (App. xiii.). They decide against him on every count. There is no question about his complicity in the surrender of the fugitive, but I cannot find it proved that he had ever fought under Montrose, though very probably Montrose assumed him to be friendly from his knowledge of his connection with Seaforth and Lemlair. For his later fate see M. and S. *loc. cit.*, and for a defence see the *Old Statistical Account of Scotland* and *Trans. of the Gaelic Society of Inverness,* XXIV. 374, etc. Ian Lom's verses are worth quoting. (*Cumha Mhontroise* in Mackenzie's *Beauties of Gaelic Poetry,* 1841; the translation is by Sheriff Nicolson):—

> 'I'll not go to Dunedin,
> Since the Graham's blood was shed,
> The manly mighty lion,
> Tortured on the gallows.

> 'That was the true gentleman,
> Who came of line not humble,
> Good was the flushing of his cheek
> When drawing up to combat.

> 'His chalk-white teeth well closing,
> His slender brow not gloomy;
> Though oft my love awakes me,
> This night I will not bear it.

> 'Neil's son of woeful Assynt,
> If I in net could take thee,
> My sentence would condemn thee,
> Nor would I spare the gibbet.

> 'If you and I encountered
> On the marshes of Ben Etive,
> The black waters and the clods
> Would then be mixed together.

> 'If thou and thy wife's father,
> The householder of Leime (Lemlair?)
> Were hanged both together
> 'Twould not atone my loss.

'Stript tree of the false apples,
Without esteem, or fame, or grace.
Ever murdering each other,
'Mid dregs of wounds and knives.

'Death-wrapping to thee, base one!
Ill didst thou sell the righteous.
For the meal of Leith,
And two-thirds of it sour!'

NOTE 94.—The whole of this complicated question has been exhaustively discussed by Mr. Lang, III. 221-6. Mr. Gardiner (*Commonwealth and Protectorate*, I. 190, etc.), takes the view given in my text.

NOTE 95.—Taylor's *Dunrobin MSS.*

NOTE 96.—This narrative, generally called the Wardlaw MS., is extensively quoted by Napier, II. 773, etc. It was in the possession of the late Sir William Fraser of Ledeclune and Morar, but I have been unable to trace its present ownership.

NOTE 97.—M. and S., 318 *n*.

NOTE 98.—Written in 1676 and published in Edinburgh in 1815.

NOTE 99.—M. and S., App. xii., No. I.

NOTE 100.—We have three accounts of Montrose's entry into Edinburgh: that of James Fraser, already quoted; that of the Wigton MS. (Maitland Club); and the report to Mazarin by the French resident in Edinburgh, M. de Graymond. See Napier, II. 776, etc., and App. iv.

NOTE 101.—Wigton MS.

NOTE 102.—Wodrow MSS. in Advocates' Library. The informant was a Mr. Patrick Simson. Napier, II. 785, etc. For Simson see Warrick's *Moderators of the Church of Scotland,* 1690-1740 (Edin. 1913). He had been for some years chaplain at Inveraray, and had formed his notions of aristocratic deportment on Argyll.

NOTE 103.—Relics of these garments were in the possession of the Napier family till 1912, when they were acquired by the Duke of Montrose.

NOTE 104.—In the Wigton MS., Napier, II. 794, etc. The account in the Wigton papers seems to embody the actual words of Montrose more than any other narrative.

NOTE 105.—Napier, II. 794 *n*.

NOTE 106.—Wardlaw MS.

NOTE 107.—The speech is from the Wardlaw MS. Besides the account in the Wigton MS., we have a description of the last scene by an English correspondent, probably a Commonwealth agent. Napier, II. 804, etc.

NOTE 108.—*Mercurius Caledonicus,* ed. by Saintserf, January 4, 1661. Napier, II. 826.

NOTE 109.—The full account is in Saintserf's *True Funerals* (1661). Napier, II., App. iii.

NOTE 110.—Napier, II., App. i.

NOTE 111.—Lang, III. 117 *n*.

NOTE 112.—For an acute study of Mackenzie's modernism, see Lang's *Sir George Mackenzie: His Life and Times.* (London, 1909.)

NOTE 113.—*Reliquiæ Baxterianæ* 51.

NOTE 114.—The quotations in the following paragraph are from the *Discourse on Sovereignty*, Napier, I. 280, etc. Compare Lord Napier's views on the subject in his *Short Discourse upon some Incongruities in Matters of Estate*, printed in *Memorials of M,* I. 70. To 'orientate' Montrose's political creed in relation to his age would require a treatise. Generally speaking, he shows a leaning to the historical and realistic school represented by Bodin, Filmer, and Hobbes, as against the speculative school of Milton and Harrington. But he never reached the rigid monarchical conclusions of the former; indeed, he was more in agreement with such men as Samuel Rutherford, whose *Lex Rex*, published in 1644, laid down Montrose's favourite doctrine that sovereignty is from the people, who may in time of extreme necessity resume their power. Rutherford's book is mainly a mosaic of Scripture texts, but he is sometimes an acute debater. Unlike his friends Napier and Drummond of Hawthornden, Montrose accepted the doctrine that a prince must be subject to the civil laws of his own dominion. But it is in his practical application that he goes beyond his contemporaries, for he saw that in a stable government the supreme power, while it must be delegated, cannot be made divisible. The Kirk was willing enough to accept the democratic doctrine of popular sovereignty, but it did not appreciate the practical conclusion—that the people cannot entrust this power to two conflicting authorities which may both claim to represent them. Church and State cannot rule conjointly over the same sphere and under the same sanctions. The nation may change at its pleasure the delegates who administer its sovereignty, but it dare not part with a fraction of the *right* of delegation.

NOTE 115.—The first quotation from Burke is from the *Thoughts on the Causes of the Present Discontents*, the second from his speech in the House of Commons on Constitutional Reform, May 7, 1782, and the third from the *Reflections on the Revolution in France*.

NOTE 116.—See page 47.

NOTE 117.—Mr. Fortescue's other comment, 'A woman in emotion and instability' (I. 228), is not very appropriate to one of the most patient and resolute of military commanders.

NOTE 118.—*Great Civil War*, II. 351.

INDEX

Aberdeen, 21-3, 64-7, 88, 97, 207, 209

Aboyne, Lord, 21-2, 63, 97, 102, 110, 111, 115, 117, 122, 133, 134, 144, 160

Airlie, Lord, 82, 87-8, 117, 122, 134, 139

Alford, Battle of, 109-12, 115, 207, 209

Antrim, 41, 43-4, 53

Arcot, Nabob of, 196

Argyll, Earl of, 56, 61, 85, 95, 131, 155, 203-4;
  character, 24-6;
  ambitions, 27, 28, 34, 39;
  campaign against Ogilvys, 28;
  the"Incident", 32;
  Convention of Estates, 38;
  in Aberdeen, 67;
  pursues Montrose, 68-70;
  Montrose harries Clan Campbell, 77-84;
  Battle of Kilsyth, 123;
  and the battle of Philiphaugh, 140;
  alliance with Cromwell, 157;
  and Montrose's capture, 187-8;
  execution, 194

Ashburnham, 153-4

Atholl, 30

Auchinbreck, 82

Auldearn, Battle of, 98-103, 105, 106, 109, 129, 207, 209

Baillie, William, 70, 79, 85, 95-6, 97, 169;
  Argyll and, 78;
  Battle of Inverlochy, 80-1;
  Montrose challenges, 89;
  and the retreat from Dundee, 92-4;
  blocks way to the Lowlands, 106;
  pursuit of Montrose, 106-9;
  and the Committee of Estates, 108;
  besieges Huntly's castle, 108;
  Battle of Alford, 109-10, 111, 112;
  resignations, 114, 117;
  Fife levies, 117-18;
  Battle of Kilsyth, 118-23

Balcarres, Earl of, 109, 110-11, 121, 122, 123, 150

Balfour, Lord, 56, 61, 63, 64, 65

Berwick, Pacification of, 22-3

Bishops' Wars, First, 18-23, 44
Bothwell, 126-7
Brechin, 89
Breda, Treaty of, 179, 181
Brereton, 105
Buccleuch, 135
Buchanan, John, 145

Callander, Earl of, 46, 47, 70
Campbell, Sir Duncan, 78-9
Campbell, Mungo, 102
Campbell clan, 73-84
Carbisdale, Battle of, 173-6,
    178, 180, 207
Careston Castle, 93
Carnwath, 45, 145
Charles I, King, 6-7;
  Scottish reforms, 11-12;
  interview with Montrose, 26-7;
  in Edinburgh, 31;
  the "Incident", 32;
  Civil War begins, 38;
  Montrose's support for, 38-41;
  hopes to come to Scotland,
    85, 95;
  defeat at Naseby, 112-13;
  war on the Border, 128;
  at Southwell, 148;
  correspondence with
    Montrose, 148-50;
  imprisonment, 153, 155;
  and Montrose in exile, 153;
  execution, 158-9, 160
Charles II, King, 157-8, 159-60,
    161-2, 163, 166-8, 178-9,
    180-2, 198, 204
Charteris of Amisfield, 137
Christian V, King of Denmark,
    153
Christina, Queen of Sweden,
    165
Church of England, 39
Colquhoun of Luss, 5
Committee of Estates, 38, 108,
    109, 119, 121, 150, 155,
    161-2, 166, 169, 185
  Covenanters, 95-6;
  Montrose joins, 13-14;

negotiations with Hamilton,
    15-17;
First Covenant Wars, 18-23;
Argyll's ambitions, 28-9, 30;
ambitions, 34-5;
and the English Civil War,
    38-9;
Montrose leaves, 40;
Battle of Tippermuir, 59-60;
defend Aberdeen, 64-7;
pursue Montrose, 68-70;
and Montrose's retreat from
    Dundee, 92-4, 95;
Battle of Auldearn, 98-103;
Battle of Alford, 109-12;
Battle of Kilsyth, 118-23;
war on the Border, 133-8, 140;
execute prisoners, 141-3;
Montrose refuses to make
    peace with, 154;
Mauchline riot, 155;
Treaty of Breda, 179;
capture Montrose, 185
Crawford, Earl of (Lord Lindsay)
    30, 106, 107, 108, 109, 112,
    133, 139, 150, 153, 154,
    170
Crieff, 96
Cromwell, Oliver, 36, 85, 101,
    113, 155, 157, 170-1, 185,
    197-8, 204, 205, 210

Dalziel, Sir John, 138, 146
Denmark, 153
Dickson, David, 141
Digby, 85, 125, 135, 145
Donald of Moidart, 121
Douglas, Marquis of, 6, 127,
    133, 134, 135, 137, 138
Douglas, Sir James, 165
Douglas, Sir Joseph, 161
Drummond, Lord, 59, 60
Drummond, Sir John, 70
Drummond, Sir Patrick, 181
Drummond of Balloch, 151
Drummond of Hawthornden,
    128
Dumfries, 45

INDEX

Dundee, 61, 63, 91–4, 95, 184, 207, 209, 210
Dunkeld, 89–91

Edinburgh, 127–8, 186–95
Elcho, Lord, 56, 58–60
Elgin, 106
Elisabeth of Bohemia, 162–3, 164
Elphinstone, Sir George, 3
Engagers, 155–6, 157–8, 161, 162
Erskine, Lord, 133, 138

Fairfax, Lord, 48, 105, 148
Farquharson, Donald, 101, 102
Ferdinand, Emperor, 156
Fettercairn, 88–9
Fleming, Lord, 138
Fleming, Sir William, 181, 185
Forbes, Sir William, 66
Forrett, William, 3–4, 60, 87
Fyvie, Battle of, 68–9

Glasgow, 126, 129, 132, 145, 209
Gordon, John, 163
Gordon, Lord, 86–7, 96, 97, 101, 102, 107, 108, 110, 111–12
Gordon, Lord Lewis, 64, 65, 86, 91, 144, 147, 160
Gordon, Nathaniel, 63–4, 65, 88, 108, 110–11, 122, 127, 128, 133, 141, 142
Gordon, Patrick, 49, 51–2, 112
Gordon clan, 18–20, 21, 22, 53, 67, 69, 87
Graham, Lord (Montrose's eldest son), 87
Graham, Lord (Montrose's second son), 88, 128
Graham, Sir Harry, 151, 163, 172, 173, 177, 194
Graham, Patrick (Black Pate), 54–5, 56, 96, 147, 194–5
Graham, Sir Richard, 45, 48
Graham, Lord Robert, 105
Graham family, 2
Gray, Thomas, 153

Gunnersen, Jens, 151
Guthrie, Andrew, 142

Haldane, Major, 121, 122
Halkerton Castle, 88–9
Hamilton, Marquis of, 6–7, 15–16, 17, 20–1, 32, 40, 156, 157, 160
Hartfell, 142
Hay, Colonel James, 65, 70
Hay, William, 139
Henderson, Alexander, 13, 39–40
Henrietta Maria, Queen, 38, 153–4, 155–6, 157, 162, 164
Hotham, Sir John, 38
Hume, Colonel, 121
Huntly, Marquis of, 18–20, 44, 51, 53, 63, 67, 107, 108, 133, 144, 146, 147–8, 160
Hurry, Sir John, 78, 79, 85, 95, 170, 172;
  at Fettercairn, 88–9;
  and the retreat from Dundee, 92, 93;
  increases army, 96, 97–8;
  Battle of Auldearn, 99–100, 102–3;
  Battle of Alford, 112;
  in exile, 150, 151;
  capture, 176, 183
Hyde, Edward, 157, 158, 159

Inchbrakie, 52, 115
India, 196
Inverlochy, Battle of, 81–4, 85, 207, 208, 209
Irvine of Drum, 144

James VI, King of Scotland, 9
Jermyn, Henry, 153, 154, 162
John of Moidart, 71
Johnston of Wariston, 13
Johnston family, 196

Kerr clan, 135
Kilpont, Lord, 61–2
Kilsyth, Battle of, 118–23, 133–4, 209

Kinnoul, Earl of, 70, 163, 164, 165
Kirk of Scotland, 9-12, 36, 85, 130, 131, 141, 198, 199
Knox, John, 8-9, 10

Lachlan of Duart, 121
Lanark, 32, 155, 161
Langdale, 145
Laud, Archbishop, 11, 12, 35
Lauderdale, 155, 161
Law, Robert, 35-6
Leopold, Archduke, 156-7
Leslie, Alexander see Leven, Lord
Leslie, David (Lord Newark), 125, 133-5, 136, 137-8, 139, 140-1, 144, 145, 147, 161, 165, 170, 172, 173
Leven, Lord (Alexander Leslie), 18, 19, 28, 67, 105, 113, 125, 148
Lindsay, Lord see Crawford, Earl of
Linton, Lord, 127, 134, 136
Lisle, Major, 151, 175
Lothian, Marquis of, 70
Loudoun, 155
Louise, Princess, 163

MacAlain Dubh, Angus, 75
Macdonald, Alastair, 67, 70, 87, 96, 109, 115, 126-7, 130;
  joins Montrose, 52-4, 55;
  Battle of Tippermuir, 58, 60;
  Battle of Aberdeen, 65, 66;
  Battle of Inverlochy, 83, 84;
  Battle of Auldearn, 99-101, 102;
  Battle of Kilsyth, 121-2;
  knighthood, 129;
  leaves Montrose, 132
Macdonald clan, 71, 115
Macdonnell clan, 115
Mackenzie of Pluscardine, 161, 170
Mackenzie clan, 53, 160-1, 170, 173

MacKinnon, Ranald, 100-1
Maclean clan, 71, 74, 115
Maclear, John, 165, 166
Macleod, Neil, 177-9
Maderty, 59
Mar, Lord, 118
Marischal, Earl, 88
Maurice, Prince, 41
Mazarin, Cardinal, 154, 156
Methven, 116, 117
Middleton, Earl of, 135, 144, 147, 148, 149-50, 155
Monro of Achnes, 175
Montrose, Marquis of:
  early life, 3-7;
  marriage, 4-5;
  character, 6;
  joins Covenanters, 13-14;
  First Covenant Wars, 18-23, 44;
  antagonism with Argyll, 26;
  interview with Charles I, 26-7;
  imprisonment, 31-2;
  views on government, 33-4;
  poetry, 36-7, 159, 191;
  support for Charles I, 38-41;
  leaves Covenanters, 40;
  raises army, 43-7, 55-6, 86-7, 96, 134;
  returns to Scotland, 48-9;
  Battle of Tippermuir, 59-61;
  captures Aberdeen, 64-7;
  Argyll pursues, 68-70;
  harries Clan Campbell, 74-84;
  retreat from Dundee, 91-4;
  Battle of Auldearn, 98-103;
  Battle of Alford, 109-12;
  Battle of Kilsyth, 118-23;
  lieutenant-governor of Scotland, 128-31;
  loses Highland supporters, 132-3;
  war on the Border, 133-8;
  after Philiphaugh, 139-51;
  correspondence with Charles I, 148-50;
  in exile, 151, 153-68;
  becomes 'fey', 158-9, 180;

and Charles II, 161-2, 166-8;
last campaign, 169-79;
capture, 177-9, 182-94;
trial, 189-90;
execution, 191-4;
funeral, 194-5;
heart, 195-6;
as a political man, 200-4;
as a statesman, 204-6;
as a soldier, 206-11
Montrose, Lady, 4-5, 105-6, 145
Montrose (town), 89
Murray, Sir John, 102
Murray, William, 142
Musgrave, Sir Philip, 85, 125

Napier, Lady, 195-6
Napier, Lilias, 154
Napier, Lord, 12, 14, 30, 105,
138, 145-6
Napier, Master of, 97, 110, 111,
127, 128, 138, 147, 150,
154-5
Naseby, Battle of, 113
National Covenant, 13-14, 15,
39, 129; see also Covenanters
Newcastle, 45, 47
Nisbet, Sir Philip, 141
Nithsdale, 145

Ogilvy, Lord, 47, 48, 133, 134,
141, 142
Ogilvy, Sir Thomas, 82, 83
Ogilvy of Inverquharity, 141
Ogilvy clan, 28, 63
O'Kean, 83, 111, 132, 140
Ormonde, Duke of, 162

Perth, 60-1, 96, 114, 115-16
Philiphaugh, Battle of, 136-8,
140, 207
Poyntz, 145
Presbyterianism, 9-14
Primrose, Sir Archibald, 129
Pym, John, 30, 38

Reay, Lord, 144
Reformation, 8-9
Retz, Cardinal de, 154
Rollo, Sir James, 4, 39-40
Rollo, Sir William, 47, 48, 65,
66, 141
Rupert, Prince, 47, 101, 113,
157, 164, 207

Saintserf, Thomas, 6, 112
Seaforth, Earl of, 78, 79, 80, 86,
87, 97-8, 102, 146, 160-1, 178
Sinclair, Lord, 46
Solemn League and Covenant,
39, 161, 189, 190, 199
Southesk, Lord, 19
Spanish Netherlands, 156-7
Spottiswoode, John, 151
Spottiswoode, Sir Robert, 128,
135, 136, 141, 142-3
Stewart, Sir Archibald, 30
Stewart, James, 61-2
Stewart, John of Ladywell, 30-1
Stewart, Walter, 30, 31
Stirling, Sir George, 30
Stirling, Lady, 46
Stormont, Lord, 30
Strachan, 173, 175, 178, 180
Strathbogie, 106, 107
Sutherland, Earl of, 172, 173

Tippermuir, Battle of, 58-61,
207, 209
Traquair, Earl of, 26, 47-8, 127,
134, 136, 139
Trot of Turriff, 21
Turner, Sir James, 46, 148

Uxbridge, Treaty of, 85

Vienna, 156